MEDICAL BILLING 101

second edition

MEDICAL BILLING 101

second edition

Crystal Clack, MS, RHIA, CCS

Adjunct Faculty, Lane Community College, Eugene, Oregon

Linda Renfroe, RHIT, CPC-P

Adjunct Instructor, Tacoma Community College, Tacoma, Washington
Coding Consultant

Michelle M. Rimmer

Owner, ABA Therapy Billing Services, LLC

✳️ Cengage

Australia • Brazil • Canada • Mexico • Singapore • United Kingdom • United States

Medical Billing 101, **Second Edition**
Crystal Clack, Linda Renfroe,
Michelle Rimmer

SVP, GM Skills & Global Product Management:
  Dawn Gerrain

Product Manager: Jadin Babin-Kavanaugh

Senior Director, Development: Marah
Bellegarde

Product Development Manager: Juliet Steiner

Senior Content Developer: Elisabeth F. Williams

Product Assistant: Mark Turner

Vice President, Marketing Services:
  Jennifer Ann Baker

Marketing Manager: Jonathan Sheehan

Senior Production Director: Wendy Troeger

Production Director: Andrew Crouth

Content Project Management and
  Art Direction: MPS Limited

Cover image(s): ©emEF/Shutterstock.com

For product information and technology assistance, contact us at
Cengage Customer & Sales Support, 1-800-354-9706
or support.cengage.com.

For permission to use material from this text or product, submit all
requests online at **www.copyright.com.**

Current Procedural Terminology (CPT) copyright © 2013 American Medical
Association. All rights reserved.

Library of Congress Control Number: 2014957976

Book Only ISBN: 978-1-133-93674-9

Package ISBN: 978-1-133-93681-7

Cengage
200 Pier 4 Boulevard
Boston, MA 02210
USA

Cengage is a leading provider of customized learning solutions with
employees residing in nearly 40 different countries and sales in more than
125 countries around the world. Find your local representative at:
www.cengage.com.

To learn more about Cengage platforms and services, register or access your
online learning solution, or purchase materials for your course, visit
www.cengage.com.

Notice to the Reader
Publisher does not warrant or guarantee any of the products described herein
or perform any independent analysis in connection with any of the product
information contained herein. Publisher does not assume, and expressly disclaims,
any obligation to obtain and include information other than that provided to it by
the manufacturer. The reader is expressly warned to consider and adopt all safety
precautions that might be indicated by the activities described herein and to avoid
all potential hazards. By following the instructions contained herein, the reader
willingly assumes all risks in connection with such instructions. The publisher
makes no representations or warranties of any kind, including but not limited to,
the warranties of fitness for particular purpose or merchantability, nor are any
such representations implied with respect to the material set forth herein, and the
publisher takes no responsibility with respect to such material. The publisher shall
not be liable for any special, consequential, or exemplary damages resulting, in
whole or part, from the readers' use of, or reliance upon, this material.

Printed in the USA
2 3 4 5 6   28 27 26 25 24

Dedication

This book is dedicated to our past, present, and future students.
It is for you that we write and because of you that we are able to live
our passion to teach.

Contents

Preface

Medical billing is an important function of a provider's office. If billing is not performed accurately, reimbursement can be negatively affected. *Medical Billing 101*, Second Edition, provides step-by-step instructions for your success as a medical biller. The material presented in this text is on an introductory level, intended to be easily comprehended by those students who are new to allied health courses and the medical field.

Medical Billing 101 is designed for the allied health student who is enrolled in a medical billing, medical coding, medical office specialist, or medical assisting program. While it can be used as a stand-alone text for a medical billing program, it can also be used to supplement other required texts in other allied health programs. Additionally, it can serve as a reference guide for medical billers on the job, both in providers' offices and in medical billing companies. Frequently, billing texts contain information on many subject areas, leaving students feeling overwhelmed or overloaded. *Medical Billing 101* maintains its focus on billing only, to support the beginning biller and enhance the learning process.

Organization of Text

The chapter order and flow of this text are designed to outline the job duties of a medical biller in the order they are performed in the provider's office setting. Chapter 1 discusses the duties required of the medical biller and the importance of maintaining certification. Chapters 2 through 5 introduce readers to the health insurance identification card, the code sets, and the various forms used to gather the data necessary for completing the medical billing function. Chapters 6 through 8 describe the types of billing the provider-based biller will be performing. Chapters 9 through 12 guide students through the processes that occur once medical claims have been submitted.

Features of the Text

- Each chapter opens with learning objectives and a list of key terms, to help orient readers to the material.
- A margin glossary defines bolded key terms for reference during the reading; all the key terms are also compiled into an end-of-book glossary.
- Many examples of real-world forms are included throughout, such as explanation of benefit (EOB) forms, aging reports, and denied claims.

- An end-of-chapter summary provides an opportunity to assess learning before moving on to the next chapter.
- Chapter review questions provide an opportunity to test learning.
- Case studies written to be completed on the CMS-1500 form allow students to practice billing for different provider service situations, including office visits and inpatient provider services.
- Space is provided in the text for students to record their answers, and blank CMS-1500 forms are included for practice.
- Appendix I contains 25 case studies (with both ICD-9 and ICD-10 codes) for CMS-1500 form completion. SimClaim software, located online at the Premium Web Site, can be used to complete the CMS-1500 form electronically or manually.
- Appendix II contains examples of several real-world forms commonly used in the billing world, including the UB-04.
- Appendix III offers a list of medical abbreviations and acronyms.
- Appendices IV and V include a state-by-state listing of Medicare carriers and insurance commissioners.
- **MindTap.** MindTap is a fully online, interactive learning platform which combines readings, multimedia activities, and assessments into a singular learning path, elevating learning by providing real-world application to better engage students. MindTap includes an interactive eBook with highlighting and note-taking capability, self-quizzes, and learning exercises such as matching activities, multiple choice questions, flash cards, and more. MindTap can be accessed at http://www.cengage.com.

Supplements

The following supplements are available to enhance the use of *Medical Billing 101*, Second Edition.

Resources for the Student

- Free Online SimClaim Software contains 25 case studies designed to help students practice and understand how to complete the CMS-1500 form. These case studies provide billing practice for different provider service situations, including office visits and inpatient provider services.
- A 59-day free trial of OptumInsight's *EncoderPro.com—Expert* is provided as a bind-in card in the front of the text. This software will allow students to look up ICD-9-CM, ICD-10-CM, CPT, and HCPCS Level II codes quickly and accurately across all code sets.
- MindTap is the first of its kind in an entirely new category: the Personal Learning Experience (PLE). This personalized program of digital products and services uses interactivity and customization to engage students, while offering a range of choice in content, platforms, devices, and learning tools. MindTap is device agnostic, meaning that it will work with any platform or learning management system and will be accessible anytime, anywhere: on desktops, laptops, tablets, mobile phones, and other Internet-enabled devices. *Medical Billing 101*, Second Edition, on MindTap includes:
  - An interactive eBook with highlighting, note-taking functions, and more
  - Drag-and-drop exercises

Flashcards for practicing chapter terms
Computer-graded activities and exercises

Resources for the Instructor

The **Instructor Resources** are housed online at the Instructor Companion Web Site found at www.cengage.com, and include:

- The *Instructor's Manual*, which contains lecture notes, classroom participation activities, homework, and answer keys to chapter review questions and to the SimClaim case studies in Appendix I.
- The *Test Bank*, which offers more than 500 questions in the powerful Cognero platform.
- Microsoft *PowerPoint* presentations, with more than 300 slides, which serve as a great teaching and lecture tool.
- In the new *Medical Billing 101*, Second Edition, on MindTap, instructors customize the learning path by selecting Cengage Learning resources and adding their own content via apps that integrate into the MindTap framework seamlessly with many learning management systems. The guided learning path demonstrates the relevance of basic principles in medical coding through engagement activities and interactive exercises, elevating the study by challenging students to apply concepts to practice. To learn more, visit www.cengage.com/mindtap.

Feedback

We welcome your feedback and success stories on *Medical Billing 101*, Second Edition. Crystal Clack can be contacted at clackc@gmail.com. Linda Renfroe can be contacted at renfroelinda@yahoo.com.

Acknowledgments

Crystal Clack would like to thank the following people:

Mary Beth, for her patience over the course of this exciting project.

My dearest husband, Scott, for his continuous support, encouragement, and love.

A loving heart-felt gratitude for my mother, grandmother, grandfather, and father.

Linda Renfroe would like to thank the following people:

Crystal Clack, for her excitement and encouragement during this project.

Robert, my husband, for cooking dinner for us when my writing took longer than I expected.

My family and friends who were always interested in how the book was coming along.

Rhonda Dearborn, who gave me the chance in the first place.

About the Authors

Crystal Clack, MS, RHIA, CCS, has over 25 years' experience working in a variety of health care settings. In the beginning, Crystal worked as a student health aide at a college clinic after graduating from high school, followed later by positions in billing, scheduling, admitting, release of information, and coding. More recently, Crystal has served as HIM manager and HIPAA privacy officer for a hospital in rural Washington, and a coding and charge capture manager for a multi-system health care provider in Oregon. She has taught adjunct coding classes for seven years, with four of those years spent teaching at Lane Community College in Eugene, Oregon. Crystal's degrees in health information informatics management and IT leadership were earned through the College of St. Scholastica in Duluth, Minnesota. In her spare time, Crystal is actively involved with Oregon Health Information Management as the Director of Education. Crystal enjoys raising and showing purebred rabbits, camping, gardening, and exploring the great outdoors with her husband Scott.

Linda Renfroe, RHIT, CPC-P, has spent the last 26 years gaining knowledge about the health information management field. As a coder, she has worked in both large and small hospitals, long-term care, and home health. Linda gained additional leadership training when working at Swedish Medical Center in Seattle, Washington, which opened the door to move her beyond the coder role. Linda returned to school after years in the health care field to earn a BA at the University of Washington. This increased education allowed Linda to be hired at several Seattle-area community colleges as an adjunct instructor, teaching medical billing, coding, and medical terminology.

In her spare time, Linda works as a volunteer for a nonprofit organization focusing on teaching young people to be leaders in their community. She has organized several local teen mission trips and helped others begin tutoring and mentoring sites for children's reading help and English as a second language.

Michelle M. Rimmer has over 20 years' experience in the medical billing industry. She has taught numerous courses and seminars at three colleges in the state of New Jersey. Her passion for teaching medical billing led to the fruition of Michelle's first textbook, *Medical Billing 101.*

Reviewers

Reviewers

Teena Gregory-Gooding, BS, MS, CPC
Medquest Facilitator and Consultant
Rapid City, South Dakota

Mariann Jeffrey, RHIT
Central Arizona College
Coolidge, Arizona

Cheryl Miller, MBA/HCM
Assistant Professor and Program Director
Westmoreland County Community College
Youngwood, Pennsylvania

Danielle Price, CPC
Acting Program Director MPMC/MOA
ATA Career Education
Spring Hill, Florida

Jose E. Santana, Jr., BS, RHIT

Technical Reviewer

Cecile R. Favreau, MBA, CPC, CHC
Business Risk Analyst
University of Virginia Physicians Group
Charlottesville, Virginia

How to Use SimClaim CMS-1500 Software

SimClaim software is an online educational tool designed to familiarize you with the basics of the CMS-1500 claims completion. Because in the real world there are many rules that can vary by payer, facility, and state, the version of SimClaim that accompanies the second edition of this textbook maps to the specific instructions found in your *Medical Billing 101* textbook.

How to Access SimClaim

To access the SimClaim student practice software program online, please refer to the information on the printed access card found in the front of this textbook. The SimClaim case studies are also available for reference in Appendix I of this textbook.

Main Menu

From the Main Menu, you can access the SimClaim program three different ways: Study Mode, Test Mode, and Blank Form Mode. You can now save your work in all three modes and return to it later.

- Click on **Study Mode** to get feedback as you fill out claim forms for the case studies. If you need help entering information in a block of the form, you may click on Block Help for block-specific instructions while in Study Mode.
- Click on **Test Mode** to fill out claim forms for the case studies to test yourself. The completed claim is graded and can be printed and e-mailed to your instructor.
- Use **Blank Form Mode** if you wish to utilize the SimClaim program to fill out a blank CMS-1500 form with another case study in the textbook.

You can access SimClaim support documentation from the Menu as well, including Block Help, a glossary, and a list of abbreviations.

General Instructions and Hints for Completing CMS-1500 Claims in SimClaim

Please read through the following general instructions before beginning work in the SimClaim program:

- **Certain abbreviations are allowed in the program**—for example, 'St' for Street, 'Dr' for Drive, 'Rd' for Road, 'Ct' for Court. No other abbreviations will be accepted as correct by the program.
- **Only one Diagnosis Pointer in Block 24E per line**—though SimClaim allows for more than one Diagnosis Pointer to be entered, only one diagnosis pointer is allowed in Block 24E for each line item.
- **No Amount Paid Indicated**—If there is no amount paid indicated on the case study, *leave the field blank.*
- **Secondary Insurance Claims**—If a Case Study indicates that a patient's Primary Insurance carrier has paid an amount, fill out a second claim for the Secondary Insurance that reflects the amount reimbursed by primary insurance when indicated.
- **Fill out Block 32** only when the facility is other than the office setting, as indicated on the Case Study.
- **Enter all dates** as listed on the Case Study.
- **For additional help using SimClaim, refer to the Block Help within SimClaim or to the specific carrier guidelines found in your textbook.**

How to Use the
EncoderPro.com—Expert
30-Day Free Trial

With the purchase of this textbook you receive free 59-day access to *EncoderPro.com—Expert*, the powerful online medical coding solution from OptumInsight©. With *EncoderPro.com—Expert*, you can simultaneously search across all code sets.

How to Access the Free Trial of *EncoderPro.com—Expert*

Information about how to access your 59-day trial of *EncoderPro.com—Expert* is included on the printed tear-out card bound into this textbook; the card contains a unique user access code and password. Once you log in, scroll down to the bottom of the License Agreement page, and click the "I Accept" link. Then, click the "I Accept" link on the Terms of Use page. Be sure to check with your instructor before beginning your free trial because it will expire 59 days after your initial login.

Features and Benefits of *EncoderPro .com—Expert*

EncoderPro.com—Expert is the essential code lookup software from OptumInsight© for CPT, HCPCS (level II), ICD-9-CM Vol. 1, ICD-9-CM Vol. 3, ICD-10-CM, and ICD-10-PCS code sets. It gives users fast searching capabilities across all code sets. *EncoderPro.com—Expert* can greatly reduce the time it takes to build or review a claim, and it helps improve overall coding accuracy.

During your free trial period to *EncoderPro.com—Expert*, the following tools will be available to you:

- Powerful CodeLogic™ search engine. Search all code sets simultaneously using lay terms, acronyms, abbreviations, and even misspelled words.
- Lay descriptions for thousands of CPT® codes. Enhance your understanding of procedures with easy-to-understand descriptions.
- Color-coded edits. Understand whether a code carries an age or sex edit, is covered by Medicare, or contains bundled procedures.

- **ICD-10 Mapping Tool.** Crosswalk from ICD-9-CM codes to the appropriate ICD-10 code quickly and easily.
- **Great value.** Get the content from over 20 code and reference books in one powerful solution.

For more information about EncoderPro.com—Expert or to become a subscriber beyond the free trial, email us at **esales@cengage.com.**

Chapter 1

Working as a Provider-Based Medical Biller

Learning Objectives

Upon completion of this chapter, the student should be able to:

- Explain the tasks and responsibilities of a medical biller.
- Explain the work environment.
- Discuss the importance of certification and maintaining CEUs.
- Define key terms.

Key Terms

Accounts
  Receivable
American Academy
  of Professional
  Coders (AAPC)
American Health
  Information
  Management
  Association
  (AHIMA)
Certification

Certified Billing
  and Coding
  Specialist (CBCS)
Certified Coding
  Associate (CCA)
Certified Medical
  Reimbursement
  Specialist (CMRS)
Certified
  Professional Biller
  (CPB)

Certified
  Professional
  Coder
Continuing
  Education Unit
  (CEU)
Home-Based
  Billing
Medical Biller
Medical Billing
  Company

National
  Healthcareer
  Association
  (NHA)
Outsource
Provider-Based
  Revenue Cycle

What is a Medical Biller?

FIGURE 1-1 Medical billers are knowledgeable about insurance payers, billing procedures, and reimbursement for services.

Medical biller

the person responsible for submitting a provider's charges to the appropriate party.

Medical billers contribute critical knowledge and subject expertise to a constantly changing health care reimbursement system, which impacts how providers are paid, and, ultimately, the cost of providing health care to the patient. Medical billers assist providers with submitting correct and compliant patient claims for reimbursement, and they have an understanding of local, state, and federal billing rules and regulations, which ensures the overall integrity of their provider's accounts receivable practices (Figure 1-1). Medical billers may also serve as subject matter experts to their provider on biller- and coding-related questions. In addition to the above skillset, highly marketable medical billers display important professional skills such as: critical thinking, superb customer service, positive attitude, team player ability, and excellent communication skills with providers and colleagues.

Revenue Cycle

A medical biller provides important knowledge and best practices to a provider's revenue cycle process (Figure 1-2). A revenue cycle starts when a patient calls to schedule an appointment with a provider and ends when payment is appropriately posted to the patient's account.

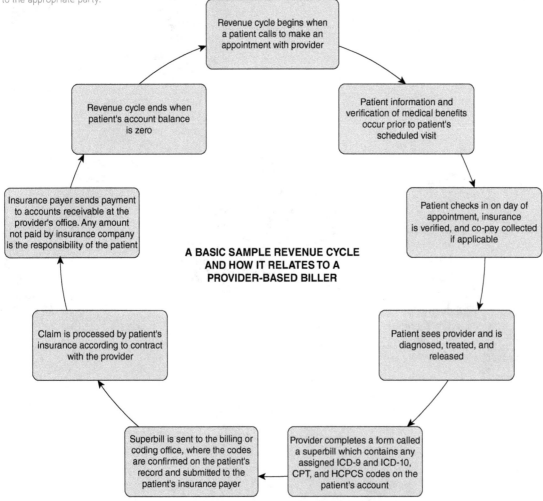

FIGURE 1-2 A sample revenue cycle and how it relates to a provider-based biller.

Skills and Attributes of a Successful Biller

Accounts receivable

monies owed to a provider for his or her services.

Revenue cycle

complete patient billing cycle that starts at the time patient makes appointment and ends when patient's account is paid in full.

Provider-based

pertaining only to a provider such as physician, nurse practitioner, physician's assistant and other clinical providers.

A medical biller must, above all, have a strong attention to detail. Working with numbers, forms, contracts, and insurance guidelines requires a medical biller's succinct ability to identify errors and correct them prior to submitting a patient claim for reimbursement. Additionally, a successful medical biller should have the following skillset:

1. Critical thinking
2. Active listening
3. Reading comprehension
4. Integrity and diplomacy
5. Phone etiquette
6. Working knowledge of computers and software
7. Team player ability
8. Ability to provide excellent customer service to a variety of patient types
9. Ability to communicate with providers, and other office staff
10. Professionalism

A medical biller must be aware of current local, state, and federal billing guidelines, and must know what to do when a claim is denied.

Work Environments

Medical billing company

an offsite company hired to process medical bills for the provider.

Home-based billing

the ability for an experienced biller to work from their home office.

Outsource

send work offsite.

An experienced and certified medical biller may work in many environments that include the following settings: hospitals, private medical practice, laboratory services, radiology departments, specialty clinics, insurance companies, attorney's offices, or a medical billing company. For those with the entrepreneurial drive and years of billing experience, a home-based billing company may be an option. With a home-based business, provider practices can outsource their billing to billers across the country who work remotely from the comforts of home. Regardless of a medical biller's working environment, all billers are encouraged to maintain their billing or coding certification and love of lifelong learning!

Importance of Certification

Certification

a professional status or level earned by successful completion of an examination; a person who is certified may subsequently list the designated credentials after her or his name.

Obtaining a medical biller or coding certification demonstrates dedication to the profession, skills, and knowledge. A certification increases the opportunity for employment and career advancement. It can also be the deciding factor for being hired over an equally qualified non-certified candidate!

In order to pursue certification, one must successfully pass an examination given by a sponsoring organization. Some exams are offered online, while others must be taken at an exam site predetermined by the sponsoring organization. Some organizations may provide study guides for use prior to taking the exam, but the majority may not. They will, however, indicate what is on the exam and what acceptable materials are allowed while taking the exam. This may include the use of ICD-9 or ICD-10-CM/PCS, CPT-4, and HCPCS coding books. Coding systems and methodologies will be further addressed in Chapter 3.

Membership in an Organization

Before one can take a certification exam, s/he is usually required to become a member of the certification exam's sponsoring organization. Membership is an important step toward demonstrating professionalism and knowledge of billing practices. Sponsoring organizations' websites are often packed with relevant information pertaining to current billing and coding trends. Furthermore, membership will expose the biller to timely profession news and trends on the organization's corresponding communications (i.e., newsletters, magazines, blogs, or virtual bulletin boards). A biller should take advantage of opportunities to network with peers and utilize the organization's resources on rules, regulations, and other guidelines more specific to medical billing and coding. Once a decision is made on which organization to join, the new member can take the credentialing examination. Credentialed billers and coders must maintain **continuing education units (CEUs)** in order to prove knowledge of current trends and changes within the medical billing profession.

Certified Billing and Coding Specialist (CBCS)

The **Certified Billing and Coding Specialist (CBCS)** exam is offered through the **National Healthcareer Association (NHA)**. A Certified Billing and Coding Specialist is mainly responsible for assigning medical diagnoses and procedures on a patient's record, and then submitting them to the insurance payer on an electronic or paper claim for reimbursement.

Certified Coding Associate (CCA)

The **Certified Coding Associate (CCA)** exam is offered through the **American Health Information Management Association (AHIMA)**. A Certified Coding Associate is responsible for assigning basic ICD codes and CPT codes to a patient's record.

Certified Medical Reimbursement Specialist (CMRS)

The **Certified Medical Reimbursement Specialist** exam is a credential created with the medical billing professional in mind. The American Medical Billing Association created this certification ten years ago to demonstrate (to providers, employers, and peers) the billing professionals' credibility and dedication to advancement of their career through education, knowledge, and skills. The exam is administered online through a secure login and contains over 800 questions. One may have up to 45 days to access and complete the exam and must pass with an 85% accuracy rate or higher to earn the CMRS credential. Sections included in the exam are:

* Medical Terminology
* Anatomy and Physiology
* Information Technology
* Web and Information Technology
* ICD-9/10-CM Coding
* CPT 4 Coding
* Clearinghouses
* CMS-1500
* Compliance
* Insurance and Insurance Carriers

Continuing Education Unit (CEU)

a level of measurement of non-credited education.

Certified Billing and Coding Specialist (CBCS)

a certification offered by the National Healthcareer Association.

National Healthcareer Association (NHA)

organization that specializes in the certification of healthcare professionals, including coders.

Certified Coding Associate (CCA)

an entry-level coding certification offered by AHIMA.

American Health Information Management Association (AHIMA)

organization of professionals dedicated to advancing the field of health information management and coding.

Certified Medical Reimbursement Specialist (CMRS)

a certification offered by the American Medical Billing Association.

- Acronyms
- Fraud and Abuse
- Managed Care
- General
- Case Study

Certified Professional Biller (CPB)

American Academy of Professional Coders (AAPC)

organization of professionals dedicated to educating physician-based coders.

Certified Professional Biller (CPB)

offered through the American Academy of Professional Coders.

The American Academy of Professional Coders (AAPC) has recently added a new credential to their list of professional certifications: Certified Professional Biller. According to the AAPC website, a CPB certified biller should be knowledgeable about the following:

- Comprehension of different types of insurance plans
- Understanding and correctly applying payer policies; Knowledge of Local Coverage Determination (LCD) and National Coverage Determination (NCD)
- Knowledge of ICD-9/10-CM, CPT-4 and HCPCS Level II coding guidelines
- Different applicable health care rules and regulations including the Health Information Portability Accountability Act (HIPAA), False Claims Act, Fair Debt Collections Act, and Stark
- Revenue life cycle
- Expertise in claims and patient follow-up, as well as denial resolution

The CPB is a proctored exam. It contains 200 multiple-choice questions, and the candidate has five hours and forty minutes to complete the exam.

Certified Professional Coder (CPC)

Certified Professional Coder

coding certification exam offered by the American Academy of Professional Coders.

The American Academy of Professional Coders offers a coding certification exam: Certified Professional Coder. According to their website, the CPC's medical billing abilities include:

- Expertise in reviewing and assigning accurate medical codes for diagnoses, procedures, and services performed by providers
- Proficiency across a wide range of services to include evaluation and management, anesthesia, surgery, radiology, pathology, and medicine
- Knowledge of ICD-9/10-CM, CPT-4 and HCPCS Level II coding guidelines
- Knowledge of compliance and reimbursement to include medical necessity, claims denials, bundling, and charge capture

The CPC is a proctored exam. It contains 150 multiple choice questions, and the candidate has five hours and forty minutes to complete the exam.

Continuing Education Units (CEUs) and Certification

Once certification is obtained, it's critical to stay on top of the required continuing education units (CEUs) in the certifying organization. Each organization's requirements are different, and the costs to maintain CEUs will vary. CEUs help maintain certifications and provide important, time-sensitive, information needed for a biller to maintain success in their chosen field.

Summary

There are many job opportunities for the provider-based medical biller. A person in this position may be physically located in a provider's office, may work for a medical billing company, or even have their own home-based business. It is important to understand that the job must be performed accurately, ethically, and diplomatically.

In order to increase the opportunity for advancement in the field of billing, certification is recommended. Obtaining certification shows dedication and professionalism to prospective employers. It also places the medical biller a step ahead of those applicants who lack certification.

REVIEW QUESTIONS

1. What are the primary job duties of a medical biller?
   a. file claims
   b. answer phones
   c. tell the provider how to assign correct codes
   d. review and submit patient visit claims to the patient's insurance payer for appropriate reimbursement

2. Provider-based billing refers to:
   a. durable medical equipment billing
   b. hospital room charges
   c. charges for a provider's services
   d. charges for copies of patient medical records

3. Professionalism is not important to a medical biller
   a. True
   b. False

4. What is the advantage of obtaining a billing or coding certification?
   a. Displays billing knowledge to an employer
   b. Shows the ability to network with peers
   c. A medical biller is told how to bill by a professional association biller
   d. Both a & b

5. Which exam is offered online?
   a. CHRS
   b. CHP
   c. CMRS
   d. none of the above

6. What does the acronym CEU stand for?
    a. continuous education understanding
    b. comprehensive evaluation unit
    c. critical evaluation understanding
    d. continuing education unit

7. Which designation is not based on passing an examination?
    a. CAP
    b. CHP
    c. CMRS
    d. none of the above

8. The _____ recently added a new credential to their certifications called Certified Professional Biller.
    a. American Academy of Professional Coders (AAPC)
    b. American Health Information Management Association (AHIMA)
    c. National Healthcareer Association (NHA)
    d. American Medical Association (AMA)

Chapter 2

Overview of the Health Insurance Payment System

Learning Objectives

Upon completion of this chapter, the student should be able to:

- Understand the Affordable Care Act and its impact on health care.
- Describe the types of health insurance and identification cards associated with the health care plans.
- Explain the difference between co-insurance and co-payments.
- Discuss how health insurance differs from a medical discount card.
- Define key terms.

Key Terms

Affordable Care Act (ACA)
Allowed Amount
Beneficiary
Carriers
Centers for Medicare and Medicaid Services (CMS)
Co-insurance
Commercial
Contract
Co-payment
Coverage
Deductible
Dependents

Disability Insurance
Eligibility Category
Emergency Room Visits
Employee
Employee/ Significant Other (E/S) Coverage
Family Coverage
Fee Schedule
Fiscal Agent
Government Plan
Group Number
Health Insurance
Health Insurance Identification Card

Health Insurance Portability and Accountability Act of 1996 (HIPAA)
Health Maintenance Organization (HMO)
Husband/Wife (H/W) Coverage
Identification Number
Indemnity Plan
Individual
In Network

Insured
Managed Care Plan
Medicaid
Medicare
Medicare Advantage
Medicare Part B
Medicare Part C (also known as Medicare Advantage)
Medigap
Military Treatment Facility (MTF)
Original Medicare
Out of Network

Out of Pocket
Outpatient
Parent/Child
 Coverage
Plan type
Point-of-Service
 (POS) Plan

Policyholder
Preferred Provider
 Network (PPN)
Preferred Provider
 Organization
 (PPO)
Prescription Drugs

Primary
Primary Care
 Provider (PCP)
Referral
Secondary
Self-pay
Specialist

Subscriber
Supplemental
Traditional
Tricare
Tricare Extra
Tricare Prime
Tricare Standard

A Bit of History

Prior to 1920, the delivery of professional medical services in the United States was very basic. House calls were made by providers to patients ill in their homes. This kept the prices of providing health care low for the patient. Those patients unable to work lost wages and struggled to maintain their lifestyle. For a patient to have two weeks without pay because of an illness was a big financial hardship. Fortunately, a newly incorporated program called disability insurance evolved, and helped workers cover lost wages due to illness.

Progression in the twentieth century led to many changes in the practice of health care. Now, instead of visiting a patient's home, practitioners perform treatments on patients in hospitals or medical offices. This shift created a need for health insurance to cover the rising costs associated with the delivery of health care in a more costly setting and increased liabilities.

Over the years, insurance in the United States developed into a highly regulated, complex, multitiered payment system. Recently, in an effort to encourage affordable health care, the Affordable Care Act (ACA) was signed into place by President Barack Obama in 2010 and was implemented on January 1, 2014. The ACA allows access to affordable, preventative health care for millions of Americans that otherwise would not have access to health insurance coverage.

Health Insurance

Most patients seen in a provider's office have health insurance, which covers the majority of costs for their personal medical care. When a patient presents for an appointment at his or her provider's office, the patient checks in at the front desk, where a receptionist asks the patient to present a health insurance identification card and complete other important paperwork. The Health Insurance Portability and Accountability Act (HIPAA) strongly suggests a photo identification confirmation prior to the patient's visit with their provider. The insurance card provides valuable information for the office staff. The photo identification, such as a driver's license or state-issued identification card, helps prevent medical fraud and abuse by confirming that the patient's identity and health insurance plans match. The patient without health insurance must pay for the entire visit out of his or her own pocket. This is known as self-pay.

The first insurance billed for the patient's care is called the primary insurance. Once the primary insurance pays on the claim, the claim's balance is submitted to the patient's secondary or supplemental insurance (called Medigap for patients whose primary insurance is Medicare). If there is a question as to which insurance is primary

Disability insurance

insurance providing income to a policyholder who is disabled and cannot work.

Health insurance

a contract between the subscriber and the insurance company to pay for medical care and preventive services.

Affordable Care Act (ACA)

landmark health reform legislation intended to lower health care costs and provide health care coverage to millions of uninsured Americans. It was signed into law by President Barack Obama in March 2010.

Health insurance identification card

card given to subscriber as proof of insurance.

Health Insurance Portability and Accountability Act of 1996 (HIPAA)

mandates government regulations that govern patient privacy, security, and electronic record transactions.

Self-pay

a patient with no health insurance who must pay out of pocket for medical care.

Primary

the insurance plan that is billed first for medical services.

Secondary

the insurance plan that is billed after the primary has paid or denied payment.

Supplemental

another name for secondary insurance. A supplemental plan usually picks up the patient's deductible and/or co-insurance.

Medigap

supplemental insurance for patients with Medicare as their primary. These plans may pick up the Medicare deductible and co-insurance.

Contract

an agreement between two or more parties.

Identification number

the number listed on the identification card that identifies the patient to the insurance company.

Group number

the number on the identification card that identifies the patient's employer group health plan.

Plan type

a specific name assigned by the insurance company designating a specific plan for that type of insurance. For example, Oxford has a "liberty" plan.

Policyholder

the person who has (carries) the health insurance.

Subscriber

another term for policyholder.

Insured

another term for policyholder or subscriber.

Beneficiary

term used for a patient who has Medicare coverage.

Co-payment

a flat fee the patient pays each time for medical services. This is associated with managed care plans.

for a patient who presents two cards upon registration, the biller must contact both insurance companies to verify who should be primary. This should not occur frequently, as patients are usually well informed regarding the order (priority) of their insurance and the benefits of each. One rule of thumb: if a patient has insurance through an employer and is also covered through a spouse's employer, the *patient's* insurance is *always* primary.

The Identification Card

The health insurance identification card will list the name and address of the insurance company. It is the responsibility of the biller or patient scheduler to verify insurance eligibility to ensure the office is contracted with the insurance plan. Once a patient checks in at the front desk, the staff member signing in the patient should confirm the following information on the patient's identity card:

- patient's identification number
- group number
- plan type
- policyholder, also known as subscriber, insured, or beneficiary
- co-payment
- co-insurance
- deductible

The receptionist or biller must scan both sides of the health insurance identification card. Because a single insurance company may have many different addresses, never assume different patients with the same insurance will have the same claims submission address and phone number.

Types of Health Insurance Plans

There are many different types of health insurance plans to choose from. It is not the *most* important job duty of a medical biller to memorize these types of plans; however, it is important to have a familiarity with the different types to ensure the medical office staff collects the correct co-payment or co-insurance amount at the time of a patient's visit.

Indemnity Plan

An indemnity plan is a type of health insurance plan that allows the participant to select his or her own provider. The insurance company usually pays 80 percent of the allowed amount based on an insurance company's fee schedule. The patient is responsible for paying the remaining 20 percent. These monies are paid only after the patient's deductible has been met. The 20 percent the patient is responsible to pay is called co-insurance. In the field of medical billing and health insurance, a biller might also hear this type of plan referred to as a traditional or commercial health insurance plan. See Figure 2-1.

Government Plan

A government plan is a health insurance plan that is funded by the federal or state government. These plans are regulated by the Centers for Medicare and Medicaid Services (CMS). Coverage may be dependent on state and federal laws, national

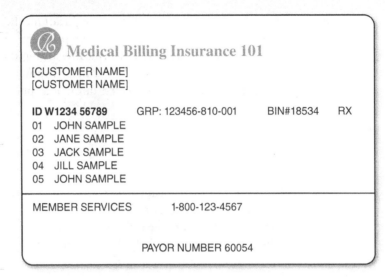

FIGURE 2-1   Sample indemnity card.

Medicare coverage decisions, and local coverage decisions (LCDs). LCDs are managed by individual companies who process Medicare claims. Each state or groups of states have different LCDs, and they must follow their guidelines on medical necessity for that patient's state. There are two types of plans that fall into the government plan category: Medicare and Medicaid.

Medicare

The Medicare health insurance coverage referred to in this text is Medicare Part B. This coverage is for provider and outpatient services, clinical research, durable medical equipment, mental health, and ambulance services. A person who has Medicare coverage is always referred to as a *beneficiary*. A person may become eligible for Medicare in several ways. Some include:

- Patient is 65 years of age or older
- Patient is disabled
- Patient has end-stage renal disease
- Patient has Medicare through spouse

Medicare billers must understand the rules and regulations regarding submission of these claims, not the reason for the patient's Medicare insurance. These rules are covered in detail in Chapter 5. There is more than one type of Medicare plan; the plan discussed in this section is called Original Medicare. Because CMS contracts with various carriers to pay Part B claims, the address to which these claims are submitted is different for each state. See Figure 2-2.

In addition to Medicare Part B, medical billers need to be aware of three other Medicare plans:

1. **Medicare Part A** – covers inpatient care in hospitals, services such as surgeries, laboratory tests, supplies and provider visits that meet medical necessity for that patient's diagnosis
2. **Medicare Part C** – Medicare Advantage Plans approved by Medicare but managed by private entities which cover all Medicare services.
3. **Medicare Part D** – Prescription drug coverage

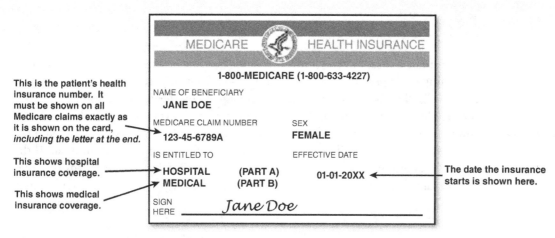

This is the patient's health insurance number. It must be shown on all Medicare claims exactly as it is shown on the card, *including the letter at the end.*

This shows hospital insurance coverage.

This shows medical insurance coverage.

The date the insurance starts is shown here.

FIGURE 2-2   Sample Medicare card.

Medicaid

a government plan for financially indigent people.

Medicare Part B

covers services such as provider exams, surgeries, lab and radiology tests, durable medical equipment supplies (such as canes, oxygen and wheelchairs) considered medically necessary to treat a patient's condition.

Outpatient

services performed at a facility where the patient stays less than 24 hours and is not admitted to the facility; also, the term for the patient receiving such services.

Original Medicare

healthcare coverage managed by the federal government.

Carrier

a company that has contracted with CMS to pay Part B claims.

Fiscal agent

a company that contracts with CMS to pay Medicaid claims.

Eligibility category

a category listing requirements for a person to be covered by a specific plan.

Managed care plan

a health insurance plan that includes financing, management, and delivery of health care services.

Medicaid

Medicaid is for a patient who is unable to pay for medical costs due to limited financial income. Medicaid is funded by both the federal government and state governments. Medicaid claims are paid through a fiscal agent. To become eligible for Medicaid, a person must fall into an eligibility category. Each state has its own guidelines; therefore, it is imperative to research the rules of the state in which the patient lives to become familiar with that state's Medicaid guidelines. Some states require that an eligible person register with a Medicaid managed care plan.

Managed Care Plans

Managed care plans are among the most common type of health insurance plans a biller will come across. With these health insurance plans, the patient is responsible for paying a co-payment at each provider encounter. Co-payment amounts vary within an insurance plan depending on the type of service that is provided. There is a co-payment for a primary care provider (PCP), a specialist, prescription drugs, emergency room visits, and other various procedures, treatments, and testing that may occur. Co-payment amounts may increase at the beginning of a calendar year. The patient will be sent a replacement health insurance identification card that lists the new co-payment amounts if there is a change in a co-payment amount.

The number and types of managed care plans can be overwhelming and confusing. This text helps students cover the basics of currently managed care plans seen from a billing perspective. These five plans are:

- health maintenance organization (HMO)
- preferred provider organization (PPO)
- point-of-service (POS) plan
- Medicare managed care plan
- Medicaid managed care plan

The HMO

With a health maintenance organization (HMO), the patient must remain in network for services to be covered. If the patient goes out of network to receive medical care, the patient is responsible to pay the entire cost of the services rendered.

The PPO

A preferred provider organization (PPO) is a group of providers and hospitals that offer insurance discounts to company clients in order to encourage more members. For example, if a person works for sporting goods company A, the insurance company, Sandy Sails PPO, wants sporting goods company A as a client. Sandy Sails PPO is willing to reduce the premiums and will pay for the company's employees' health insurance coverage, *if* a large number of the employees choose the Sandy Sails PPO plan and the preferred providers in it. The co-payment amount the patient pays is minimal. If the patient goes out of network, however, reimbursement by the insurance company is at a lower rate; therefore, going out of network increases the patient's out-of-pocket cost.

The POS Plan

The point-of-service (POS) plan is one in which a member can choose to stay in network and pay the designated co-payment amount, or go out of network and pay a deductible and co-insurance for the services rendered. If the patient goes out of network in a POS plan, reimbursement to the provider is still very good, and the patient's co-insurance amount is usually between 20 to 30 percent. If offered by their employer, many employees choose this type of plan because of its flexibility.

Medicare Managed Care Plans

When a person becomes eligible for Medicare benefits, that person has an option to choose a Medicare managed care plan, known as Medicare Advantage or Medicare Part C. Medicare managed care plans are offered by the same insurance companies that offer managed care plans to non-Medicare patients. When a person chooses this plan, s/he is responsible for the monthly Medicare Part B premiums. If selected, the Medicare managed care plan is the patient's primary insurance. Original Medicare is *not billed* if a patient opts for a Medicare managed care plan.

The advantages of these plans vary. Some do not charge their members monthly premiums, while others do not require the patient to obtain a referral to see a specialist or to have certain testing or procedures done. With this kind of plan, the patient does not pay a 20 percent co-insurance of the allowed amount, as required with Original Medicare, but does pay a flat co-payment for each medical encounter. This is financially beneficial to the patient who may have several procedures or services done in the office during a single visit. See Figure 2-3.

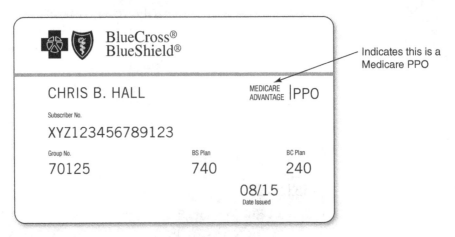

FIGURE 2-3 Sample Medicare managed care plan card.

Medicaid Managed Care Plan

Because Medicaid guidelines vary by state, it's important for the medical biller to refer to the state's rules and regulations regarding a Medicaid managed care plan. If a state requires eligible Medicaid recipients to choose from a variety of managed care plans, then the state's Medicaid website will list the managed care plans to choose from. The income guidelines determining monthly premiums and co-payment amounts will be listed as well.

Tricare

Tricare is health insurance provided for retired military personnel, active military personnel, and their dependents. There are three Tricare regions throughout the United States: West, North, and South. Tricare-eligible beneficiaries have the opportunity to choose from three Tricare plans:

* Tricare Prime
* Tricare Standard
* Tricare Extra

Tricare Prime

With the Tricare Prime plan, active-duty service members are not required to pay an enrollment fee. Medical services for this plan are given at a military treatment facility (MTF). Members receive treatment at these facilities from a Tricare-contracted civilian medical provider that is a preferred provider network (PPN). Tricare Prime members also have a POS option, as described earlier in the managed care section. If members use the POS option under this plan, there is a deductible to meet and additional charges may apply.

Tricare Prime advantages include:

* No enrollment fee for active-duty service members or their families
* Small co-payment for a visit to civilian providers and no fee for active-duty service members
* Guaranteed appointments
* Away-from-home emergency coverage
* POS option

Tricare Prime disadvantages include:

* Enrollment fee for retirees and their families
* Limited provider choice
* Specialty care by referral only
* Not universally available

Tricare Standard

The Tricare Standard plan is available only to retired military service members and their families. This plan option is considered the most flexible of the three plans. It is a fee-for-service plan that gives beneficiaries the opportunity to see any Tricare-authorized provider. The Standard plan covers most of the costs of medical care received from civilian providers when care from an MTF is unavailable.

Tricare Standard advantages include:

* Broadest choice of providers

Medicare Part C

plans run by private companies that combine coverage for both hospital and provider visits for an out-of-pocket fee.

Referral

permission from the primary care provider to seek services from a specialist for an evaluation, testing, and/or treatment. Managed care plans require this.

Tricare

health insurance provided for retired military personnel, active military personnel, and their dependents.

Tricare Prime

the only Tricare plan offering coverage for active-duty service members. Retired members may also select this plan.

Military Treatment Facility (MTF)

a place where Tricare members receive medical treatment.

Preferred Provider Network (PPN)

a group of civilian medical providers that has contracted with Tricare.

Tricare Standard

a Tricare plan available only to retired military service members and their families. This plan is available both in the United States and overseas.

- Wide availability
- No enrollment fee
- Members may also use Tricare Extra

  Tricare Standard disadvantages include:

- No primary care provider
- Members must pay a deductible and 25 percent of the allowed charges for service
- If provider is nonparticipating, members may pay an additional 15 percent of fees if the bill exceeds the allowed charges
- Members may have to file their own health insurance claims

Tricare Extra

Tricare Extra

a Tricare plan available only to retired military service members and their families. This plan is not available overseas.

Like the Standard plan, the Tricare Extra plan is also available only to retired military service members and their families. The deductible and cost-sharing rules are similar to those of the Tricare Standard plan. Tricare Extra, however, is not available overseas. This plan may also be used on a case-by-case basis by Tricare Standard members.

Tricare Extra advantages include:

- Co-payment is 5 percent less than that of Tricare Standard
- No enrollment fee
- No deductible when using a retail pharmacy network
- No form to file
- Members may also use Tricare Standard

Tricare Extra disadvantages include:

- No primary care provider
- Limited provider choice
- Patient pays deductible and co-payment
- Not universally available

Types of Coverage

Regardless of whether a patient has health insurance through a job or has to pay out of pocket for health insurance premiums, the coverage falls into one of four types:

- Individual or employee coverage
- Husband/wife or employee/significant other coverage
- Parent/child coverage
- Family coverage

Individual or Employee Coverage

Coverage

existence and scope of the existing health insurance.

Individual

the one and only person covered under a health insurance plan.

Employee

a person employed who is covered under an employer's group health plan.

Individual or employee coverage is usually for a single person. The person may or may not have a child, but if s/he does, and the child is not covered under the plan, the coverage is under an individual or employee coverage. The individual is the only person covered under the plan.

Husband/Wife or Employee/Significant Other Coverage

Husband/Wife (H/W) coverage

health insurance covering both the husband and wife.

When an individual has health insurance that covers himself and his spouse, or himself and a significant other, the coverage is called husband/wife (H/W) or employee/ significant other (E/S) coverage.

Employee/Significant other (E/S) coverage

health insurance covering the employee and the employee's significant other.

Parent/Child Coverage

Parent/Child coverage

health insurance coverage for a parent and child.

The single parent who insures both her/himself and her/his children through a health insurance plan has parent/child coverage. This coverage is very common for men who are divorced and required by the divorce decree to carry insurance coverage for their children.

Family Coverage

Family coverage

health insurance coverage for the individual employee, the employee's spouse, and the employee's children.

Dependents

persons covered under the policyholder's plan.

Family coverage is health insurance that covers the individual employee, the employee's spouse, and the employee's children. For the most part, health insurance premiums will remain the same regardless of how many children are covered or added to the policy. The only time this may not be true is in a Medicaid managed care plan. Depending on the state and the size of the family, premiums may increase as the family size increases. Most family coverage plans now include adopted children and stepchildren. Persons covered under the policyholder's plan are called dependents.

Summary

The health insurance identification card contains important information that is needed for a biller to verify a patient's health care coverage. It is always necessary to confirm current eligibility and benefits prior to a patient's visit. When the health insurance identification card is presented, a biller or receiving staff member must scan both the front and back of the card.

Because there are so many different types of health insurance plans, a biller is not expected to memorize them all. A biller is expected to know the difference between indemnity, government, and managed care plans and the difference between co-insurance and co-payment. A co-payment is a flat fee the patient pays for each provider encounter. Co-payments are used in managed care plans. Co-insurance is defined as a percentage the patient is responsible for paying at each provider visit. Co-insurance relates to indemnity plans and Original Medicare. Medicaid is for the low-income patient who has limited funds to pay for their health care expenses. Depending on the state in which a patient lives, Medicaid may require the patient to use a managed care plan. Active and retired military personnel have health insurance through Tricare. Three types of Tricare plans are offered; eligibility depends on the patient's status as active or retired military, and on family coverage.

Lastly, it's a biller's responsibility not to confuse health insurance identification cards with medical discount cards. It is wise for the provider to determine in advance whether to accept discount cards.

REVIEW QUESTIONS

1. It is not important to copy/scan both the front and back of the health insurance identification card.

   a. True
   b. False

2. A patient who has no health insurance is called a/an:

   a. self-referral
   b. indigent
   c. dependent
   d. self-pay

3. The insurance that is billed first for the patient is called:

   a. principal
   b. primary
   c. presenting
   d. none of the above

4. Another name for secondary insurance is:

   a. duplicate
   b. supplemental
   c. co-insurance
   d. primary

5. A nongovernmental plan that usually pays 80 percent and makes the patient responsible for 20 percent is called a(n) _____ plan.

   a. PPO
   b. HMO
   c. POS
   d. self-pay

6. The acronym ACA stands for:

   a. Accountable Care Association
   b. American Care Act
   c. Affordable Care Act
   d. Affordable Care Association

7. CMS stands for:

   a. Centers for Medical Supervisors
   b. Centers for Medical Services
   c. Centers for Medicare and Medicaid Services
   d. none of the above

8. The Health Information Portability and Accountability Act strongly suggests seeing _____ prior to the patient's visit with their provider.

   a. consent
   b. identification
   c. authorization
   d. photo id

9. _____ is a type of health insurance plan that allows the participant to select his or her own provider.

    a. Government plan

    b. Medicaid

    c. PPO

    d. Indemnity plan

10. Medicare Part B is for provider and _____ services.

    a. inpatient

    b. outpatient

    c. rehabilitation

    d. surgical

Chapter 3

The Codes (ICD-9, ICD-10, CPT, HCPCS Level II, and Modifiers)

Learning Objectives

Upon completion of this chapter, the student should be able to:

- Recognize an ICD-9 and ICD-10 code.
- Differentiate between a CPT code and a HCPCS national code.
- Explain modifier usage.
- Define key terms.

Key Terms

Audit	E codes	ICD-9-CM	Superbill
Codes	HCPCS	ICD-10-CM	V Codes
Current Procedural Technology (CPT)	HCPCS Modifier	Modifier	
	HCPCS National Codes	Place of Service (POS)	
CPT Modifier			

Learning a New Language

Codes

assigned letters, numbers, or a combination of both used to report procedures, services, supplies, durable medical equipment, and diagnoses.

Understanding the terms associated with medical billing is similar to learning a new language. A huge part of medical billing lingo is comprised primarily of numbers and letters called codes. These codes represent descriptions of:

- Services
- Diagnoses

- Procedures
- Supplies
- Medicine
- Durable Medical Equipment (DME)

Fluency in any language requires practice; the language of medical billing is no different.

ICD-9-CM Coding System

Volume 1 (Tabular List)

ICD-9-CM

International Classification of Diseases, 9th Revision, Clinical Modification. The ICD-9 codes are used to report diagnoses, signs, and symptoms of a patient's illness or disease.

V codes

used exclusively in ICD-9 for conditions and factors influencing a patient's health and subsequent care with a health services agency.

E codes

used exclusively in ICD-9 to explain causes of patient injuries and poisonings.

Codes in Volume 1 of the ICD-9-CM manual are listed numerically, according to diseases and disorders of the body systems. This volume also contains V codes, which are used for Supplementary Classification of Factors Influencing Health Status and Contact with Health Service Codes and E codes, which are Supplementary Classification of External Causes of Injury and Poisoning Codes. Because Volume 1 contains the fourth-digit subcategories and fifth-digit subclassification descriptions, the coder in the provider's office should always refer to this volume to be certain whether an ICD-9-CM code requires further subdivision.

V Codes (V01–V91)

V codes are assigned when a patient is seen in the office for a reason other than injury or disease. Preventive medicine for both children and adults is always designated with a V code as a diagnosis. For example, the ICD-9-CM code for a well-baby checkup is V20.2, and the ICD-9-CM code for an annual physical examination is V70.0.

E Codes (E000–E999)

E codes are assigned to describe external causes of injury, poisoning, or other adverse reactions affecting the patient's health. When a code from this section is applicable, it is intended to be used *in addition to* the main numeric ICD-9-CM code indicating the nature of the condition. This means that E codes are never listed as primary codes.

For example, a child falls while running around the bases at his baseball game. He is diagnosed with a closed fracture of the wrist (814.00). The additional E code E849.4 would follow to indicate the location where the injury occurred.

Volume 2 (Index to Diseases)

This volume of the ICD-9-CM manual is an alphabetical listing of diseases and injuries. The novice medical biller may at first experience some difficulty when looking for an ICD-9-CM code in this section, because diagnoses with more than one word are not always listed alphabetically by the first term.

For example, a patient is diagnosed with back pain. When searching in Volume 2 of the ICD-9-CM manual under the letter B, the main term "back" is located. The biller will find the following words, *"see condition."* This means that the ICD-9-CM code is listed by the condition first. In this example, the condition is "pain." Once the main term for the condition "pain" is located, the subterm is found directly under the main term. Here the ICD-9 code for back pain is 724.5.

Volume 2 of the ICD-9-CM manual is usually referenced first, followed by verifying in Volume 1 to see if the code requires further subdivision. If it does, an additional fourth or fifth digit must be included in order to accurately assign a diagnosis.

 Note: *Because this text is not an instructional coding text, information given on the ICD-9-CM, ICD-10-CM, and CPT coding manuals are very basic. To see a complete list of codes and appendices in these manuals, check with the course instructor, or visit the local library if copies are not available.*

ICD-10-CM/PCS Coding System

A new coding system called ICD-10-CM and ICD-10-PCS will replace the ICD-9-CM and ICD-9 Volume 3 coding systems in the near future. ICD-10-CM allows for code expansion in response to newly discovered diseases and treatments. It also embraces a greater level of specificity and laterality, which means that the ability to code is more specific to a body part and/or side of the body. This change is due to ICD-9-CM's inability to accommodate an increased need for updated diagnostic and procedural codes. Currently, ICD-9-CM contains 3–5 digit placeholders and over 14,000 codes. ICD-10-CM contains 3–7 character spaces and over 68,000 codes!

ICD-10-CM and ICD-10-PCS Codes

ICD-10-CM codes are used to report a patient's diagnosis and health status. ICD-10 codes can be found in ICD-10-CM and ICD-10-PCS coding manuals. The manuals are arranged in sections as follows:

ICD-10-CM

The ICD-10 codes are used to report diagnoses, signs, and symptoms of a patient's illness or disease.

* ICD-10-CM Index to Diseases and Injuries
* ICD-10-CM Tabular List of Diseases and Injuries
* ICD-10-PCS Index
* ICD-10-PCS Tables

Medical billing performed in the provider's office uses only ICD-10-CM codes. ICD-10-PCS codes are used in hospitals for procedures, and they will not be addressed in this book.

To further explain, an ICD-10-CM code book is a combination of alphanumeric code sections divided into the Index and the Tabular List. The Index contains the Index to Diseases and Injuries and the Index to External Causes of Injuries, a Neoplasm Table, and a Table of Drug and Chemicals. The Tabular List contains the alphanumeric codes and their descriptions. The first character of the code is a letter followed by numbers or alpha characters. Codes may be between three and seven characters in length. Some codes use X as a fifth character placeholder. The X allows for further expansion of codes without interrupting the six-character structure.

Superbill

a form listing CPT, HCPCS, and ICD-10 codes used to record services performed for the patient and the patient's diagnosis(es) for a given visit.

A provider's office will track patient visits and consequential diagnostic and CPT codes on a form called a **superbill** that contains the most common ICD-10-CM and CPT codes for the provider's specific practice and specialty. After a patient is seen, the provider will mark the correct diagnosis associated with the documentation that the provider has written on the patient's chart. It is critical that a definitive diagnosis is supported by provider documentation and is recorded in the patient's medical record. See Figure 3-1.

ENCOUNTER FORM

Tel: (101) 555-1111
Fax: (101) 555-2222

Kim Donaldson, M.D.
INTERNAL MEDICINE
101 Main Street, Suite A
Alfred, NY 14802

EIN: 11-9876543
NPI: 1234567890

OFFICE VISITS	NEW	EST	OFFICE PROCEDURES		INJECTIONS	
☐ Level I	99201	99211	☐ EKG with interpretation	93000	☐ Influenza virus vaccine	____
☐ Level II	99202	99212	☐ Oximetry with interpretation	94760	☐ Admin of Influenza vaccine	G0008
☐ Level III	99203	99213	**LABORATORY TESTS**		☐ Pneumococcal vaccine	90732
☐ Level IV	99204	99214	☐ Blood, occult (feces)	82270	☐ Admin of pneumococcal vaccine	G0009
☐ Level V	99205	99215	☐ Skin test, Tb, intradermal (PPD)	86580	☐ Hepatitis B vaccine	90746
					☐ Admin of Hepatitis B vaccine	G0010
					☐ Tetanus toxoid vaccine	90703
					☐ Immunization administration	90471

DIAGNOSIS

☐ Abnormal heart sounds	R00.9	☐ Chronic ischemic heart disease	I25.9	☐ Hypertension	I10
☐ Abdominal pain	R10.8_	☐ Chronic obstructive lung disease	J44.9	☐ Hormone replacement	Z79.890
☐ Abnormal feces	R19.5	☐ Congestive heart failure	I50.9	☐ Hyperlipidemia	E78.5
☐ Allergic rhinitis	J30.9	☐ Cough	R05	☐ Hyperthyroidism	E05.9_
☐ Anemia, pernicious	D51.0	☐ Depressive disorder	F32.9	☐ Influenza	J11.1
☐ Anxiety	F41.9	☐ Diabetes mellitus, type 2	E11.____	☐ Loss of weight	R63.4
☐ Asthma	J45.909	☐ Diarrhea	R19.7	☐ Nausea	R11.0
☐ Atrophy, cerebral	G31.9	☐ Dizziness	R42	☐ Nausea with vomiting	R11.2
☐ B-12 deficiency	D51.9	☐ Emphysema	J43._	☐ Pneumonia	J18._
☐ Back pain	M54.9	☐ Fatigue	R53.83	☐ Sore throat	J02.9
☐ Bronchitis	J40	☐ Fever	R50.9	☐ Vaccine, hepatitis B	Z23
☐ Cardiovascular disease	I25.1_	☐ Gastritis	K29.50	☐ Vaccine, influenza	Z23
☐ Cervicalgia	M54.2	☐ Heartburn	R12	☐ Vaccine, pneumococcus	Z23
☐ Chest pain	R07.9	☐ Hematuria	R31.9	☐ Vaccine, tetanus toxoid	Z23
☐	____	☐	____	☐	____

PATIENT IDENTIFICATION

PATIENT NAME:	
PATIENT NUMBER:	
DATE OF BIRTH:	

ENCOUNTER DATE

DATE OF SERVICE:	/ /

RETURN VISIT DATE

DATE OF RETURN VISIT:	/ /

FINANCIAL TRANSACTION DATA

INVOICE NO.	
ACCOUNT NO.	
TOTAL FOR SERVICE:	$
AMOUNT RECEIVED:	$
PAID BY:	☐ Cash ☐ Check ☐ Credit Card
CASHIER'S INITIALS:	

FIGURE 3-1 Sample superbill using ICD-10-CM codes.

When reviewing diagnosis codes, the Diagnosic Coding and Reporting Guidelines for Outpatient Services, found in the beginning of an ICD-10 coding book, are important guidelines for correct diagnostic coding practices. The ICD-10 codes are updated October 1 of each year. While it is unnecessary to memorize the ICD-10 codes, it is very important to know and understand the coding guidelines, and how to look up a code. Some offices may have encoders, which are automated coding software programs, which a biller may also have to learn as a new employee.

Current Procedural Terminology (CPT) Coding System

Current Procedural Technology (CPT)

codes used to report services and procedures. These are level I codes under HCPCS.

Current Procedural Terminology (CPT) codes, also known as *level I codes*, are five-digit numeric codes. They are used to describe procedures and services provided by a health care professional. These codes are used in conjunction with the diagnostic codes previously explained in order to communication what has happened during a patient's visits, and any consequential treatment. Used together, these codes are submitted to a contracted payor for reimbursement.

Like the ICD-9-CM and the ICD-10-CM manuals, the CPT manual contains an index and a table of contents for the following services and procedures:

- Evaluation and Management (E/M) (99201–99499)
- Anesthesia (00100–01999, 99100–99140, 00100–01999)
- Surgery (10021–69990)
- Radiology (70010–79999)
- Pathology and Laboratory (81099–88299, 88399–88398, 80047–89398)
- Medicine (90281–91299, 92002–92014, 92015–92140, 99225–99607)

Evaluation and management (E/M) codes are "visit" codes that are used extensively in outpatient settings. Billers may encounter these codes and need to identify a New versus Established patient, which quantifies the amount of time and resources used to help diagnose and treat a patient's concern. Other things that billers should be aware of is the place of services, such as office or hospital, and the type of visit, such as office visit or inpatient admissions. These codes are very important to providers. Their reimbursement can be impacted by incorrect coding practices.

Anesthesia codes are used primarily by anesthesiologists who perform procedures in an ambulatory surgery center or in a hospital operating room.

The surgery section of the CPT book is divided into subsections based on body systems, and while many of the procedures indicated are performed in an ambulatory surgery center or hospital operating room, some of the procedures may be performed in a provider's office.

Radiology CPT codes are used for diagnostic and screening exams such as x-rays, ultrasound, MRI, CT scans, and mammography. Additionally, they may be used for administration of contrast materials used in conjunction with MRI or CT scans. These CPT codes are also used for radiation treatment management.

Pathology and Laboratory are used for any specimen, or disease-oriented testing. This may include testing for drugs, diseases, or in reproductive medicine.

The Medicine section contains many services. Some examples of services included in the medicine section are immunizations, vaccinations, psychiatry, dialysis, ophthalmology, and cardiovascular.

The CPT manual containing these codes is updated and published every year on January 1 by the American Medical Association.

Modifiers

There are occasions in medical billing when a code description does not contain all of the information needed to describe the service completely. When specific or additional information is needed to be able to accurately bill with a CPT or

HCPCS

a coding system used to report procedures, services, supplies, medicine, and durable medical equipment. Comprised of CPT (level I) and national (level II) codes.

Modifier

a two-character alphabetic, numeric, or alphanumeric descriptor used to signify that a procedure or service has been altered by an unusual or specific circumstance, although the code itself has not changed. Additional use includes referencing a specific body site.

CPT modifier

a two-character numeric descriptor used only with CPT codes.

HCPCS national code, a CPT or HCPCS modifier may be added to the CPT or HCPCS codes. In these instances, the medical biller must attach a modifier to the appropriate code.

Modifiers are used when:

- A service or procedure has a technical component
- A service or procedure has a professional component
- A service or procedure was performed by more than one provider
- A service or procedure was increased or reduced
- Only part of a service was performed
- An additional service was performed
- A bilaterial procedure was performed more than once
- Referencing a specific body site
- Unusual events occurred

CPT Modifiers

It is extremely important that the medical biller use the most accurate CPT modifier in a given situation. Incorrect modifier usage can result in denial of the claim or, worse, an audit by the insurance company. Each provider's office should have a CPT manual on hand for the medical biller to refer to. See Table 3-1.

TABLE 3-1 CPT Modifiers

22	Unusual procedural service—Surgeries for which services performed are significantly greater than usually required; may be billed with the 22 modifier added to the CPT code. Include a concise statement about how the service differs from the usual. Supportive documentation (e.g., operative reports, pathology reports, etc.) must be submitted with the claim.
23	Unusual anesthesia.
24	Unrelated evaluation and management (E&M) service by the same provider during a postoperative period.
25	Significant, separately identifiable E&M service by the same provider on the same day of the procedure or other therapeutic service that has a 0- to 10-day global period. A separate diagnosis is not needed. This modifier is used on the E&M service.
26	Professional component—Certain procedures that are combined with a provider's professional component may be identified by adding the modifier 26 to the usual procedure number. All diagnostic testing with a technical or professional component, whether done in an outpatient or inpatient setting, must reflect the 26 modifier. The fiscal intermediary (Part A Medicare) will reimburse the facility for the technical component.
50	Bilateral procedure—*Bilateral services* are procedures performed on both sides of the body during the same operative session or on the same day. Medicare will approve 150 percent of the fee-schedule amount for those services.
51	Multiple procedures—For internal use by carrier only.
52	Reduced services—Use modifier 52 (reduced service) to indicate a service or procedure that was partially reduced or eliminated at the provider's election. If claims are submitted electronically with modifier 52, the insurer or payor will request medical records from the provider before processing the claims.
53	Discontinued procedure—Under certain circumstances, the provider may elect to terminate a surgical or diagnostic procedure. Due to extenuating circumstances, or those that threaten the well-being of the patient, it may be necessary to indicate that a surgical or diagnostic procedure was started but discontinued. If claims are

Continues

TABLE 3-1 CPT Modifiers (Continued)	
	submitted electronically with modifier 53, the insurer or payor will request medical records from the provider before processing the claims. One of the most common examples of the use of modifier 53 is when an incomplete colonoscopy is performed. Add modifier 53 to CPT code 45378. No documentation is required (this is an exception to the rule).
54	Surgical care only—When one provider performs a surgical procedure and another provider provides preoperative and/or postoperative management, the surgical service should be identified by adding modifier 54 to the usual procedure code.
55	Postoperative management only—Used for a provider's postoperative services when one provider performs the postoperative management and another provider has performed the surgical procedure.
57	Initial decision for surgery (90-day global period)—This modifier is used on E&M service, the day before or the day of surgery, to exempt it from the global surgery package.
58	Staged or related procedure or service by the same provider during the postoperative period—If a less extensive procedure fails and a more extensive procedure is required, the second procedure is payable separately. Modifier 58 must be reported with the second procedure.
59	Distinct procedural service—The provider may need to indicate that a procedure or service was distinct or separate from other services performed on the same day. This may represent a different session or patient encounter, different procedure or surgery, different site, separate lesion, or separate injury. However, when another already established modifier is appropriate, it should be used rather than modifier 59.
62	Two surgeons (co-surgery)—Under certain circumstances, the skills of two surgeons (usually different skills) may be required in the management of a specific surgical procedure. Adding modifier 62 to the procedure code used by each surgeon should identify the separate service.
66	Surgical team—Under some circumstances, highly complex procedures requiring the accompanying services of several providers, often of different specialties, plus other highly skilled or specially trained personnel, and also various types of complex equipment, are carried out under the surgical team concept. Claims with modifier 66 cannot be processed without a copy of the operative report.
73	Discontinued outpatient hospital/ambulatory surgery center (ASC) procedure prior to the administration of anesthesia.
74	Discontinued outpatient hospital/ambulatory surgery center (ASC) procedure after administration of anesthesia.
76	Repeat procedure by same provider—Indicate the reason or the different times for the repeat procedure in item 19 of the CMS-1500 form or the electronic equivalent.
77	Repeat procedure by another provider—Indicate the reason or the different times for the repeat procedure in item 19 of the CMS-1500 form or the electronic equivalent.
78	Return to the operating room for a related procedure during the postoperative period—The provider may need to indicate that another procedure was performed during the postoperative period of the initial procedure. When this subsequent procedure is related to the first, and requires use of the operating room, it should be reported by adding modifier 78 to the related procedure.
79	Unrelated procedure or service by the same provider during the postoperative period—The provider may need to indicate that the performance of a procedure or service during the postoperative period was unrelated to the original procedure.
80	Assistant surgeon—Add modifier 80 to the usual procedure in a nonteaching setting to identify surgical assistant services.
82	Assistant surgeon when qualified resident surgeon not available in a teaching setting.

Continues

TABLE 3-1 CPT Modifiers (Continued)

90	Reference (outside) laboratory—When laboratory procedures are performed by a party other than the treating or reporting provider, the procedure may be identified by adding the modifier 90 to the usual procedure number. For the Medicare program, this modifier is used by independent clinical laboratories when referring tests to a reference laboratory for analysis.
91	Repeat clinical diagnostic lab tests performed on same day to obtain subsequent reportable test value(s)—This modifier is used to report a separate specimen(s) taken at a separate encounter.
99	The Multi-Carrier System (MCS) now allows the biller to send up to four modifiers per line of service on claims, for both electronically submitted and paper claims. Please indicate the pricing modifiers in the first two positions and processing or informational modifiers in the third and fourth positions. Use modifier 99 when more than four modifiers are needed on a line of service. In situations that require five or more modifiers, indicate modifier 99 in the first modifier field on the line of service and enter the remaining modifiers in the narrative field of an EMC claim or item 19 of a CMS-1500 claim form. For example: 79, RT, LT, QU, GA—99 in the first modifier field on the line of service, and 79, RT, LT, QU, GA in the narrative field of an EMC claim or item 19 of a CMS-1500 claim form.

Audit

a formal examination of an individual's or organization's accounts.

HCPCS national codes

alphanumeric codes used to identify categories not included in HCPCS level I codes. These codes are considered level II codes.

HCPCS modifier

a two-character alphabetic or alphanumeric descriptor used with both CPT level I and level II national codes.

HCPCS National Coding System

HCPCS national codes, or *level II codes*, are five-digit alphanumeric codes. The codes always begin with a letter followed by four numbers. Level II codes cover:

- Supplies
- Durable medical equipment
- Materials
- Injections/drugs
- Services

The **HCPCS modifier** can be used with both a CPT level I and level II national code. It is in this list of modifiers that the biller will find reference to specific body sites. See Table 3-2.

TABLE 3-2 HCPCS Modifiers

AA	Anesthesia services personally furnished by an anesthesiologist.
AD	Medical supervision by provider: more than four concurrent anesthesia services.
AQ	Provider providing a service in a health professional shortage area (HPSA) (for dates of service on or after January 1, 2006).
AR	Provider providing services in a provider scarcity area.
AS	Provider assistant, nurse practitioner, or clinical nurse specialist service for assistant at surgery.
AT	Acute or chronic active/corrective treatment (effective October 1, 2004).
CB	Services ordered by a dialysis-facility provider as part of the ESRD (end-stage renal disease) beneficiary's dialysis benefit; this is not part of the composite rate and is separately reimbursable.
CC	Procedure code change (the carrier uses CC when the procedure code submitted was changed either for administrative reasons or because an incorrect code was filed).

Continues

TABLE 3-2   HCPCS Modifiers (Continued)

CR	Catastrophe-/disaster-related.
EJ	Subsequent claim for EPO (epoetin alfa) course of therapy.
E1	Upper left, eyelid.
E2	Lower left, eyelid.
E3	Upper right, eyelid.
E4	Lower right, eyelid.
FA	Left hand, thumb.
F1	Left hand, second digit.
F2	Left hand, third digit.
F3	Left hand, fourth digit.
F4	Left hand, fifth digit.
F5	Right hand, thumb.
F6	Right hand, second digit.
F7	Right hand, third digit.
F8	Right hand, fourth digit.
F9	Right hand, fifth digit.
GA	Advance Beneficiary Notification on file.
GC	This service has been performed in part by a resident under the direction of a teaching provider.
GE	This service has been performed by a resident without the presence of a teaching provider, under the primary care exception.
GG	Performance and payment of screening mammogram and diagnostic mammogram on the same patient, same day (effective for dates of service on or after January 1, 2002).
GJ	"OPT OUT" provider or practitioner emergency or urgent service.
GM	Multiple patients on one ambulance trip.
GN	Service delivered under an outpatient speech-language pathology plan of care.
GO	Service delivered under an outpatient occupational therapy plan of care.
GP	Service delivered under an outpatient physical therapy plan of care.
GQ	Via asynchronous telecommunications system.
GT	Via interactive audio and video telecommunications system.
GV	Attending provider not employed or paid under arrangement by the patient's hospice provider (effective for dates of service on or after January 1, 2002).

Continues

TABLE 3-2 HCPCS Modifiers (Continued)

GW	Service not related to the hospice patient's terminal condition (effective for dates of service on or after January 1, 2002).
GY	Item or service statutorily excluded or does not meet the definition of any Medicare benefit.
GZ	Item or service expected to be denied as not reasonable and necessary and Advance Beneficiary Notification has not been signed.
J1	Competitive acquisition program (CAP) no-pay submission for a prescription number.
J2	CAP restocking of emergency drugs after emergency administration.
J3	CAP drug not available through CAP as written; reimbursed under average sales price methodology.
KD	Infusion drugs furnished through implanted durable medical equipment (effective January 1, 2004).
KX	Claims for therapy services that have exceeded therapy caps (either by automatic exception or by approved request), for which specific required documentation is on file.
KZ	New coverage not implemented by managed care.
LC	Left circumflex coronary artery.
LD	Left anterior descending coronary artery.
LR	Laboratory round trip.
LT	Left side (use to identify procedures performed on the LEFT side of the body).
QA	FDA investigational device exemption.
QB	Provider providing service in a rural HPSA.
QC	Single-channel monitoring (recording device for Holter monitoring).
QD	Recording and storage in solid-state memory by a digital recorder (digital recording/storage for Holter monitoring).
QJ	Services/items provided to a prisoner or patient in state or local custody. However, the state or local government, as applicable, meets the requirements in 42 C.F.R. § 411.4.
QK	Medical direction of two, three, or four concurrent anesthesia procedures involving qualified individuals.
QL	Patient pronounced dead after ambulance called.
QP	Documentation is on file showing that the laboratory test(s) was ordered individually or ordered as a CPT-recognized panel other than automated profile codes.
QR	Services that are covered under a clinical study/trial.
QS	Monitored anesthesia care service.

Continues

TABLE 3-2 HCPCS Modifiers (Continued)

QT	Recording and storage on tape by an analog tape recorder.
QU	Provider providing services in an urban HPSA (for dates of service prior to January 1, 2006).
QV	Item or service provided as routine care in a Medicare qualifying clinical trial.
QW	CLIA waived test.
QX	Certified registered nurse anesthetist (CRNA) service with medical direction by a provider.
QY	Medical direction of one CRNA by an anesthesiologist.
QZ	CRNA service without medical direction by a provider.
Q3	Live kidney donor surgery and related services.
Q5	Service furnished by a substitute provider under a reciprocal billing arrangement.
Q6	Service furnished by a locum tenens provider.
Q7	One class "A" finding.
Q8	Two class "B" findings. Class "B" findings: Absent posterior tibial pulse; advanced tropic changes (hair growth, nail changes, pigmentary changes, or skin texture—three required); absent dorsalis pedis pulse.
Q9	One class "B" and two class "C" findings. Class "C" findings: Claudication; temperature changes, edema, paresthesias; burning.
RC	Right coronary artery.
RT	Right side (use to identify procedures performed on the RIGHT side of the body).
SG	Ambulatory surgical center (ASC) facility charges. This modifier is used only by the ASC for identifying the facility charge. It should not be reported by the provider when reporting the provider's professional service rendered in an ASC.
TA	Left foot, great toe.
T1	Left foot, second digit.
T2	Left foot, third digit.
T3	Left foot, fourth digit.
T4	Left foot, fifth digit.
T5	Right foot, great toe.
T6	Right foot, second digit.
T7	Right foot, third digit.
T8	Right foot, fourth digit.
T9	Right foot, fifth digit.

Continues

TABLE 3-2 HCPCS Modifiers (Continued)

TC	Technical component. Under certain circumstances, a charge may be made for the technical component of a diagnostic test only. Under those circumstances, the technical component charge is identified by adding modifier TC to the usual procedure number.
TS	Pre-diabetic screening is paid twice within a rolling 12-month period. Second screening should be billed with TS modifier.
UN	Transportation of portable X-rays, two patients served (effective January 1, 2004).
UP	Transportation of portable X-rays, three patients served (effective January 1, 2004).
UQ	Transportation of portable X-rays, four patients served (effective January 1, 2004).
UR	Transportation of portable X-rays, five patients served (effective January 1, 2004).
US	Transportation of portable X-rays, six or more patients served (effective January 1, 2004).

See Table 3-3 for a sample of HCPCS level II DME codes, and Table 3-4 for a sample of HCPCS level II injection codes.

- An additional service was performed
- A bilateral procedure was performed more than once
- Referencing a specific body site
- Unusual events occurred

TABLE 3-3 Sample of HCPCS Level II DME Codes

HCPCS Code	Description
AMBULATION DEVICES	
Canes and Crutches	
A4635	Underarm pad, crutch, replacement, each
A4636	Replacement handgrip, cane, crutch, or walker, each
A4637	Replacement tip, cane, crutch, or walker, each
E0100	Cane; includes canes of all materials, adjustable or fixed, with tip
E0105	Cane, quad or three-prong; includes canes of all materials, adjustable or fixed, with tips
E0111	Crutch, forearm; includes crutches of various materials, adjustable or fixed, each, with tip and handgrips
E0113	Crutch, underarm, wood, adjustable or fixed, each, with pad, tip, and handgrip
E0116	Crutch, underarm, other than wood, adjustable or fixed, each, with pad, tip, and handgrip
E0117	Crutch, underarm, articulating, spring-assisted, each

Continues

TABLE 3-3 Sample of HCPCS Level II DME Codes (Continued)

Walkers

E0130	Rigid (pick-up), adjustable or fixed height
E0135	Folding (pick-up), adjustable or fixed height
E0144	Enclosed, framed folding walker, wheeled, with posterior seat
E0147	Heavy-duty, multiple-braking-system, variable-wheel-resistance walker
E0148	Walker, heavy-duty, without wheels, rigid or folding, any type, each
E0149	Walker, heavy-duty, wheeled, rigid or folding, any type, each
E0155	Wheel attachment, rigid pick-up walker, per pair
E0159	Brake attachment for wheeled walker, replacement, each

BATHROOM EQUIPMENT

E0163	Commode chair, mobile or stationary, with fixed arms
E0165	Commode chair, mobile or stationary, with detachable arms
E0167	Pail or pan for use with commode chair, replacement only

TABLE 3-4 Sample of HCPCS Level II Injection Codes

J1460	Gamma globulin, intramuscular, 1 cc, injection
J1470	Gamma globulin, intramuscular, 2 cc, injection
J9999	Abarelix, 100 mg, injection (Plenaxis)
J0128	Abarelix, 10 mg, injection (Plenaxis)
J0130	Abciximab, 10 mg, injection (ReoPro)
J1120	Acetazolamide sodium, up to 500 mg, injection (Diamox)
J0133	Acyclovir, 5 mg, injection
J0150	Adenosine, 6 mg, injection (not to be used to report any adenosine phosphate compounds; instead use A9270) (Adenocard)
J0152	Adenosine, 30 mg, injection (not to be used to report any adenosine phosphate compounds; use A9270)
J0180	Agalsidase beta, 1 mg, injection (Fabrazyme)
J9015	Aldesleukin, per single-use vial (Proleukin, etc.)
J0215	Alefacept, 0.5 mg, injection (Amevive)
J9010	Alemtuzumab, 10 mg, injection (Campath)
J0205	Alglucerase, per 10 units, injection (Ceredase)
J2997	Alteplase recombinant, 1 mg, injection (Activase)

Continues

TABLE 3-4	Sample of HCPCS Level II Injection Codes (Continued)
J0278	Amicacin sulfate, 100 mg, injection
J0207	Amifostine, 500 mg, injection (Ethyol)
J0280	Aminophylline, up to 250 mg, injection
J1320	Amitriptyline HCl, up to 20 mg, injection (Elavil, Enovil)
J0300	Amobarbital, up to 125 mg, injection (Amytal)
J0285	Amphotericin B, 50 mg, injection
J0288	Amphotericin B cholesteryl sulfate complex, 10 mg, injection (Amphotee)
J0287	Amphotericin B lipid complex, 10 mg, injection
J0289	Amphotericin B liposome, 10 mg, injection (Ambisome)
J0290	Ampicillin sodium, 500 mg, injection (Omnipen-N, Totacillin-N)
J0295	Ampicillin sodium/sulbactam sodium, per 1.5 g, injection (Unasyn)
J0350	Anistreplase, per 30 units, injection (Eminase)
J7197	Antithrombin III (human), per IU (Throbate III, ATnativ)
J0395	Arbutamine HCl, 1 mg, injection
J9017	Arsenic trioxide, 1 mg, injection (Trisenox)
J9020	Asparaginase, 10,000 units (Elspar)
J9025	Azacitidine, 1 mg, injection (Vidaza)
J0456	Azithromycin, 500 mg, injection (Zithromax)

Place of Service

Place of Service (POS)

location where service was provided to a patient. This information is used for billing purposes.

Place of service (POS) codes are usually located on the first page inside the CPT manual. These codes indicate the location that the service was provided; an example of this is an office visit, which would have a place of service of 11.

It takes many years of practice to be an expert biller and coder. There are many other books that explain coding and billing to a greater level of specificity. Because this text is not an instructional coding text, information given on the CPT and ICD-10 coding is very basic. To see a complete list of codes and appendices in these manuals, visit online the Centers for Medicare Studies, for additional information.

A Word about Fraud

Fraud is a word that no one wants to hear. But, as a medical biller, it is important to be aware of fraud and to be alert for the most common signs of fraud. Most important, when seeing fraud occur, it's critical to know where to go for help. Fraud appears in many forms. Up-coding is assigning a code because of higher reimbursement. Unbundling codes is assigning an individual code for everything done in a procedure when there is only one code warranted. Billing for services that were not done, or even undercoding, can signal potential problems. The Office of Inspector General (OIG) is the health care watchdog. Every year, they create a work plan that determines specific codes and/or modifiers to be on the lookout for. They then visit providers across the United States in order to review coding, documentation, and billing practices. If the OIG finds fraud, fines and imprisonment may occur. If there is any suspicion of fraud in a workplace, it's important to take this information to a trusted manager or supervisor. They will help determine if there is a problem, and how to take care of it.

Summary

The novice medical biller must practice the language of codes repeatedly to become proficient, and use the correct codes consistently and accurately. The three types of codes used by the provider-based medical biller include ICD-9-CM or ICD-10-CM, CPT, and HCPCS Level II codes. ICD-9-CM and ICD-10-CM codes are used to describe the sign or symptom the patient is experiencing. CPT and HCPCS national level II codes are used to determine what was done *to* and *for* the patient (office visits, medicine, supplies, and so on).

It is not the medical biller's job to assign ICD-9-CM or ICD-10-CM, CPT, or HCPCS codes; the provider or the coder will complete this specialized task. However, it is important for the medical biller to become familiar with all of the coding manuals, including CPT and HCPCS modifiers. It is the medical biller's job to attach these modifiers when needed in specific billing scenarios. Accurate use of codes and modifiers when billing reduces the chance of the provider's office being audited by an insurance company, or worse, the Office of Inspector General.

REVIEW QUESTIONS

1. Numbers, letters, or a combination of both describing procedures, services, and diagnoses are called ___.

2. The coding system used to report procedures, services, supplies, medicine, and durable medical equipment is called:
    a. ICD-10-CM
    b. HCPCS
    c. level II
    d. none of the above

3. The coding manual that includes Evaluation and Management codes (99201–99499) is the ___ manual.

4. A durable medical equipment code is called a ___ or ___ code.

5. Five-digit numeric codes are called ___ codes.

6. A modifier is a ___ character ___, ___, or ___ descriptor.

7. Give four examples of modifier usage.

8. Two types of modifiers are ___ and ____.

9. The ___ modifier can be used with either a CPT or a national code.

10. A code used to report a diagnosis is called a(n) ___or _____ code.

11. Which volume of the ICD-9-CM manual is listed alphabetically?

12. Codes used to report external causes of injury are called ___ codes.

13. Accurate coding reduces the risk of a(n) ___ by an insurance company.

14. What does the accronym OIG stand for?

15. ICD-10-CM embraces a greater level of _____ and _____.

Chapter 4

The Forms (Patient Registration, Superbill, and Hospital Sheet)

Learning Objectives

Upon completion of this chapter, the student should be able to:

- Describe the use of various forms in the office.
- Decipher data from the superbill and hospital sheet.
- Explain the importance of a completed patient registration form.
- Define key terms.

Key Terms

Admit	Consultation	Hospital Billing Sheet	Protected Health
Admit/Discharge	Established	New Patient	Information (PHI)
Sheet	Patient	Patient Registration	Superbill
Authorization	Follow-up Visit	Form	

Patient Registration Form

Patient registration form

a form used to gather all patient information, including demographics and insurance information.

When a new patient comes into your office to obtain care, he will be asked to release some information about himself to begin a smooth transition through your facility. The patient will need to completely fill out the patient registration form, which is a form used to gather all patient information, including demographics and insurance information. There are many types and brands of patient registration forms available on the market; each one can be geared to specific details for your provider's office, which could include topics such as allergies or referrals. (See Figure 4-1 for one example.)

There are three key elements to each registration form, the patient's demographics, guarantor, and health insurance information. The demographics are the statistical information about a patient, like name, address, and date of birth. The guarantor information section of the form tells who is responsible financially for the patient's account. The health insurance information section lists primary and secondary insurance policies and names the primary policyholders on each insurance plan the patient has. A new patient, who has never been seen before, or who has not been seen in the past 36 months, will need to give detailed information so that your office can best meet the patient's health care requirements. The established patient, who has been seen in the past 36 months, needs only to review previous personal information for any changes. Be sure you photocopy the front and back of the patient's health insurance card for accurate billing. It is very important to encourage the patient to fill out the patient registration form as completely as possible. A completed form will provide more contact information, which will save you a lot of time if insurance eligibility questions arise.

Authorization to Release Protected Health Information

The information a patient gives you on the registration form or relays to the provider during the health care encounter is confidential and is required by law to be protected. The patient will need to sign an authorization, which is a patient's signed approval to release their protected health information (PHI) for billing the health insurance company. If the patient is a minor, the authorization can be signed by a parent or guardian. The authorization can be printed on the bottom of the patient registration form or it can be an additional form given to the patient at registration. This authorization is signed only once, and remains in the patient's medical chart.

HIPAA Release

Offices will also have a new patient sign a variety of Health Insurance Portability and Accountability Act (HIPAA) forms. These will include a form regarding the office's privacy policies and a form asking the patient to whom their medical information may be released in case of an emergency, including names, relationship to the patient, and telephone numbers. Some offices update these forms at the beginning of the calendar year, in case the patient wishes to change the previous information.

The Superbill

The superbill, also called an encounter form, is used to record services performed for a patient during a given visit (see Figure 4-2). The superbill contains the patient's name, date of service, any insurance co-pays that need to be satisfied for the visit, and a list of procedural (CPT), HCPCS, and diagnostic, (ICD-9 or ICD-10) codes used specifically by that office or provider's specialty. As an example, a superbill for a cardiologist would list only CPT and ICD-9 or ICD-10 codes relating to the heart and its function, whereas a family practice superbill will have codes for the many different body systems listed.

The provider is usually responsible for completing the superbill after a patient has been seen in the office. This process includes checking off the level of office visit, which is the CPT evaluation and management level (E/M code), procedures (if any), and any diagnosis for that patient on a given day. Some offices, particularly large group practices, may employ

New patient

a patient who has never been seen before, or who has not been seen in the past 36 months.

Established patient

a patient who has been seen in the past 36 months.

Authorization

a patient's signed approval for the medical office to use the PHI for billing purposes when submitting a health insurance claim to the insurance company.

Protected Health Information (PHI)

any information that identifies a patient, including age, sex, ethnicity or demographics, or describes his or her health status.

Superbill

a form listing CPT, HCPCS, and ICD-9 codes used to record services performed for the patient and the patient's diagnosis(es) for a given visit.

Practice Name
PATIENT REGISTRATION

Welcome to our office. In order to serve you properly, we will need the following information. **(Please Print)**
All information will be strictly confidential.

Patient's Name	Sex M F	Birth Date ____/____/____ Age_____	Marital Status Single [ ] Married [ ] Widowed [ ] Divorced [ ]

Residence address City State Zip	Home Phone:	Patient's Social Security #

Person financially responsible for this account	Self Spouse Parent	Responsible Party's Birthdate ____/____/____	Responsible Party's Social Security #

Responsible Party Drivers License # State: Number	Occupation	How Long at current Employer?

Credit Card: Number: Type [ ] Mastercard [ ] Visa [ ] Discover	Expiration Date:	Name On Card

Name of employer Address	Business Phone	Occupation

Name of Spouse/Parent	Birth date	Social security #	Business phone

Reason for Visit:	Referred by: (include address and phone)

Person to contact in case of emergency:	Relationship to patient	Phone

Medicare Yes [ ]
            No [ ]
	Medicare #	Medicaid Yes [ ]
		            No [ ]
			Medicaid #	Effective Date

Medicare Secondary insurance name Address	Policy #	Group #

Workers' Yes [ ] Motor Yes [ ] Compensation? No [ ] Vehicle? No [ ] **If Yes-put W/C or MVA carrier below**	Date of Accident	Treatment authorized by	Claim #	W/C or MVA Insurance Phone #

Primary insurance company Address	Is insurance through your employer?

Subscriber Name	Subscriber birth date	Policy #	Group #

Secondary insurance name Address	Policy #	Group #

Medicare Lifetime Signature on File:
I request that payment of authorized Medicare benefits be made on my behalf to Practice Name for any services furnished me by the physician. I authorize any holder of medical information about me to release to the Health Care Financing Administration and its agents any Information to determine these benefits payable for related services

_____   _____
            Patient Signature   Date

Private Insurance Authorization for Assignment of Benefits/Information Release:
I, the undersigned authorize payment of medical benefits to Practice Name for any services furnished me by the physician. I understand that I am financially responsible for any amount not covered by my contract. I also authorize you to release to my insurance company or their agent information concerning health care, advice, treatment or supplies provided to me. This information will be used for the purpose of evaluating and administering claims of benefits.

_____   _____
Patient, Parent or Guardian Signature (if child is under 18 years old)   Date

FIGURE 4-1 Sample patient registration form.

Office Codes

New Pt	Established Pt	Consult
_____99201	_____99211	_____99241
_____99202	_____99212	_____99242
_____99203	_____99213	_____99243
_____99204	_____99214	_____99244
_____99205	_____99215	_____99245

CPT Codes

_____93000 EKG	_____85014 Hemocult
_____36415 Venipuncture	_____J3420 Vitamin B-12 injection
_____71010 Chest X-ray, single view	_____J1030 Depo-Medrol
_____69210 Cerumen removal	_____87070 Throat culture
_____99000 Specimen handling	_____90471 Immunization admin
_____81002 Urinalysis	_____11200 Skin tag removal

ICD-9 Codes

_____789.00 Abdominal pain	_____V70.0 Routine visit
_____477.9 Allergies	_____784.0 Headache
_____285.9 Anemia	_____401.1 Hypertension
_____427.9 Arrhythmia	_____458.9 Hypotension
_____466.0 Bronchitis, acute	_____272.4 Hyperlipidemia
_____436 Cardiovascular accident	_____410.91 Myocardial infarction
_____414.00 Coronary artery disease	_____382.90 Otitis media
_____250.00 DM–controlled	_____462 Pharyngitis
_____782.3 Edema	_____482 Pneumonitis
_____780.79 Fatigue	_____461.9 Sinusitis
_____530.81 GERD	_____599.0 Urinary tract infection

Name _____   Date _____
Prim ins _____   Sec ins _____
Self-pay _____   Co-pay _____   Pd-ck _____   Chg _____   Cash _____

FIGURE 4-2   Sample superbill.

a coder, whose job it is to assign billing codes based on the provider's documentation in the medical chart, and/or to add codes not listed on the superbill, if needed.

Hospital Billing

Admit

term used when the patient is checked in to the hospital.

Follow-up visit

subsequent visit made by the provider following an admission.

Consultation

term used when a provider calls upon another provider to evaluate and make an assessment on a patient in the hospital setting.

The medical biller is responsible for submitting health insurance claims, not only for patients seen in the office, but also for patients who are seen by the provider in the hospital. These visits include admits, follow-up visits, consultations, and discharges. The hospital billing sheet or an admit/discharge sheet lists the evaluation and management CPT codes used for the provider's visits for each day the patient was in the hospital, as well as insurance information and a space for noting the patient's diagnosis. The hospital sheet usually will not list ICD-9 or ICD-10 codes; therefore, the provider will either write in the ICD-9 or ICD-10 codes or write out the diagnosis for the coder to assign. (See Figure 4-3.) The hospital billing sheet is much more convenient to use for an inpatient stay because there is only one form for the month instead of a

Name _____							Date Admitted _____								Date Discharged _____														

Month _____   Year _____   Patient's Insurance _____

01	02	03	04	05	06	07	08	09	10	11	12	13	14	15	16	17	18	19	20	21	22	23	24	25	26	27	28	29	30	31	CPT Codes
																															99221
																															99222
																															99223
																															99231
																															99232
																															99233
																															99251
																															99252
																															99253
																															99254
																															99255
																															99238
																															99239

Diagnosis(es)

1 _____
2 _____
3 _____
4 _____

FIGURE 4-3 Sample hospital billing sheet.

Hospital billing sheet

form used by the provider to record hospital codes for inpatient visits.

Admit/discharge sheet

a sheet generated by the hospital listing all patient information, including demographics and insurance information.

separate encounter form to fill out for each day, which would happen if a billing office used the patient registration form designed for a provider's office.

The admit/discharge sheet (see Figure 4-4) is similar to the office version of the patient registration form. It includes patient demographics, insurance information and the names of providers involved with admitting and attending the patient. Some providers will attach the hospital billing sheet directly to the admit/discharge sheet. Other providers will write the CPT and ICD-9 or ICD-10 codes directly on the admit/discharge sheet, and the medical biller will gather claims submission information directly from these sheets. Regardless of how your provider prepares hospital billing, the codes will be the same for an inpatient visit as an outpatient visit.

Nursing Home Visits

If the provider you are billing for visits patients who live in nursing homes, you will submit claims for these visits and services also. There are special evaluation and management CPT codes for nursing home visits that differ from those listed on your superbill or hospital sheet. Your office may have a special encounter sheet designed for these visits, or the provider may use an admit/discharge sheet from the nursing home and write the CPT codes directly on that sheet.

Home Visits

Home visits to a patient are rare these days, but you may nonetheless end up working for a provider who performs them. Again, check your CPT book for the set of evaluation and management codes made just for home visits. A provider who performs home visits will most likely have these codes listed on the superbill or encounter form used in the office.

MedRec#:22-000478

Admit Date_____ Discharge Date_____
Physician Signature_____

Patient Name: Admit Date and Time:

Address: Discharge Date and Time:

City: State: Zip code: Phone#:

Soc sec#:   Date of Birth: Sex: M/S:

Emp. Status:

Emp. Address:

Guarantor Name: Rel: DOB:

Soc sec#:   Address:

Phone:

Insurance #1:   ID#:   Gr#:

Insured: Rel to patient:

Insurance #2:   ID#:   Gr#:

Insured: Rel to patient:

Admitting Physician: Attending Physician:

Admitting Diagnosis:
Comments:

Principal Diagnosis: Procedures:
Secondary Diagnosis:

ABC Hospital
125 Rt 70
Brick, NJ 08724

FIGURE 4-4   Sample admit/discharge sheet.

Frequency of Billing

The frequency with which an office submits health insurance claims can vary. Some medical billers submit claims on a daily basis, while others may submit once or twice per week. It is important for the coder or medical biller to understand the billing process and procedures in their facility. If working for a medical billing company, the biller will most likely receive the assigned work for the provider accounts to process on a weekly basis. If you work for a provider working in a hospital, you might get billing forms on a daily basis after hospital rounds are complete. Remember, the biller will not bill for the patient's entire stay at the hospital, but for each day the patient is seen by the provider.

Summary

Although the medical biller must become familiar with many forms, three very important ones are the patient registration form, the superbill, and the hospital sheet, if working in a hospital setting. It is appropriate to emphasize to the front-desk staff the importance of a completed registration form to eliminate trying to obtain needed data after the fact. The CPT codes listed on the superbill will vary from those on the hospital sheet or admit/discharge sheet. It is the medical biller's job to understand the codes recorded on the superbill, to ensure that the codes are correct when submitting a health insurance claim. The billing process for both medical offices and medical billing companies is the same; however, the frequency of claims submission may vary. Never make an assumption about missing information on a form. Call the patient if need be, or ask the provider if you are unsure of a code. It is the medical biller's responsibility to create and submit accurate insurance claims.

REVIEW QUESTIONS

1. A new patient is one who has never been seen in the office, or who has not been seen in the past:
   a. 12 months
   b. 24 months
   c. 36 months
   d. none of the above

2. Another name for the superbill is:
   a. bill form
   b. payment form
   c. encounter form
   d. none of the above

3. Privacy enforcement in the office is regulated by:
    a. HIPPA
    b. HIPPO
    c. HIPAA
    d. none of the above

4. Two types of codes found on the superbill are:
    a. CPT and ICD-9
    b. ICD-9 and ICD-10
    c. CPT and CMA
    d. none of the above

5. The history, physical exam information, and diagnoses related to a patient are kept in the:
    a. file
    b. superbill
    c. medical chart
    d. HIPAA envelope

6. The person responsible for assigning an ICD-9 code on a superbill is the:
    a. biller
    b. coder
    c. provider
    d. nurse
    e. b or c

7. Codes used for hospital visits are found on the:
    a. superbill
    b. encounter form
    c. hospital sheet
    d. none of the above

8. Explain the importance of a thoroughly completed patient registration form.

    _____

    _____

9. How might a provider present his hospital billing to the medical biller if a hospital sheet is not used?

    _____

    _____

10. Explain how the frequency of billing may vary from office to office, or if working for a medical billing company.

    _____

    _____

    _____

See Figure 4-5 to answer the following questions.

Practice Name
PATIENT REGISTRATION

Welcome to our office. In order to serve you properly, we will need the following information. **(Please Print)**
All information will be strictly confidential.

Patient's Name	Sex	Birth Date	Marital Status
Sarah Jones	M __ F **X**	04 / 18 / 1940	Single [ ] Married [X] Widowed [ ] Divorced [ ]

Residence address	City	State	Zip	Home Phone:	Cell phone:	Patient's Social Security #
999 Apple Lane	Brick	NJ	08724	732-999-9999	848-999-9999	999-99-9999

Person financially responsible for this account	X Self __Spouse __Parent	Responsible Party's Birthdate 04/18/1940	Responsible Party's Social Security # 999-99-9999
Sarah Jones			

Responsible Party Drivers License # State: NJ Number 4478-9978-7788-7440	Relation to patient: self	Phone:

Patient Employer Address	Occupation retired	How Long at current Employer?

Name of Spouse/Parent	Birth date	Home phone	Cell phone	Social security #
Michael Jones	01/28/1940	same	848-222-0000	888-77-9999

Name of Spouse employer Address	Business Phone	Occupation

Reason for Visit:	Referred by: (include address and phone)

Person to contact in case of emergency:	Relationship to patient	Phone

Medicare Yes [X] No [ ]	Medicare # 999-99-9999A	Medicaid Yes [ ] No [X]	Medicaid #		Effective Date

Medicare Secondary insurance name Address		Policy #	Group #

Workers' Yes [ ] Motor Yes [ ] Compensation? No [X] Vehicle? No [X] **If Yes-put W/C or MVA carrier below**	Date of Accident	Treatment authorized by	Claim #	W/C or MVA Insurance Phone #

Primary insurance company Address	Is insurance through your employer?

Subscriber Name	Subscriber birth date	Policy #	Group #

Secondary insurance name Address	Policy #		Group #
BCBS			

Subscriber Name	Subscriber birth date	Policy #	Group #

Medicare Lifetime Signature on File:
I request that payment of authorized Medicare benefits be made on my behalf to Practice Name for any services furnished me by the physician. I authorize any holder of medical information about me to release to the Health Care Financing Administration and its agents any information to determine these benefits payable for related services

Sarah Jones	05/01/XX
Patient Signature	Date

Private Insurance Authorization for Assignment of Benefits/Information Release:
I, the undersigned authorize payment of medical benefits to Practice Name for any services furnished me by the physician. I understand that I am financially responsible for any amount not covered by my contract. I also authorize you to release to my insurance company or their agent information concerning health care, advice, treatment or supplies provided to me. This information will be used for the purpose of evaluating and administering claims of benefits.

Patient, Parent or Guardian Signature (if child is under 18 years old)	Date

FIGURE 4-5 Sample completed registration form.

11. What is the patient's work telephone number?

_____

12. Which insurance is primary for this patient?

_____

13. Who is the policyholder for the secondary insurance plan?

_____

14. Is there a group number for the primary insurance plan?

_____

15. What important piece of insurance information is missing from this patient registration form?

_____

See Figure 4-6 to answer the following questions.

Office Codes

New Pt	Established Pt	Consult
_____99201	_____99211	_____99241
_____99202	_____99212	_____99242
_____99203	_X__99213	_____99243
_____99204	_____99214	_____99244
_____99205	_____99215	_____99245

CPT Codes

_____93000 EKG	_____85014 Hemocult
_____36415 Venipuncture	_____J3420 Vitamin B-12 injection
_____71010 Chest X-ray, single view	_____J1030 Depo-Medrol
_____69210 Cerumen removal	_____87070 Throat culture
_X__99000 Specimen handling	_____90471 Immunization admin
_X__81002 Urinalysis	_____11200 Skin tag removal

ICD-9 Codes

_____789.00 Abdominal pain	_____V70.0 Routine visit
_____477.9 Allergies	_____784.0 Headache
_____285.9 Anemia	_____401.1 Hypertension
_____427.9 Arrhythmia	_____458.9 Hypotension
_____466.0 Bronchitis, acute	_____272.4 Hyperlipidemia
_____436 Cardiovascular accident	_____410.91 Myocardial infarction
_____414.00 Coronary artery disease	_____382.90 Otitis media
_____250.00 DM–controlled	_____462 Pharyngitis
_____782.3 Edema	_____482 Pneumonitis
_____780.79 Fatigue	_____461.9 Sinusitis
_____530.81 GERD	_X__599.0 Urinary tract infection

Name __Patty Patient__   Date __April 19, 20XX__
Prim ins __Great West__   Sec ins _____
Self-pay _____ Co-pay _$20_ Pd-ck _____ Chg _____ Cash _$20_

FIGURE 4-6 Sample completed superbill.

16. Which CPT codes will be billed out for this visit?

_____

_____

17. What are the patient's diagnoses for this visit?

_____

18. What type and level of patient was seen for this date of service?

_____

See Figure 4-7 to answer the following questions.

19. What date was the patient admitted?

_____

20. What are the diagnosis codes for this admission?

_____

21. What is the primary insurance for this patient? What is the secondary insurance?

_____

22. According to this hospital sheet, has the patient been discharged?

_____

23. How many total visits will be billed from this hospital sheet?

_____

Name __Sarah Jones__   Date Admitted __10/15/20XX__   Date Discharged __10/19/20XX__

Month __October__   Year __20XX__   Patient's Insurance __Medicare-pri BCBS-sec__

01	02	03	04	05	06	07	08	09	10	11	12	13	14	15	16	17	18	19	20	21	22	23	24	25	26	27	28	29	30	31	CPT Codes
																															99221
																															99222
														X																	99223
																	X														99231
															X	X															99232
																															00200
																															99251
																															99252
																															99253
																															99254
																															99255
																		X													99238
																															99239

Diagnosis(es)
1 __786.50__
2 __272.4__
3 _____
4 _____

FIGURE 4-7 Sample completed hospital billing sheet.

Chapter 5

The Heart of Medical Billing: The CMS-1500 Form

Learning Objectives

Upon completion of this chapter, the student should be able to:

- Differentiate between patient and insured data fields and provider or supplier data fields on the CMS-1500 form.
- Discuss requirements for specific blocks on the CMS-1500 form.
- Explain multiple uses for different blocks on the CMS-1500 form.
- Define key terms.

Key Terms

Assignment of Benefits	National Provider Identifier (NPI)	National Uniform Claim Committee (NUCC)	Payer
Intelligence-free			

National Uniform Claim Committee (NUCC)

is a voluntary organization that represents providers, payers, designated standards maintenance organizations, and vendors. It is chaired by the American Medical Association (AMA), with the Centers for Medicare and Medicaid Services (CMS) as a critical partner.

Introduction

The **National Uniform Claim Committee (NUCC)** is a voluntary organization that represents providers, payers, designated standards maintenance organizations, and vendors. It is chaired by the American Medical Association (AMA), with the Centers for Medicare and Medicaid Services (CMS) as a critical partner.

The NUCC began the implementation of the newest CMS-1500 form, 02/12, released April 1, 2014. (See Figure 5-1). The NUCC worked with the health care

HEALTH INSURANCE CLAIM FORM

APPROVED BY NATIONAL UNIFORM CLAIM COMMITTEE (NUCC) 02/12

| | PICA | | | | | | | PICA | |

1. MEDICARE (Medicare#)   MEDICAID (Medicaid#)   TRICARE (ID#/DoD#)   CHAMPVA (Member ID#)   GROUP HEALTH PLAN (ID#)   FECA BLK LUNG (ID#)   OTHER (ID#)

1a. INSURED'S I.D. NUMBER (For Program in Item 1)

2. PATIENT'S NAME (Last Name, First Name, Middle Initial)

3. PATIENT'S BIRTH DATE   MM DD YY   SEX   M   F

4. INSURED'S NAME (Last Name, First Name, Middle Initial)

5. PATIENT'S ADDRESS (No., Street)

6. PATIENT RELATIONSHIP TO INSURED   Self   Spouse   Child   Other

7. INSURED'S ADDRESS (No., Street)

CITY   STATE

8. RESERVED FOR NUCC USE

CITY   STATE

ZIP CODE   TELEPHONE (Include Area Code) ( )

ZIP CODE   TELEPHONE (Include Area Code) ( )

9. OTHER INSURED'S NAME (Last Name, First Name, Middle Initial)

10. IS PATIENT'S CONDITION RELATED TO:

11. INSURED'S POLICY GROUP OR FECA NUMBER

a. OTHER INSURED'S POLICY OR GROUP NUMBER

a. EMPLOYMENT? (Current or Previous)   YES   NO

a. INSURED'S DATE OF BIRTH   MM DD YY   SEX   M   F

b. RESERVED FOR NUCC USE

b. AUTO ACCIDENT?   YES   NO   PLACE (State)

b. OTHER CLAIM ID (Designated by NUCC)

c. RESERVED FOR NUCC USE

c. OTHER ACCIDENT?   YES   NO

c. INSURANCE PLAN NAME OR PROGRAM NAME

d. INSURANCE PLAN NAME OR PROGRAM NAME

10d. CLAIM CODES (Designated by NUCC)

d. IS THERE ANOTHER HEALTH BENEFIT PLAN?   YES   NO   If yes, complete items 9, 9a, and 9d.

READ BACK OF FORM BEFORE COMPLETING & SIGNING THIS FORM.
12. PATIENT'S OR AUTHORIZED PERSON'S SIGNATURE I authorize the release of any medical or other information necessary to process this claim. I also request payment of government benefits either to myself or to the party who accepts assignment below.

SIGNED _____   DATE _____

13. INSURED'S OR AUTHORIZED PERSON'S SIGNATURE I authorize payment of medical benefits to the undersigned physician or supplier for services described below.

SIGNED _____

14. DATE OF CURRENT ILLNESS, INJURY, or PREGNANCY (LMP)   MM DD YY   QUAL.

15. OTHER DATE   QUAL.   MM DD YY

16. DATES PATIENT UNABLE TO WORK IN CURRENT OCCUPATION   FROM MM DD YY   TO MM DD YY

17. NAME OF REFERRING PROVIDER OR OTHER SOURCE

17a.
17b. NPI

18. HOSPITALIZATION DATES RELATED TO CURRENT SERVICES   FROM MM DD YY   TO MM DD YY

19. ADDITIONAL CLAIM INFORMATION (Designated by NUCC)

20. OUTSIDE LAB?   YES   NO $ CHARGES

21. DIAGNOSIS OR NATURE OF ILLNESS OR INJURY Relate A-L to service line below (24E)   ICD Ind.

A. _____ B. _____ C. _____ D. _____
E. _____ F. _____ G. _____ H. _____
I. _____ J. _____ K. _____ L. _____

22. RESUBMISSION CODE   ORIGINAL REF. NO.

23. PRIOR AUTHORIZATION NUMBER

24. A. DATE(S) OF SERVICE					B. PLACE OF SERVICE	C. EMG	D. PROCEDURES, SERVICES, OR SUPPLIES (Explain Unusual Circumstances) CPT/HCPCS MODIFIER	E. DIAGNOSIS POINTER	F. $ CHARGES	G. DAYS OR UNITS	H. EPSDT Family Plan	I. ID. QUAL.	J. RENDERING PROVIDER ID. #
From MM DD YY			To MM DD YY										
1												NPI	
2												NPI	
3												NPI	
4												NPI	
5												NPI	
6												NPI	

25. FEDERAL TAX I.D. NUMBER   SSN EIN

26. PATIENT'S ACCOUNT NO.

27. ACCEPT ASSIGNMENT? (For govt. claims, see back)   YES   NO

28. TOTAL CHARGE $

29. AMOUNT PAID $

30. Rsvd for NUCC Use

31. SIGNATURE OF PHYSICIAN OR SUPPLIER INCLUDING DEGREES OR CREDENTIALS (I certify that the statements on the reverse apply to this bill and are made a part thereof.)

SIGNED _____   DATE _____

32. SERVICE FACILITY LOCATION INFORMATION

a.   b.

33. BILLING PROVIDER INFO & PH # ( )

a.   b.

NUCC Instruction Manual available at: www.nucc.org   *PLEASE PRINT OR TYPE*   APPROVED OMB-0938-1197 FORM 1500 (02-12)

CARRIER

PATIENT AND INSURED INFORMATION

PHYSICIAN OR SUPPLIER INFORMATION

From www.cms.gov

FIGURE 5-1 Blank CMS-1500 form (02/12 version).

industry to identify two priorities that were included in the revision of the prior CMS-1500, 08/05 claim form to the 02/12 version.

* The first was the addition of an indicator in Item Number 21 to identify the version of the diagnosis code set being reported, i.e., ICD-9 or ICD-10. The need to identify which version of the code set is being reported will be important during the implementation period of ICD-10.
* The second priority was to expand the number of diagnosis codes that can be reported in Item Number 21, which was increased from 4 to 12.

Additional revisions will improve the accuracy of the data reported, such as being able to identify the role of the provider reported in Item Number 17 and the specific dates reported in Item Number 14.

It is advisable for the medical biller to check the NUCC website frequently to stay abreast of current changes and new requirements. This site also offers a free NUCC 1500 instruction manual to help a biller understand how each data element of the form is correctly filled out.

Claim Filing Instructions

Payer

synonym for insurance company.

The following CMS-1500 claim form instructions are generic; that is, they are not specific to any one individual **payer** (a synonym for insurance company). For specific payer guidelines, contact the individual payer in question.

Carrier or Payer Block

Payer block: Enter the name and address of the payer in the upper right-hand side of the form. Enter the name and address in the following format:

* Line 1 Name
* Line 2 First line of address
* Line 3 Second line of address or leave blank if not needed
* Line 4 City, state (two characters), and ZIP code

HEALTH INSURANCE CLAIM FORM
APPROVED BY NATIONAL UNIFORM CLAIM COMMITTEE (NUCC) 02/12
☐☐☐ PICA

PICA ☐☐☐

From www.cms.gov

Blocks 1–13: Patient and Insured Information

Block 1: Check the payer type for the claim by marking an "X" in the appropriate box. Only one box can be checked.

* Options are Medicare, Medicaid, Tricare, CHAMPVA, Group Health Plan, FECA BLK Lung, and Other.
* The "OTHER" box can include HMO, commercial, motor vehicle, liability, or workers' compensation insurance.
* Add the insured ID number in Block 1a.

From www.cms.gov

Block 2: Enter the patient's full legal name, beginning with the last name, first name, and middle initial. Insert a comma between the last name and first name and before the middle initial.

- If patient's last name includes a suffix (e.g., Jr. or Sr.), enter the suffix after the last name.
- Do not enter professional credentials or designations (e.g., M.D., Esq.) in this box.
- A hyphen may be inserted for hyphenated last names.
- Do not enter a period in this block.

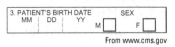

From www.cms.gov

Block 3: Enter the patient's date of birth in an eight-digit format (MM/DD/YYYY). Enter an "X" in the appropriate box for the patient's gender.

From www.cms.gov

Block 4: Enter the insured's full legal name, beginning with last name, first name, and middle initial. The "Insured's Name" identifies the person who holds the policy, which would be the employee for employer-provided health insurance.

- Do not insert professional credentials, titles, or periods in this block.
- If the insured is the patient, you may enter "Same" in this block.

From www.cms.gov

Block 5: Enter the patient's permanent address and telephone number.

- If using a nine-digit Zip Code to include the rural route, use a hyphen.
- Do not use commas, periods, or other punctuation marks in this block.
- If the patient's address is the same as the insured's address, it is not necessary to report the patient's address again in block 7.

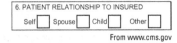

From www.cms.gov

Block 6: Enter an "X" in the correct box indicating the patient's relationship to the insured if block 4 is completed.

- For workers' compensation claims, check the "Other" box. The insured is always the patient's employer.
- Only one box can be checked.

From www.cms.gov

Block 7: Enter the insured's address, if Block 4 is completed with a name other than the patient's name.

- Do not use commas, periods, or other punctuation in this block.
- If the insured's address is the same as the patient's, you may enter "Same."
- For workers' compensation claims, enter the patient's employer's address.

From www.cms.gov

Block 8: Reserved for NUCC Use
The NUCC will provide instructions for any use of this field.

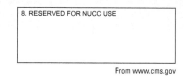

From www.cms.gov

Block 9: If Block 11d is checked "YES", complete Block 9, 9a, and 9d, otherwise leave blank.

- Enter the full, legal name of the insured that holds the secondary/supplemental insurance.
- If the insured's name is the same as in Block 2, you may leave this block blank.

Block 9a: Enter the policy and/or group number of the secondary/supplemental insurance.

- It is not necessary to include a hyphen or space between the policy and group number for handwritten claims; however, most software programs are formatted to indicate a space between the two numbers.

Block 9b: Reserved for NUCC Use
The NUCC will provide instructions for any use of this field.

Block 9c: Reserved for NUCC Use
The NUCC will provide instructions for any use of this field.

Block 9d: Enter the name of the secondary/supplemental insurance plan or program.

9. OTHER INSURED'S NAME (Last Name, First Name, Middle Initial)
a. OTHER INSURED'S POLICY OR GROUP NUMBER
b. RESERVED FOR NUCC USE
c. RESERVED FOR NUCC USE
d. INSURANCE PLAN NAME OR PROGRAM NAME

From www.cms.gov

Blocks 10a–10c: Place an "X" in the "NO" box if the patient's condition is not related to employment injury, an automobile accident, or another accident. Any item marked "YES" would indicate that another insurance coverage would be primary, such as automobile liability insurance. Enter the other insurance coverage in block 11.

- If the patient's condition is the result of an injury that occurred on the job, place an "X" in the "YES" box in 10a.
- If the patient's condition is the result of an automobile accident, place an "X" in the "YES" box in 10b and enter the two-character Postal Service abbreviation in the "(State)" line for the state in which the accident occurred.
- If the patient's condition is the result of another accident (e.g., a fall on the ice outside a condominium complex), place an "X" in the "YES" box in 10c.

10. IS PATIENT'S CONDITION RELATED TO:
a. EMPLOYMENT? (Current or Previous)
[ ] YES   [ ] NO
b. AUTO ACCIDENT?   PLACE (State)
[ ] YES   [ ] NO
c. OTHER ACCIDENT?
[ ] YES   [ ] NO

From www.cms.gov

Block 10d: When applicable, this block is reserved to report appropriate claim codes approved by the NUCC. Contact individual payers for their guidelines.

```
10d. CLAIM CODES (Designated by NUCC)
```
From www.cms.gov

Block 11: Enter the primary insurance policy's group number as listed on the health insurance identification card (if one is listed). If Item 4 is completed, then this field should be completed.

- For workers' compensation claims, enter the insured's policy, group, or FECA number (a nine-digit alphanumeric identifier assigned to a patient claiming a work-related condition).
- For Medicare claims, enter the word "None" here.

Block 11a: Enter the insured's (person named in Block 4) date of birth in an eight-digit (MM/DD/YYYY) format. Enter an "X" in the correct box for the insured's gender.

Block 11b: Enter the "Other Claim ID". Applicable claim identifiers are designated by the NUCC.

The following qualifier and accompanying identifier has been designated for use:
Y4   Property Casualty Claim Number

- Enter the qualifier to the left of the vertical, dotted line. Enter the identifier number to the right of the vertical, dotted line.
- For Workers' Compensation or Property & Casualty claims, this block is required, if known. Enter the claim number assigned by the payer.

Block 11c: Enter the primary insurance payer's plan or program name of the insured (this may be listed on the health insurance identification card).

- Some payers require an identification number here (contact the individual payer for specific guidelines).
- If no plan or program name is listed on the health insurance identification card and the payer in question does not require data in this block, leave this block blank.

Block 11d: Enter an "X" in the "YES" box if there is health insurance coverage other than the insurance checked in Block 1. (For primary claims, checking "YES" indicates that there is a secondary/supplemental plan.)

- If "YES" is checked, complete blocks 9 through 9d.
- If there is no other health insurance coverage, mark an "X" in the "NO" box.

```
11. INSURED'S POLICY GROUP OR FECA NUMBER

a. INSURED'S DATE OF BIRTH        SEX
   MM   DD   YY          M     F

b. OTHER CLAIM ID (Designated by NUCC)

c. INSURANCE PLAN NAME OR PROGRAM NAME

d. IS THERE ANOTHER HEALTH BENEFIT PLAN?
   YES    NO    If yes, complete items 9, 9a, and 9d
```
From www.cms.gov

Block 12: This block is for the patient's or authorized person's signature.

- If a legal signature is not available, enter "Signature on file" or "SOF" in this field, as long as the patient's or authorized person's signature is on file in the medical chart.
- If there is no signature on file, leave blank or enter "No signature on file."
- Enter the date the form was signed or the date of service, in either a six-digit (MM/DD/YY) or an eight-digit (MM/DD/YYYY) format.

From www.cms.gov

Block 13: Enter the insured's or authorized person's signature here. When signed, the person is requesting that benefits be paid directly to the provider. This is known as **assignment of benefits**.

13. INSURED'S OR AUTHORIZED PERSON'S SIGNATURE I authorize payment of medical benefits to the undersigned physician or supplier for services described below.

SIGNED _____

From www.cms.gov

Blocks 14–33: Physician or Supplier Information

Block 14: This block is used to enter the six-digit (MM/DD/YY) or eight-digit (MM/DD/YYYY) format for the first date of the present illness, injury, or pregnancy.

Enter the applicable qualifier to identify which date is being reported.
- 431   Onset of Current Symptoms or illness
- 484   Last Menstrual Period

- For workers' compensation, motor vehicle accidents, or other accidents, enter the date of the injury or accident here.
- For pregnancy claims, enter the date of the patient's last menstrual period (LMP) here.

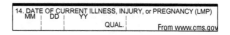

Block 15: Enter a six-digit (MM/DD/YY) or an eight-digit (MM/DD/YYYY) date in this block to show another date related to the patient's condition or treatment.

Enter the applicable qualifier to identity which date is being reported.
- 454   Initial Treatment
- 304   Latest Visit or Consultation
- 453   Acute Manifestation of a Chronic Condition
- 439   Accident
- 455   Last X-ray
- 471   Prescription
- 090   Report Start (Assumed Care Date)
- 091   Report End (Relinquished Care Date)
- 444   First Visit or Consultation

- This block is *not* a required field.
- Leave block blank if original illness date is unknown.

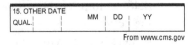

Block 16: If the patient is employed and is unable to work in the current occupation, enter a six-digit (MM/DD/YY) or an eight-digit (MM/DD/YYYY) date in both the "FROM" and "TO" sections of this block, indicating the dates the patient was unable to work. If the "TO" date is unknown, some software programs will allow "N/A" (not applicable) or no date at all in this field.

- Entry in this block is usually related to a workers' compensation claim.

Block 17: This block is used for a referring provider, ordering provider, or other source that referred or ordered the service, or procedures rendered on the claim.

If multiple providers are involved, enter one provider using the following priority order:

1. Referring Provider
2. Ordering Provider
3. Supervising Provider

Enter the applicable qualifier to identify which provider is being reported.

DN	Referring Provider
DK	Ordering Provider
DQ	Supervising Provider

- Enter the first name, middle initial, last name, and credentials of the professional who referred or ordered the service(s) or supplies on the claim. Do not enter commas or periods in this block.
- May enter hyphen for hyphenated names.

Block 17a: In the small box to the left, enter the two-character qualifier designated for the ID (identification) number of the referring, ordering, or supervising provider.

The provider legacy qualifiers according to the NUCC are as follows:

0B	State License Number
1G	Provider UPIN Number
G2	Provider Commercial Number
LU	Location Number (This qualifier is used for Supervising Provider only.)

National Provider Identifier (NPI)

a 10-digit, intelligence-free, numeric identifier.

Block 17b: Enter the 10-digit NPI number of the referring provider, ordering, or supervising provider in 17b. The National Provider Identifier (NPI) number is

Intelligence-free

does not carry information about health care providers, such as the state in which they practice or their specialization.

issued to all HIPAA-covered entities. It is a 10-digit, intelligence-free, numeric identifier that identifies the provider to all payers. Intelligence-free means it does not carry information about health care providers, such as the state in which they practice or their specialization.

From www.cms.gov

Block 18: Enter the six-digit (MM/DD/YY) or eight-digit (MM/DD/YYYY) hospitalization dates related to current services here.

* This block relates to inpatient stays only. If the patient has not yet been discharged, may enter "N/A" or leave the "TO" field blank.

18. HOSPITALIZATION DATES RELATED TO CURRENT SERVICES						
	MM	DD	YY	MM	DD	YY
FROM				TO		

From www.cms.gov

Block 19: Additional Claim Information (designated by NUCC). Please refer to the most current instructions from the public or private payer regarding the use of this field.

19. ADDITIONAL CLAIM INFORMATION (Designated by NUCC)

From www.cms.gov

Block 20: Enter an "X" in the "YES" box when billing for purchased services.

* Checking "YES" indicates that the service was performed by an entity other than the billing provider. The independent provider of these services will be named on block 32. Enter the dollar amount under "CHARGES" for the purchased services. Enter "00" to the right of the vertical line if the dollar amount is a whole number.
* Do not enter dollar signs.
* Enter an "X" in the "NO" box when no purchased services are reported on the claim, or leave the field blank.

20. OUTSIDE LAB?		$ CHARGES	
☐ YES	☐ NO		

From www.cms.gov

Block 21: Enter the applicable ICD indicator to identify which version of ICD codes is being reported between the vertical, dotted lines in the upper right-hand portion of the block.

    9   ICD-9-CM
    0   ICD-10-CM

* List no more than 12 ICD-9-CM or ICD-10-CM diagnosis codes. Relate lines A-L to the lines of service in 24E by the letter of the line. Use highest level of specificity. Do not provide narrative descriptions in this block. For ICD-9 codes containing more than three digits, enter the first three digits before the period, and the fourth and fifth (if required) digits after the period.

21. DIAGNOSIS OR NATURE OF ILLNESS OR INJURY Relate A-L to service line below (24E)			ICD Ind.
A. _____	B. _____	C. _____	D. _____
E. _____	F. _____	G. _____	H. _____
I. _____	J. _____	K. _____	L. _____

From www.cms.gov

Block 22: This block is used to resubmit a claim. List the original reference number assigned by the destination payer or receiver to indicate a previously submitted claim or encounter. When resubmitting a claim, enter the appropriate bill frequency to the left justified in the left-hand side of the field.

    7   Replacement of a prior claim

    8   Void/cancel prior claim

22. RESUBMISSION CODE	ORIGINAL REF. NO.

From www.cms.gov

Block 23: Enter any of the following in this block:

- Prior authorization number, if assigned by payer.
- Mammography Precertification number, if assigned by payer.
- Clinical Laboratory Improvement Amendments (CLIA) number, if billing for lab services.
- Referral number

23. PRIOR AUTHORIZATION NUMBER

From www.cms.gov

Section 24

The six service lines in Section 24 have been divided horizontally to accommodate submission of both the NPI and another/proprietary identifier and to accommodate the submission of supplemental information to support the billed service. The top area of the six service lines is shaded and is the location for reporting supplemental information.

Block 24A: Enter the "From" and "To" dates for service(s) rendered.

- Some payers may require a "To" date even when it is the same as the "From" date; it is advisable always to enter both sections to reduce the risk of claim rejection.
- If billing for multiple units for the same service (e.g., follow-up hospital visits for same level of service), you may reflect this by listing the "From" date as the first day of the service and the "To" date as the last date this same service was rendered. The multiple units must be for consecutive days and must correspond to the number of units in Block 24G.

Block 24B: Enter the appropriate two-digit place-of-service code for each billable item or service performed. The place of service codes are available at www.cms.gov/physicianfeesched/downloads/Website POS database.pdf.

24. A. DATE(S) OF SERVICE						B. PLACE OF SERVICE
From			To			
MM	DD	YY	MM	DD	YY	
1						
2						
3						
4						
5						
6						

From www.cms.gov

Block 24C: This block is used if the service rendered is deemed an "emergency service."

- Check the individual payer's requirements for completion of this block. If deemed an emergency, usually a "Y" will be required in this block; if not an emergency, leave blank.

Block 24D: Enter the CPT or HCPCS code (s) and modifier(s) (if applicable) from the appropriate code set in effect on the date of service. CPT/HCPCS codes are listed to the left; up to four two-digit modifiers may be listed per line item.

- Up to six CPT/HCPCS line items may be billed on one claim form.
- If payers require additional anesthesia services information (e.g., begin and end times) or a narrative description of an unspecified code, enter this information in the shaded area of the block, directly above the CPT/HCPCS code.
- If payers require specific codes (e.g., NCD code for drugs) for durable medical equipment or supplies, enter these codes in the shaded area of the block.

Block 24E: Enter the diagnosis reference number (pointer) from Block 21 that pertains to each billable line item.

- When multiple services are provided, the primary reference number should always be listed first, and then other services should follow.
- The reference letter (s) should be A–L or multiple letters as applicable. This block can contain an "A", "B", "C", or "D", etc., or any combination of up to four diagnosis reference letters.
- Do not list the actual ICD-9 or ICD-10 code in this block.
- Do not use commas to separate the numbers.

Block 24F: Enter the dollar amount for each billable service, procedure, or item.

- Do not enter dollar signs or commas.
- Enter "00" in the cents field to the right of the perforated line if the amount is a whole number.

Block 24G: Enter the number of days or units for the CPT/HCPCS code listed in Block 24D.

- The most common use of this block is for multiple visits, units of supplies, anesthesia units or minutes, or oxygen volume.
- If only one day or unit was needed, enter "1" in this block. If reporting a fraction of a unit, use a decimal point.
- Anesthesia services must be reported in minutes. Units may only be reported for anesthesia services when the code description includes a time period (such as "daily management").

Block 24H: This block is to report Early & Periodic Screening, Diagnosis, and Treatment related services, if required (e.g., state requirement).

If the claim is related to family planning, enter "Y" for Yes or N for No only.

Block 24I: Enter the non-NPI qualifier as directed in Block 17a (refer to list of qualifiers).

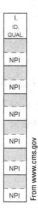

Block 24J: Enter the non-NPI ID number in the shaded area of the field. Enter the 10-digit NPI number in the unshaded area of the field. The Rendering Provider is the person or company (laboratory or other facility) who rendered or supervised the care. Report the Identification Number in Items 24I and 24J only when different from data recorded in Block 33A and 33B.

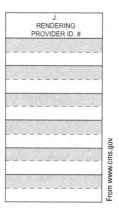

Block 25: Enter the provider or supplier's federal tax identification number (employer ID or SSN) here with an "X" in the appropriate box.

- For rendering providers who are part of a group practice, enter the *group's* tax identification number.
- Do not enter hyphens with numbers. Enter number left justified in the field. Only one box can be marked.

From www.cms.gov

Block 26: Enter the patient's account number assigned by the provider or supplier's accounting system.

From www.cms.gov

Block 27: Enter an "X" in the appropriate box.

- An "X" in the "YES" box indicates that the provider has agreed to accept assignment on the claim. An "X" in the "NO" box indicates that the provider does not accept assignment on the claim (a "NO" would indicate that the provider does not have a contract with or does not participate with the payer in question).

From www.cms.gov

Block 28: Enter the total charges from lines 1 through 6 in Block 24F.

- Do not enter dollar signs.
- Enter "00" to the right of the perforated line if the total amount is a whole number.

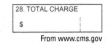

From www.cms.gov

Block 29: Enter amount the patient and/or other payers paid on the covered services only.

- Do not use commas, dollar signs, or negative dollar amounts in this field.
- If no payment is made, you may leave blank or enter "0" to the left of the perforated line and "00" to the right of the perforated line.

From www.cms.gov

Block 30: Reserved for NUCC use.

From www.cms.gov

The NUCC will provide instructions for any use of this field.

Block 31: Enter the legal signature of the practitioner or supplier, or signature of the practitioner or supplier representative. Include degrees or credentials after the name.

- "Signature on file" or "SOF" is acceptable in this block.
- Enter the six-digit (MM/DD/YY) or eight-digit (MM/DD/YYYY) date on which the claim was signed or billed (for computerized claims).

```
31. SIGNATURE OF PHYSICIAN OR SUPPLIER
    INCLUDING DEGREES OR CREDENTIALS
    (I certify that the statements on the reverse
    apply to this bill and are made a part thereof.)



SIGNED                              DATE
```
From www.cms.gov

Block 32: Enter the name and address of the location where billed items (Block 24D) were rendered. Enter the name and address in this format:

1st Line	Name
2nd Line	Address
3rd Line	City, State and ZIP Code

- If the provider is billing for purchased diagnostic tests, enter the supplier's name and address here. When more than one supplier is used, a separate 1500 Claim Form should be used for each supplier.
- If the provider is part of a group practice, enter the name of the group here.
- Do not use commas, periods, or other punctuation in the address. Enter a space between town name and state code.

Block 32a: Enter the NPI of the provider, supplier, or facility listed in Block 32. Report a Service Facility Location NPI only when it is different from the Billing Provider NPI.

Block 32b: Enter the two-digit qualifier identifying the non-NPI number by the ID number. The non-NPI ID number of the service facility is the payer assigned unique identifier of the facility.

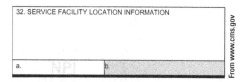

```
32. SERVICE FACILITY LOCATION INFORMATION




a.         NPI          b.
```
From www.cms.gov

Block 33: Enter the provider's or supplier's name, address, and telephone number in the format listed for Block 32. If the provider is part of a group practice, enter the group's name here. This block identifies the provider that is requesting to be paid for the services rendered and should always be completed.

Block 33a: Enter the NPI number of the billing entity listed in Block 33a. If the billing entity is a group practice, enter the group's NPI number here.

Block 33b: Enter the two-digit qualifier (see instructions for Block 17a) followed by ID number.

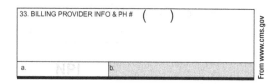

```
33. BILLING PROVIDER INFO & PH #    (          )




a.         NPI          b.
```
From www.cms.gov

Several sample bills and claims on the CMS-1500 form appear in Chapters 6 and 7, and in Appendix I at the back of this textbook.

Summary

The NUCC began the implementation of the newest CMS-1500 form, 02/12, April 1, 2014. The changes in this form were needed to accommodate the arrival of ICD-10-CM in the United States, and also, to expand the number of diagnoses that can be reported on each claim. Each time the CMS-1500 claim form is updated, it allows a more complete picture of the patient's encounter.

Each payer may require completion of certain blocks, boxes, or items, or may require specific information to be listed in different blocks on this form. If the medical biller is in doubt about a payer's requirements regarding a block or box, the biller should contact the payer to get its claim filing instructions.

REVIEW QUESTIONS

1. Which fields of the CMS-1500 form require information about the patient and insured?

2. Which fields require information about the provider or supplier?

3. Where on the CMS-1500 form are the name and address of the payer placed?

4. True or False: Is the term "signature on file" or "SOF" acceptable in all blocks requiring a signature?

5. If you check the "yes" box in field 20, what are you saying? ___

6. Why was the NPI number developed?

Chapter 6

Billing for Office Services and Procedures

Learning Objectives

Upon completion of this chapter, the student should be able to:

- Distinguish between new patient and established patient office visit codes.
- Accurately complete a CMS-1500 form for a patient encounter in the provider's office.
- Determine codes used for an encounter at a specialist's office and the important CMS-1500 form box requirements for such.
- Define key terms.

Key Terms

Electronic Health
  Record (EHR)
Electronic Medical
  Record (EMR)

Office Visit
Referral
Specialist

Gathering Data

Medical billers working in providers' offices extract data from the patient registration form and the superbill (introduced in Chapter 4).

    The CPT codes from the evaluation and management (E/M) section will be utilized on most practices' superbills, with the exception of psychiatrists, for new, established, and consult visits. Pediatricians will have additional preventive medicine evaluation and management codes on their superbills to reflect services that are relevant to their offices, such as well-baby and well-child visits. See Figure 6-1.

New		Established		Consult	
Level 1	99201	Level 1	99211	Level 1	99241
Level 2	99202	Level 2	99212	Level 2	99242
Level 3	99203	Level 3	99213	Level 3	99243
Level 4	99204	Level 4	99214	Level 4	99244
Level 5	99205	Level 5	99215	Level 5	99245

FIGURE 6-1 CPT codes for office visits.

Billing for a New Patient

Electronic Medical Record (EMR)

digital version of a patient record, usually limited to its location site.

Electronic Health Record (EHR)

digital version of a patient record, one that is easily shared with other location sites.

Office visit

an encounter in the provider's office.

Before submitting a claim to an insurance payer for a new patient, the data gathered from the patient registration form must be entered into the practice's computer software program or electronic medical record (EMR). The photocopies, or scans, of the patient's insurance card(s) will be placed in the patient's medical chart. The chart can be paper but is now more commonly in an electronic format. The electronic patient record is called an electronic medical record (EMR) or electronic health record (EHR). The medical biller will need to reference these records in order to submit correct claims, also known as clean claims.

Once all the data are entered into the practice's medical software system, the medical biller enters the claim information after a coder reviews and codes the chart. Claims are submitted electronically to the insurance payer once the biller finalizes all of the necessary information such as adding appropriate modifiers. This creates an efficient turnaround time for reimbursement from the payer to the payee, which is the medical practice.

The CPT codes used for billing an office visit for a new patient vary in levels ranging from 99201–99205. The shortest visit would be demonstrated by the use of E/M code 99201, which is a straightforward visit, it is problem-focused, and the time spent with a patient face-to-face is about 10 minutes, this is known as a level 1 office visit. On the other hand, 99205 is a high-complexity visit, it is comprehensive, and it can last up to 60 minutes face-to-face with the provider. This visit is known as a level 5 office visit. A new patient is defined as one that has not received any professional services, from the provider/qualified health care professional or another provider/qualified health care professional of the exact same specialty and subspeciality who belongs to the same group practice, within the past three years. The E/M level assigned to the patient's visit is determined by the provider or coder, based on detailed documentation in the patient's medical chart. See Figure 6-2.

Code	Description	
99201	Level I	New Patient
99202	Level II	New Patient
99203	Level III	New Patient
99204	Level IV	New Patient
99205	Level V	New Patient

FIGURE 6-2 Office visit codes for a new patient.

Code	Description	
99211	Level I	Est. Patient
99212	Level II	Est. Patient
99213	Level III	Est. Patient
99214	Level IV	Est. Patient
99215	Level V	Est. Patient

FIGURE 6-3 Office visit codes for an established patient.

Billing for an Established Patient

Billing for established patients is less time-consuming, as their patient and insurance information has already been entered into the computer's software program. The E/M level codes range from 99211—simple, straightforward visits that can last five minutes—up to 99215, which, like 99205, is a highly complex visit, and the time spent face-to-face with a provider can be up to 40 minutes. Occasionally, the medical biller may need to add or edit the patient's information if the patient has moved or switched insurance carriers; however, the process of submitting a claim to the insurance carrier remains the same as with a new patient visit.

The CPT codes for established patients are similar to those for new patients, with the exception of the fourth digit in each level. The "0" in new patient codes is replaced by a "1" in established patient codes. See Figure 6-3.

Billing for a Consult

A consultation is a type of evaluation and management service provided at the request of another provider or appropriate source, to either recommend care for a specific condition or problem or to determine whether to accept responsibility for ongoing management of the patient's entire care, or for the care of a specific condition or problem. When a provider sends a patient to seek treatment of a specific condition or problem to another specialist, the patient is referred to another provider, and this does not qualify as a consultation but as a referral.

All specialists should have consultation E/M visit codes on superbills that could be used in their offices. Occasionally, primary care providers will also have consultation codes on their superbills. These are used when the patient is at the office for referrals of a service, such as diagnostic, therapeutic, or surgical clearance prior to surgery.

The reimbursement amounts for consultation codes are usually higher than those for office visits. Specialists can expect to receive more for their services because of their additional training and experience in a particular area of medicine. As of 2010, Medicare discontinued paying for consultation codes. If providers are providing consultation services to Medicare patients, they are to bill the appropriate office visit codes depending on the documentation.

Note that there is no distinction in consultation codes between new patients and established patients. The codes used are the same for both, yet they are distinct based

Specialist

provider who concentrates on a particular area of medicine (e.g., cardiology or gastroenterology).

Referral

patient is sent to a specialist for evaluation and testing.

Code	Description
99241	Level I Consult
99242	Level II Consult
99243	Level III Consult
99244	Level IV Consult
99245	Level V Consult

FIGURE 6-4   Consultation codes used for office encounters (same for both new and established patients).

on their location of the consultations, such as outpatient or inpatient consultation. See Figure 6-4.

Billing for Procedures and HCPCS Level II Codes

Office visits and consultations are not the only items to be billed from the superbill. Depending on the type of practice, there will also be codes for services such as:

- Immunizations
- Injections
- Minor procedures

It is important not to miss any of these services when preparing to submit the claim.

Determining Modifier Usage

Because most superbills in providers' offices do *not* have the modifiers listed on the superbill next to the appropriate CPT or HCPCS level II code, the medical biller's knowledge of modifier usage is critical to the process of submitting clean claims. Examples of modifiers can be found in Chapter 3, or in any CPT reference manual.

Billing for services and procedures performed in the provider's office becomes easier with practice and time. The same codes are used on a daily basis, which enables the medical biller to become familiar with these codes fairly quickly.

Note:

For the purpose of completing CMS-1500 forms for billing exercises, the patient registration form and superbill have been combined into one form called a case study form (see Figure 6-5). A biller can gather the information needed to prepare the claim for submission from each case study form. Sample case study forms requiring modifiers are listed in Appendix I at the back of this textbook.

Case Study

PATIENT INFORMATION:

Name:

Social Security #:

Address:

City:

State:

Zip Code:

Home Telephone:

Date of Birth:

Gender:

Occupation:

Employer:

Employer Telephone:

Spouse:

Spouse's Social Security #:

Spouse's Employer:

Spouse's Date of Birth:

INSURANCE INFORMATION:

Patient Number:

Place of Service:

Primary Insurance Plan:

Primary Insurance Plan ID #:

Group #:

Primary Policyholder:

Policyholder Date of Birth:

Relationship to Patient:

Secondary Insurance Plan:

Secondary Insurance Plan ID #:

Secondary Policyholder:

Patient Status   ☐ Married   ☐ Divorced   ☐ Single   ☐ Student   ☐ Other

DIAGNOSIS INFORMATION

	Diagnosis	Code		Diagnosis	Code
1.			5.		
2.			6.		
3.			7.		
4.			8.		

PROCEDURE INFORMATION

	Description of Procedure or Service	Date	Code	Charge
1.				
2.				
3.				
4.				
5.				
6.				

SPECIAL NOTES:

FIGURE 6-5   Sample blank case study form.

Summary

There are many challenges working in a provider's office. The biller must learn about new processes and computer systems, policies and procedures, and, in some cases, electronic medical records (EMR). A biller will start slowly with their training, and as they become more proficient, they will be able to process more complex and advanced claims. The greatest challenge as a new biller is to learn how to use modifiers and append a modifier to a CPT code for correct reimbursement.

REVIEW QUESTIONS

1. From which two forms are data extracted to prepare a claim?

2. What is the difference between an office visit code and a consult code for the office?

3. What is the only difference between new patient and established patient office visit codes?

4. Define:
   a. office visit
   b. referred
   c. specialist

5. What is normally not found on a superbill that may present a challenge for the biller?

Before completing the following exercises, see Figure 6-6 and Figure 6-7.

6. Using the case study form in Figure 6-8a, complete the CMS-1500 form in Figure 6-8b, using ICD-9-CM coding.

7. Using the case study form in Figure 6-9a, complete the CMS-1500 form in Figure 6-9b, using ICD-10-CM coding.

Michael Rowe, M.D.

Case Study

123 Apple Lane • Brick, NJ 08723 • (732) 222-3333
Tax ID# 11-2345678
NPI# 9933993399

PATIENT INFORMATION:

Name:	Anne Adams
Social Security #:	000-11-0000
Address:	111 Rail Road
City:	Brick
State:	New Jersey
Zip Code:	08724
Home Telephone:	(732) 000-1111
Date of Birth:	04-12-1972
Gender:	Female
Occupation:	Cashier
Employer:	Groceries 'R' Us
Employer Telephone:	(732) 111-2222
Spouse:	
Spouse's Social Security #:	
Spouse's Employer:	
Spouse's Date of Birth:	

INSURANCE INFORMATION:

Patient Number:	Adaan000
Place of Service:	Office
Primary Insurance Plan:	Aetna
Primary Insurance Plan ID #:	723Z92660
Group #:	9800-00
Primary Policyholder:	Anne Adams
Policyholder Date of Birth:	04-12-1972
Relationship to Patient:	Self
Secondary Insurance Plan:	
Secondary Insurance Plan ID #:	
Secondary Policyholder:	

Patient Status   ☐ Married   ☐ Divorced   ☒ Single   ☐ Student   ☐ Other

DIAGNOSIS INFORMATION

Diagnosis	Code		Diagnosis	Code
1. Headache	784.0	5.		
2.		6.		
3.		7.		
4.		8.		

PROCEDURE INFORMATION

Description of Procedure or Service	Date	Code	Charge
1. Level 2 office visit - new patient	04-01-YYYY	99202	$75.00
2.			
3.			
4.			
5.			
6.			

SPECIAL NOTES:

FIGURE 6-6   Case study form for new patient Anne Adams (using ICD-9 coding).

HEALTH INSURANCE CLAIM FORM

APPROVED BY NATIONAL UNIFORM CLAIM COMMITTEE (NUCC) 02/12

PICA ☐☐   **PICA** ☐☐

1. MEDICARE ☐ (Medicare#)   **MEDICAID** ☐ (Medicaid#)   **TRICARE** ☐ (ID#/DoD#)   **CHAMPVA** ☐ (Member ID#)   **GROUP HEALTH PLAN** ☒ (ID#)   **FECA BLK LUNG** ☐ (ID#)   **OTHER** ☐ (ID#)

1a. INSURED'S I.D. NUMBER (For Program in Item 1): 723Z92660

2. PATIENT'S NAME (Last Name, First Name, Middle Initial): ADAMS, ANNE

3. PATIENT'S BIRTH DATE: 04 12 1972   **SEX** M☐ F☒

4. INSURED'S NAME (Last Name, First Name, Middle Initial): SAME

5. PATIENT'S ADDRESS (No., Street): 111 RAIL ROAD

6. PATIENT RELATIONSHIP TO INSURED: Self☐ Spouse☐ Child☐ Other☐

7. INSURED'S ADDRESS (No., Street): SAME

CITY: BRICK   **STATE:** NJ

8. RESERVED FOR NUCC USE

CITY: **STATE:**

ZIP CODE: 08724   **TELEPHONE (Include Area Code):** (732)000 1111

ZIP CODE: **TELEPHONE (Include Area Code):** ( )

9. OTHER INSURED'S NAME (Last Name, First Name, Middle Initial):

10. IS PATIENT'S CONDITION RELATED TO:

11. INSURED'S POLICY GROUP OR FECA NUMBER:

a. OTHER INSURED'S POLICY OR GROUP NUMBER:

a. EMPLOYMENT? (Current or Previous) YES☐ NO☒

a. INSURED'S DATE OF BIRTH: **SEX** M☐ F☐

b. RESERVED FOR NUCC USE

b. AUTO ACCIDENT? YES☐ NO☒ **PLACE (State)**

b. OTHER CLAIM ID (Designated by NUCC):

c. RESERVED FOR NUCC USE

c. OTHER ACCIDENT? YES☐ NO☒

c. INSURANCE PLAN NAME OR PROGRAM NAME:

d. INSURANCE PLAN NAME OR PROGRAM NAME:

10d. CLAIM CODES (Designated by NUCC):

d. IS THERE ANOTHER HEALTH BENEFIT PLAN? YES☐ NO☒ If yes, complete items 9, 9a, and 9d.

12. PATIENT'S OR AUTHORIZED PERSON'S SIGNATURE SIGNED SOF DATE 0401YYYY

13. INSURED'S OR AUTHORIZED PERSON'S SIGNATURE SIGNED SOF

14. DATE OF CURRENT ILLNESS, INJURY, or PREGNANCY (LMP): QUAL.

15. OTHER DATE: QUAL.

16. DATES PATIENT UNABLE TO WORK IN CURRENT OCCUPATION: FROM TO

17. NAME OF REFERRING PROVIDER OR OTHER SOURCE: 17a. / 17b. NPI

18. HOSPITALIZATION DATES RELATED TO CURRENT SERVICES: FROM TO

19. ADDITIONAL CLAIM INFORMATION (Designated by NUCC):

20. OUTSIDE LAB? YES☐ NO☒ **$ CHARGES**

21. DIAGNOSIS OR NATURE OF ILLNESS OR INJURY ICD Ind. R51: A. 784.0

22. RESUBMISSION CODE ORIGINAL REF. NO.

23. PRIOR AUTHORIZATION NUMBER

24.A. DATE(S) OF SERVICE From / To	B. PLACE OF SERVICE	C. EMG	D. CPT/HCPCS / MODIFIER	E. DIAGNOSIS POINTER	F. $ CHARGES	G. DAYS OR UNITS	H. EPSDT	I. ID. QUAL.	J. RENDERING PROVIDER ID.#
1. 04 01 YY 04 01 YY	11		99202	1	75 00	1			NPI
2									NPI
3									NPI
4									NPI
5									NPI
6									NPI

25. FEDERAL TAX I.D. NUMBER: 112345678 SSN☐ EIN☒

26. PATIENT'S ACCOUNT NO.: ADAAN000

27. ACCEPT ASSIGNMENT? YES☒ NO☐

28. TOTAL CHARGE: $ 75 00

29. AMOUNT PAID: $ 0 00

30. Rsvd for NUCC Use: 75 00

31. SIGNATURE OF PHYSICIAN OR SUPPLIER: MICHAEL ROWE MD   DATE 0402YY

32. SERVICE FACILITY LOCATION INFORMATION: MICHAEL ROWE MD / 123 APPLE LANE / BRICK NJ 08723   a. 9933993399

33. BILLING PROVIDER INFO & PH #: (732)222-3333 MICHAEL ROWE MD / 123 APPLE LANE / BRICK NJ 08723   a. 9933993399

FIGURE 6-7 Completed CMS-1500 form for Anne Adams (using ICD-9 coding).

Michael Rowe, M.D.

123 Apple Lane • Brick, NJ 08723 • (732) 222-3333
Tax ID# 11-2345678
NPI# 9933993399

Case Study

PATIENT INFORMATION:

Name:	Bella Berry
Social Security #:	111-22-3333
Address:	001 Trail Terrace
City:	Brick
State:	New Jersey
Zip Code:	08723
Home Telephone:	(732) 111-0000
Date of Birth:	01-28-1969
Gender:	Female
Occupation:	Teacher
Employer:	Burns Elementary School
Employer Telephone:	(732) 999-2222
Spouse:	Bernie Berry
Spouse's Social Security #:	222-33-4444
Spouse's Employer:	QTA Corporation
Spouse's Date of Birth:	11-07-1968

INSURANCE INFORMATION:

Patient Number:	Berbe000
Place of Service:	Office
Primary Insurance Plan:	Cigna
Primary Insurance Plan ID #:	33B427A16
Group #:	624700
Primary Policyholder:	Bernie Berry
Policyholder Date of Birth:	11-07-1968
Relationship to Patient:	Spouse
Secondary Insurance Plan:	
Secondary Insurance Plan ID #:	
Secondary Policyholder:	

Patient Status   ☒ Married   ☐ Divorced   ☐ Single   ☐ Student   ☐ Other

DIAGNOSIS INFORMATION

	Diagnosis	Code		Diagnosis	Code
1.	UTI	599.0	5.		
2.			6.		
3.			7.		
4.			8.		

PROCEDURE INFORMATION

	Description of Procedure or Service	Date	Code	Charge
1.	Level 3 office visit - est. patient	03-15-YYYY	99213	$60.00
2.	Urinalysis	03-15-YYYY	81002	$15.00
3.				
4.				
5.				
6.				

SPECIAL NOTES:

FIGURE 6-8a Case study form for an established patient (using ICD-9 coding).

HEALTH INSURANCE CLAIM FORM

APPROVED BY NATIONAL UNIFORM CLAIM COMMITTEE (NUCC) 02/12

PICA

1. MEDICARE	MEDICAID	TRICARE	CHAMPVA	GROUP HEALTH PLAN	FECA BLK LUNG	OTHER
(Medicare#)	(Medicaid#)	(ID#/DoD#)	(Member ID#)	(ID#)	(ID#)	(ID#)

1a. INSURED'S I.D. NUMBER (For Program in Item 1)

2. PATIENT'S NAME (Last Name, First Name, Middle Initial)

3. PATIENT'S BIRTH DATE MM DD YY SEX M F

4. INSURED'S NAME (Last Name, First Name, Middle Initial)

5. PATIENT'S ADDRESS (No., Street)

6. PATIENT RELATIONSHIP TO INSURED Self Spouse Child Other

7. INSURED'S ADDRESS (No., Street)

CITY STATE

8. RESERVED FOR NUCC USE

CITY STATE

ZIP CODE TELEPHONE (Include Area Code) ( )

ZIP CODE TELEPHONE (Include Area Code) ( )

9. OTHER INSURED'S NAME (Last Name, First Name, Middle Initial)

10. IS PATIENT'S CONDITION RELATED TO:

11. INSURED'S POLICY GROUP OR FECA NUMBER

a. OTHER INSURED'S POLICY OR GROUP NUMBER

a. EMPLOYMENT? (Current or Previous) YES NO

a. INSURED'S DATE OF BIRTH MM DD YY SEX M F

b. RESERVED FOR NUCC USE

b. AUTO ACCIDENT? YES NO PLACE (State)

b. OTHER CLAIM ID (Designated by NUCC)

c. RESERVED FOR NUCC USE

c. OTHER ACCIDENT? YES NO

c. INSURANCE PLAN NAME OR PROGRAM NAME

d. INSURANCE PLAN NAME OR PROGRAM NAME

10d. CLAIM CODES (Designated by NUCC)

d. IS THERE ANOTHER HEALTH BENEFIT PLAN? YES NO If yes, complete items 9, 9a, and 9d.

READ BACK OF FORM BEFORE COMPLETING & SIGNING THIS FORM.
12. PATIENT'S OR AUTHORIZED PERSON'S SIGNATURE I authorize the release of any medical or other information necessary to process this claim. I also request payment of government benefits either to myself or to the party who accepts assignment below.

SIGNED DATE

13. INSURED'S OR AUTHORIZED PERSON'S SIGNATURE I authorize payment of medical benefits to the undersigned physician or supplier for services described below.

SIGNED

14. DATE OF CURRENT ILLNESS, INJURY, or PREGNANCY (LMP) MM DD YY QUAL.

15. OTHER DATE QUAL. MM DD YY

16. DATES PATIENT UNABLE TO WORK IN CURRENT OCCUPATION FROM MM DD YY TO MM DD YY

17. NAME OF REFERRING PROVIDER OR OTHER SOURCE

17a. 17b. NPI

18. HOSPITALIZATION DATES RELATED TO CURRENT SERVICES FROM MM DD YY TO MM DD YY

19. ADDITIONAL CLAIM INFORMATION (Designated by NUCC)

20. OUTSIDE LAB? YES NO $ CHARGES

21. DIAGNOSIS OR NATURE OF ILLNESS OR INJURY Relate A-L to service line below (24E) ICD Ind.

A. B. C. D.
E. F. G. H.
I. J. K. L.

22. RESUBMISSION CODE ORIGINAL REF. NO.

23. PRIOR AUTHORIZATION NUMBER

24. A. DATE(S) OF SERVICE From To MM DD YY MM DD YY	B. PLACE OF SERVICE	C. EMG	D. PROCEDURES, SERVICES, OR SUPPLIES (Explain Unusual Circumstances) CPT/HCPCS MODIFIER	E. DIAGNOSIS POINTER	F. $ CHARGES	G. DAYS OR UNITS	H. EPSDT Family Plan	I. ID. QUAL.	J. RENDERING PROVIDER ID. #
1									NPI
2									NPI
3									NPI
4									NPI
5									NPI
6									NPI

25. FEDERAL TAX I.D. NUMBER SSN EIN

26. PATIENT'S ACCOUNT NO.

27. ACCEPT ASSIGNMENT? (For govt. claims, see back) YES NO

28. TOTAL CHARGE $

29. AMOUNT PAID $

30. Rsvd for NUCC Use

31. SIGNATURE OF PHYSICIAN OR SUPPLIER INCLUDING DEGREES OR CREDENTIALS (I certify that the statements on the reverse apply to this bill and are made a part thereof.)

SIGNED DATE

32. SERVICE FACILITY LOCATION INFORMATION

a. NPI b.

33. BILLING PROVIDER INFO & PH # ( )

a. NPI b.

NUCC Instruction Manual available at: www.nucc.org

PLEASE PRINT OR TYPE

CARRIER — PATIENT AND INSURED INFORMATION — PHYSICIAN OR SUPPLIER INFORMATION

From www.cms.gov

FIGURE 6-8b Blank CMS-1500 form for case study exercise (use ICD-9 coding).

Thomas Shue, M.D.

111 Peach Blvd • Brick, NJ 08723 • (732) 999-0000
Tax ID# 11-1122334
NPI# 1122223333

Case Study

PATIENT INFORMATION:

Name:	Cameron Carle
Social Security #:	222-33-4444
Address:	001 Queenie Road
City:	Brick
State:	New Jersey
Zip Code:	08724
Home Telephone:	(732) 002-0009
Date of Birth:	03-28-1975
Gender:	Male
Occupation:	IT Specialist
Employer:	BMB Industries
Employer Telephone:	(732) 003-2600
Spouse:	
Spouse's Social Security #:	
Spouse's Employer:	
Spouse's Date of Birth:	

INSURANCE INFORMATION:

Patient Number:	Carca000
Place of Service:	Office
Primary Insurance Plan:	Healthnet
Primary Insurance Plan ID #:	002003ZZQ
Group #:	H 12300
Primary Policyholder:	Cameron Carle
Policyholder Date of Birth:	03-28-1975
Relationship to Patient:	Self
Secondary Insurance Plan:	
Secondary Insurance Plan ID #:	
Secondary Policyholder:	

Patient Status   ☐ Married   ☐ Divorced   ☒ Single   ☐ Student   ☐ Other

DIAGNOSIS INFORMATION

Diagnosis	Code	Diagnosis	Code
1. Stomach pain	R10.9	5.	
2.		6.	
3.		7.	
4.		8.	

PROCEDURE INFORMATION

Description of Procedure or Service	Date	Code	Charge
1. Level 2 office consultation	05 12 YYYY	99242	$125.00
2.			
3.			
4.			
5.			
6.			

SPECIAL NOTES:

Patient was referred by Dr. Michael Rowe; NPI# 9933993399

FIGURE 6-9a Case study form for a consult visit (using ICD-10 coding).

HEALTH INSURANCE CLAIM FORM

APPROVED BY NATIONAL UNIFORM CLAIM COMMITTEE (NUCC) 02/12

	PICA						PICA	

1. MEDICARE MEDICAID TRICARE CHAMPVA GROUP HEALTH PLAN FECA BLK LUNG OTHER **1a. INSURED'S I.D. NUMBER** (For Program in Item 1)

☐ (Medicare#) ☐ (Medicaid#) ☐ (ID#/DoD#) ☐ (Member ID#) ☐ (ID#) ☐ (ID#) ☐ (ID#)

2. PATIENT'S NAME (Last Name, First Name, Middle Initial)

3. PATIENT'S BIRTH DATE MM DD YY SEX M ☐ F ☐

4. INSURED'S NAME (Last Name, First Name, Middle Initial)

5. PATIENT'S ADDRESS (No., Street)

6. PATIENT RELATIONSHIP TO INSURED Self ☐ Spouse ☐ Child ☐ Other ☐

7. INSURED'S ADDRESS (No., Street)

CITY STATE **8. RESERVED FOR NUCC USE** CITY STATE

ZIP CODE TELEPHONE (Include Area Code) ( ) ZIP CODE TELEPHONE (Include Area Code) ( )

9. OTHER INSURED'S NAME (Last Name, First Name, Middle Initial)

10. IS PATIENT'S CONDITION RELATED TO:

11. INSURED'S POLICY GROUP OR FECA NUMBER

a. OTHER INSURED'S POLICY OR GROUP NUMBER

a. EMPLOYMENT? (Current or Previous) ☐ YES ☐ NO

a. INSURED'S DATE OF BIRTH MM DD YY SEX M ☐ F ☐

b. RESERVED FOR NUCC USE

b. AUTO ACCIDENT? ☐ YES ☐ NO PLACE (State)

b. OTHER CLAIM ID (Designated by NUCC)

c. RESERVED FOR NUCC USE

c. OTHER ACCIDENT? ☐ YES ☐ NO

c. INSURANCE PLAN NAME OR PROGRAM NAME

d. INSURANCE PLAN NAME OR PROGRAM NAME

10d. CLAIM CODES (Designated by NUCC)

d. IS THERE ANOTHER HEALTH BENEFIT PLAN? ☐ YES ☐ NO *If yes*, complete items 9, 9a, and 9d.

READ BACK OF FORM BEFORE COMPLETING & SIGNING THIS FORM.

12. PATIENT'S OR AUTHORIZED PERSON'S SIGNATURE I authorize the release of any medical or other information necessary to process this claim. I also request payment of government benefits either to myself or to the party who accepts assignment below.

SIGNED _____ DATE _____

13. INSURED'S OR AUTHORIZED PERSON'S SIGNATURE I authorize payment of medical benefits to the undersigned physician or supplier for services described below.

SIGNED _____

14. DATE OF CURRENT ILLNESS, INJURY, or PREGNANCY (LMP) MM DD YY QUAL.

15. OTHER DATE QUAL. MM DD YY

16. DATES PATIENT UNABLE TO WORK IN CURRENT OCCUPATION MM DD YY FROM TO MM DD YY

17. NAME OF REFERRING PROVIDER OR OTHER SOURCE 17a. 17b. NPI

18. HOSPITALIZATION DATES RELATED TO CURRENT SERVICES MM DD YY FROM TO MM DD YY

19. ADDITIONAL CLAIM INFORMATION (Designated by NUCC)

20. OUTSIDE LAB? ☐ YES ☐ NO $ CHARGES

21. DIAGNOSIS OR NATURE OF ILLNESS OR INJURY Relate A-L to service line below (24E) ICD Ind. R10.9

A. ____ B. ____ C. ____ D. ____
E. ____ F. ____ G. ____ H. ____
I. ____ J. ____ K. ____ L. ____

22. RESUBMISSION CODE ORIGINAL REF. NO.

23. PRIOR AUTHORIZATION NUMBER

24. A. DATE(S) OF SERVICE		B. PLACE OF SERVICE	C. EMG	D. PROCEDURES, SERVICES, OR SUPPLIES (Explain Unusual Circumstances)		E. DIAGNOSIS POINTER	F. $ CHARGES	G. DAYS OR UNITS	H. EPSDT Family Plan	I. ID. QUAL.	J. RENDERING PROVIDER ID. #
From MM DD YY	To MM DD YY			CPT/HCPCS	MODIFIER						
1											NPI
2											NPI
3											NPI
4											NPI
5											NPI
6											NPI

25. FEDERAL TAX I.D. NUMBER SSN ☐ EIN ☐

26. PATIENT'S ACCOUNT NO.

27. ACCEPT ASSIGNMENT? (For govt. claims, see back) ☐ YES ☐ NO

28. TOTAL CHARGE $

29. AMOUNT PAID $

30. Rsvd for NUCC Use

31. SIGNATURE OF PHYSICIAN OR SUPPLIER INCLUDING DEGREES OR CREDENTIALS (I certify that the statements on the reverse apply to this bill and are made a part thereof.)

SIGNED _____ DATE _____

32. SERVICE FACILITY LOCATION INFORMATION

a. NPI b.

33. BILLING PROVIDER INFO & PH # ( )

a. NPI b.

NUCC Instruction Manual available at: www.nucc.org *PLEASE PRINT OR TYPE*

FIGURE 6-9b Blank CMS-1500 form for case study exercise (use ICD-10 coding).

Chapter 7
Billing for Inpatient and Nursing Facility Services

Learning Objectives

Upon completion of this chapter, the student should be able to:

- Differentiate between initial and subsequent visit codes.
- Distinguish between admitting and consulting codes.
- Comprehend the use of critical care codes for inpatient services.
- Accurately complete the CMS-1500 form for inpatient and nursing facility services.
- Define key terms.

Key Terms

Consulting Provider	Initial Hospital Care	Long-Term Care Facility	Subsequent Hospital Care
Critical Care	Inpatient	Nursing Facility	
Discharge	Intermediate Care Facility		

Inpatient Billing For Provider Services

Inpatient

a patient who has been admitted to a hospital.

As used in this text, the term **inpatient** billing refers to the billing done for evaluation and management services performed by providers for patients who have been admitted to a hospital. This type of billing is not the same as performed by medical billers working at the hospital and billing for the hospital's services (such as a private or semi-private room charge).

Billing for the Admitting Provider

Providers will charge with an initial hospital care code for all evaluation and management services provided to a patient that are related to that patient's admission.

This code can be used only once and *only* by the admitting provider.

There are three CPT evaluation and management codes to choose from when billing for initial hospital care:

- 99221 (level one)
- 99222 (level two)
- 99223 (level three)

Remember, it is *not* the medical biller's job to select the level of care provided by the provider. The provider will choose the appropriate level, and the code will be listed on the hospital billing sheet given to the medical biller to prepare the claim.

Billing for the Consulting Provider

Very often, an admitting provider will place a call to a specialist and request a consult on a patient who has been admitted to the hospital. The type of specialist called will depend on the nature of the patient's problems. For example, if the patient is experiencing persistent chest pains, a cardiologist will be called as a consulting provider.

A primary care provider can also be called upon to perform a consult on an inpatient if the admitting provider seeks that doctor's advice or second opinion on a patient's care or diagnosis.

There are five CPT evaluation and management codes for the initial inpatient consultation:

- 99251 (level one)
- 99252 (level two)
- 99253 (level three)
- 99254 (level four)
- 99255 (level five)

Again, the level of care is chosen by the consulting provider.

Subsequent Hospital Care

The evaluation and management of a patient following the initial hospital care is considered subsequent hospital care. These visits made to the inpatient are frequently referred to as *follow-ups*.

Follow-ups do not necessarily occur on the day after admission, nor must they occur on a daily basis for the patient in the hospital. The frequency of these visits is determined by the provider, based on the patient's condition and need.

Although the initial hospital care codes for admitting and consulting providers differ, the subsequent hospital care CPT evaluation and management codes for both doctors are the same. These CPT codes are:

- 99231 (level one)
- 99232 (level two)
- 99233 (level three)

Critical Care Services

The precedents for use of critical care service codes, when billing for a patient in the hospital setting, include:

- The injury or illness acutely impairs one or more vital organ systems with threat of possible failure to an organ system. Vital organ system problems include, but are not limited to:
  - Central nervous system failure
  - Circulatory failure
  - Shock
  - Renal failure
  - Hepatic failure
  - Metabolic failure
  - Respiratory failure
- High-complexity decision making
- Assessment to treat single or multiple vital organ system failure
- Assessment to prevent further life-threatening deterioration of the patient's condition

These evaluation and management CPT codes are based on the total duration of time spent by a provider in providing the critical care services. The time spent on these services can be devoted to a single patient only. Therefore, for billing purposes, the provider cannot perform critical care services for multiple critically ill or injured patients in a given time period. The length of time spent with or on an individual patient must be documented in that patient's medical record. The total duration of time spent can include:

- Time spent engaged in work directly related to the individual patient's care (at immediate bedside or elsewhere on the hospital floor or unit)
- Time spent discussing the patient's care with other medical staff
- Time spent in discussions with family members or surrogate decision makers

The codes used to report these services are:

- 99291 (30–74 minutes)
- 99292 (additional block of time of up to 30 minutes each beyond the first 74 minutes)
- 99291 × 1 and 99292 × 1 75–104 minutes
- 99291 × 1 and 99292 × 2 105–304 minutes

Critical care codes can be used in conjunction with initial hospital and subsequent hospital care evaluation and management codes. However, critical care services totaling less than 30 minutes are not reported. Instead, the provider should only charge for the initial and/or subsequent evaluation and management, using the appropriate E&M codes.

Hospital Discharge Services

The management of a patient's discharge is reported with hospital-day discharge management codes. These, too, are based on the duration of time spent by the provider on a patient's discharge. Qualifiers for discharge services include:

- Final examination of the patient
- Discussion of the hospital stay

Admitting Physician		Consulting Physician	
Initial Visit	Subsequent/Follow-up Visit	Initial Visit	Subsequent/Follow-up Visit
99221	99231	99251	99231
99222	99232	99252	99232
99223	99233	99253	99233
		99254	
		99255	
Critical Care Codes		Hospital Discharge	
99291 - 30 to 74 minutes		99238 - 30 minutes or under	
99292 - each additional 30 minutes		99239 - more than 30 minutes	

FIGURE 7-1   Inpatient hospital visit codes.

- Instructions on continuing care to relevant caregivers
- Preparation of discharge records, prescriptions, and referral forms

Evaluation and management codes for hospital discharge services are:

- 99238 (30 minutes or less)
- 99239 (more than 30 minutes)

Unlike critical care codes, CPT code 99239 is *not* used in addition to CPT code 99238. Only one discharge-day management code can be billed for a patient.

A reference sheet used by the medical biller who is billing for inpatient hospital services might look like the sample in Figure 7-1.

Billing For Nursing Facility Services

Medical billers will bill out using nursing facility service evaluation and management codes when the provider visits a patient in:

- A nursing facility (formerly called a skilled nursing facility)
- An intermediate care facility
- A long-term care facility

Codes used for the initial care of a patient for admission (new patient) or readmission (established patient) to a facility are:

- 99304 (low severity)
- 99305 (moderate severity)
- 99306 (high severity)

Codes used for subsequent care in a facility are:

- 99307 (straightforward decision making)
- 99308 (low-complexity decision making)
- 99309 (moderate-complexity decision making)
- 99310 (high-complexity decision making)

Evaluation and management codes used for discharge services from a nursing facility involve the same criteria as those used for discharging a patient from the hospital. Discharge service codes are:

- 99315 (30 minutes or less)
- 99316 (more than 30 minutes)

A reference sheet used by the medical biller who is billing for nursing facility services might look like the sample in Figure 7-2.

Nursing facility

a facility that provides continuous medical supervision via 24-hour-a-day nursing care and related services, in addition to food, shelter, and personal care.

Intermediate care facility

an institution that provides health-related care and services to individuals who do not require the degree of care and treatment that a hospital or nursing facility is designed to provide.

Long-term care facility

a facility that provides medical services and assistance to patients over an extended period of time and is designed to meet the medical, personal, and social needs of the patient.

Initial (New/Est.)	Subsequent	Discharge
99304	99307	99315 30 minutes or less
99305	99308	99316 more than 30 minutes
99306	99309	
	99310	

FIGURE 7-2   Nursing facility services codes.

Summary

It is important for the medical biller who is billing for inpatient, nursing facility, or critical care services to become familiar with these codes and their appropriate use. Providers are human, so they might make errors such as reporting an initial visit two days in a row, instead of day one as the admission and day two as a follow-up. An astute medical biller will pick up this error and bring it to the provider's attention. Failure to notice such an error could result in rejection of the claim and therefore could delay payment to the provider.

REVIEW QUESTIONS

1. Define the following key terms:
   a. inpatient
   b. initial hospital care
   c. subsequent hospital care
   d. critical care
   e. discharge
   f. nursing facility
   g. intermediate care facility
   h. long-term care facility

2. Which evaluation and management codes introduced in this chapter are based on time?

3. List three vital organ systems involved in billing for critical care services.

4. Why is it important for the medical biller to become familiar with inpatient, critical care, and nursing facility services codes?

5. Using the case study form in Figure 7-3a, complete the CMS-1500 form in Figure 7-3b using ICD-9-CM coding.

6. Using the case study form in Figure 7-4a, complete the CMS-1500 form in Figure 7-4b using ICD-10-CM coding.

7. Using the case study form in Figure 7-5a, complete the CMS-1500 form in Figure 7-5b using ICD-10-CM coding.

8. Using the case study form in Figure 7-6a, complete the CMS-1500 form in Figure 7-6b using ICD-10-CM coding.

Case Study

Rindy Rain, M.D.

0072 Route 79 • Brick, NJ 08724 • (732) 999-9999
Tax ID# 11-9436799
NPI# 0001112223

PATIENT INFORMATION:

Name:	Wendy Winters
Social Security #:	999-88-7777
Address:	009 Queen Court
City:	Neptune
State:	NJ
Zip Code:	00001
Home Telephone:	(732) 888-7777
Date of Birth:	12-01-1970
Gender:	Female
Occupation:	Clerk
Employer:	XYZ Gardens
Employer Telephone:	(732) 000-3333
Spouse:	Wayne Winters
Spouse's Social Security #:	333-44-5555
Spouse's Employer:	Marks Corporation
Spouse's Date of Birth:	07-30-1969

INSURANCE INFORMATION:

Patient Number:	Win We000
Place of Service:	In-patient hospital
Primary Insurance Plan:	Healthchoice
Primary Insurance Plan ID #:	A9723649
Group #:	0026
Primary Policyholder:	Wayne Winters
Policyholder Date of Birth:	07-30-1969
Relationship to Patient:	Spouse
Secondary Insurance Plan:	
Secondary Insurance Plan ID #:	
Secondary Policyholder:	

Patient Status ☒ Married   ☐ Divorced   ☐ Single   ☐ Student   ☐ Other

DIAGNOSIS INFORMATION

Diagnosis	Code	Diagnosis	Code
1. Chest pain	786.50	5.	
2. Shortness of breath	786.05	6.	
3.		7.	
4.		8.	

PROCEDURE INFORMATION

Description of Procedure or Service	Date	Code	Charge
1. Initial hospital care - level 2	04-07-YY	99222	$150.00
2.			
3.			
4.			
5.			
6.			

SPECIAL NOTES: Ocean Grove Hospital
080 Route 99
Ocean Grove, NJ 00008
Facility NPI# 0006600001

FIGURE 7-3a Case study form for services provided by the admitting physician (using ICD-9 coding).

HEALTH INSURANCE CLAIM FORM

APPROVED BY NATIONAL UNIFORM CLAIM COMMITTEE (NUCC) 02/12

| | PICA | | | | | | | | PICA | |

| 1. | MEDICARE | MEDICAID | TRICARE | CHAMPVA | GROUP HEALTH PLAN | FECA BLK LUNG | OTHER | 1a. INSURED'S I.D. NUMBER | (For Program in Item 1) |

(Medicare#) (Medicaid#) (ID#/DoD#) (Member ID#) (ID#) (ID#) (ID#)

2. PATIENT'S NAME (Last Name, First Name, Middle Initial)

3. PATIENT'S BIRTH DATE MM DD YY SEX M F

4. INSURED'S NAME (Last Name, First Name, Middle Initial)

5. PATIENT'S ADDRESS (No., Street)

6. PATIENT RELATIONSHIP TO INSURED Self Spouse Child Other

7. INSURED'S ADDRESS (No., Street)

CITY STATE

8. RESERVED FOR NUCC USE

CITY STATE

ZIP CODE TELEPHONE (Include Area Code) ( )

ZIP CODE TELEPHONE (Include Area Code) ( )

9. OTHER INSURED'S NAME (Last Name, First Name, Middle Initial)

10. IS PATIENT'S CONDITION RELATED TO:

11. INSURED'S POLICY GROUP OR FECA NUMBER

a. OTHER INSURED'S POLICY OR GROUP NUMBER

a. EMPLOYMENT? (Current or Previous) YES NO

a. INSURED'S DATE OF BIRTH MM DD YY SEX M F

b. RESERVED FOR NUCC USE

b. AUTO ACCIDENT? PLACE (State) YES NO

b. OTHER CLAIM ID (Designated by NUCC)

c. RESERVED FOR NUCC USE

c. OTHER ACCIDENT? YES NO

c. INSURANCE PLAN NAME OR PROGRAM NAME

d. INSURANCE PLAN NAME OR PROGRAM NAME

10d. CLAIM CODES (Designated by NUCC)

d. IS THERE ANOTHER HEALTH BENEFIT PLAN? YES NO *If yes*, complete items 9, 9a, and 9d.

READ BACK OF FORM BEFORE COMPLETING & SIGNING THIS FORM.

12. PATIENT'S OR AUTHORIZED PERSON'S SIGNATURE I authorize the release of any medical or other information necessary to process this claim. I also request payment of government benefits either to myself or to the party who accepts assignment below.

SIGNED _____ DATE _____

13. INSURED'S OR AUTHORIZED PERSON'S SIGNATURE I authorize payment of medical benefits to the undersigned physician or supplier for services described below.

SIGNED _____

14. DATE OF CURRENT ILLNESS, INJURY, or PREGNANCY (LMP) MM DD YY QUAL.

15. OTHER DATE QUAL. MM DD YY

16. DATES PATIENT UNABLE TO WORK IN CURRENT OCCUPATION FROM MM DD YY TO MM DD YY

17. NAME OF REFERRING PROVIDER OR OTHER SOURCE

17a.

17b. NPI

18. HOSPITALIZATION DATES RELATED TO CURRENT SERVICES FROM MM DD YY TO MM DD YY

19. ADDITIONAL CLAIM INFORMATION (Designated by NUCC)

20. OUTSIDE LAB? YES NO $ CHARGES

21. DIAGNOSIS OR NATURE OF ILLNESS OR INJURY Relate A-L to service line below (24E) ICD Ind.

A. |_____ B. |_____ C. |_____ D. |_____
E. |_____ F. |_____ G. |_____ H. |_____
I. |_____ J. |_____ K. |_____ L. |_____

22. RESUBMISSION CODE ORIGINAL REF. NO.

23. PRIOR AUTHORIZATION NUMBER

24. A. DATE(S) OF SERVICE		B. PLACE OF SERVICE	C. EMG	D. PROCEDURES, SERVICES, OR SUPPLIES (Explain Unusual Circumstances)		E. DIAGNOSIS POINTER	F. $ CHARGES	G. DAYS OR UNITS	H. EPSDT Family Plan	I. ID. QUAL.	J. RENDERING PROVIDER ID. #
From MM DD YY	To MM DD YY			CPT/HCPCS	MODIFIER						
1										NPI	
2										NPI	
3										NPI	
4										NPI	
5										NPI	
6										NPI	

25. FEDERAL TAX I.D. NUMBER SSN EIN

26. PATIENT'S ACCOUNT NO.

27. ACCEPT ASSIGNMENT? (For govt. claims, see back) YES NO

28. TOTAL CHARGE $

29. AMOUNT PAID $

30. Rsvd for NUCC Use

31. SIGNATURE OF PHYSICIAN OR SUPPLIER INCLUDING DEGREES OR CREDENTIALS (I certify that the statements on the reverse apply to this bill and are made a part thereof.)

SIGNED _____ DATE _____

32. SERVICE FACILITY LOCATION INFORMATION

a. NPI b.

33. BILLING PROVIDER INFO & PH # ( )

a. NPI b.

NUCC Instruction Manual available at: www.nucc.org *PLEASE PRINT OR TYPE*

CARRIER — PATIENT AND INSURED INFORMATION — PHYSICIAN OR SUPPLIER INFORMATION

From www.cms.gov

FIGURE 7-3b Blank CMS-1500 form for case study exercise (use ICD-9 coding).

Case Study

Autumn Anderson, M.D.

0873 Route 10 • Lakewood, NJ 08701 • (732) 888-8888
Tax ID# 11-1122999
NPI# 5522998877

PATIENT INFORMATION:

Name:	Frank Fields
Social Security #:	888-77-8888
Address:	002 Cherry Blvd
City:	Lakewood
State:	NJ
Zip Code:	08701
Home Telephone:	(732) 000-6652
Date of Birth:	06-27-1932
Gender:	Male
Occupation:	Retired
Employer:	
Employer Telephone:	
Spouse:	
Spouse's Social Security #:	
Spouse's Employer:	
Spouse's Date of Birth:	

INSURANCE INFORMATION:

Patient Number:	Fiefr000
Place of Service:	In-patient hospital
Primary Insurance Plan:	Medicare
Primary Insurance Plan ID #:	888-77-8888A
Group #:	
Primary Policyholder:	
Policyholder Date of Birth:	06-27-1932
Relationship to Patient:	Self
Secondary Insurance Plan:	AARP
Secondary Insurance Plan ID #:	BB 279639
Secondary Policyholder:	Frank Fields

Patient Status ☐ Married ☐ Divorced ☒ Single ☐ Student ☐ Other

DIAGNOSIS INFORMATION

Diagnosis	Code	Diagnosis	Code
1. GI bleeding	578.9	5.	
2.		6.	
3.		7.	
4.		8.	

PROCEDURE INFORMATION

Description of Procedure or Service	Date	Code	Charge
1. Initial In-patient consultation - level 4	11-22-YY	99254	$250.00
2. Subsequent hospital care - level 3	11-23-YY	99233	$175.00
3.			
4.			
5.			
6.			

SPECIAL NOTES: Referring physician: Rindy Rain M.D., NPI# 0001112223
Kendrall Hospital
0930 Route 10
Lakewood, NJ 08701
Facility NPI# 0202020211

FIGURE 7-4a Case study form for services provided by a consulting physician (using ICD-9 coding).

HEALTH INSURANCE CLAIM FORM

APPROVED BY NATIONAL UNIFORM CLAIM COMMITTEE (NUCC) 02/12

| | PICA | PICA | |

1. MEDICARE (Medicare#) MEDICAID (Medicaid#) TRICARE (ID#/DoD#) CHAMPVA (Member ID#) GROUP HEALTH PLAN (ID#) FECA BLK LUNG (ID#) OTHER (ID#)   **1a.** INSURED'S I.D. NUMBER (For Program in Item 1)

2. PATIENT'S NAME (Last Name, First Name, Middle Initial)   **3.** PATIENT'S BIRTH DATE MM DD YY SEX M F   **4.** INSURED'S NAME (Last Name, First Name, Middle Initial)

5. PATIENT'S ADDRESS (No., Street)   **6.** PATIENT RELATIONSHIP TO INSURED Self Spouse Child Other   **7.** INSURED'S ADDRESS (No., Street)

CITY   STATE   **8.** RESERVED FOR NUCC USE   CITY   STATE

ZIP CODE   TELEPHONE (Include Area Code) ( )   ZIP CODE   TELEPHONE (Include Area Code) ( )

9. OTHER INSURED'S NAME (Last Name, First Name, Middle Initial)   **10.** IS PATIENT'S CONDITION RELATED TO: **11.** INSURED'S POLICY GROUP OR FECA NUMBER

a. OTHER INSURED'S POLICY OR GROUP NUMBER   **a.** EMPLOYMENT? (Current or Previous) YES NO   **a.** INSURED'S DATE OF BIRTH MM DD YY SEX M F

b. RESERVED FOR NUCC USE   **b.** AUTO ACCIDENT? YES NO PLACE (State)   **b.** OTHER CLAIM ID (Designated by NUCC)

c. RESERVED FOR NUCC USE   **c.** OTHER ACCIDENT? YES NO   **c.** INSURANCE PLAN NAME OR PROGRAM NAME

d. INSURANCE PLAN NAME OR PROGRAM NAME   **10d.** CLAIM CODES (Designated by NUCC)   **d.** IS THERE ANOTHER HEALTH BENEFIT PLAN? YES NO If yes, complete items 9, 9a, and 9d.

READ BACK OF FORM BEFORE COMPLETING & SIGNING THIS FORM.
12. PATIENT'S OR AUTHORIZED PERSON'S SIGNATURE I authorize the release of any medical or other information necessary to process this claim. I also request payment of government benefits either to myself or to the party who accepts assignment below.
SIGNED _____ DATE _____   **13.** INSURED'S OR AUTHORIZED PERSON'S SIGNATURE I authorize payment of medical benefits to the undersigned physician or supplier for services described below. SIGNED _____

14. DATE OF CURRENT ILLNESS, INJURY, or PREGNANCY (LMP) MM DD YY QUAL.   **15.** OTHER DATE QUAL. MM DD YY   **16.** DATES PATIENT UNABLE TO WORK IN CURRENT OCCUPATION FROM MM DD YY TO MM DD YY

17. NAME OF REFERRING PROVIDER OR OTHER SOURCE   **17a.**   **17b.** NPI   **18.** HOSPITALIZATION DATES RELATED TO CURRENT SERVICES FROM MM DD YY TO MM DD YY

19. ADDITIONAL CLAIM INFORMATION (Designated by NUCC)   **20.** OUTSIDE LAB? YES NO $ CHARGES

21. DIAGNOSIS OR NATURE OF ILLNESS OR INJURY Relate A-L to service line below (24E) ICD Ind.
A. B. C. D. E. F. G. H. I. J. K. L.   **22.** RESUBMISSION CODE ORIGINAL REF. NO.   **23.** PRIOR AUTHORIZATION NUMBER

24. A. DATE(S) OF SERVICE From To MM DD YY MM DD YY **B.** PLACE OF SERVICE **C.** EMG **D.** PROCEDURES, SERVICES, OR SUPPLIES (Explain Unusual Circumstances) CPT/HCPCS MODIFIER **E.** DIAGNOSIS POINTER **F.** $ CHARGES **G.** DAYS OR UNITS **H.** EPSDT Family Plan **I.** ID. QUAL. **J.** RENDERING PROVIDER ID. #

1 NPI
2 NPI
3 NPI
4 NPI
5 NPI
6 NPI

25. FEDERAL TAX I.D. NUMBER SSN EIN   **26.** PATIENT'S ACCOUNT NO.   **27.** ACCEPT ASSIGNMENT? (For govt. claims, see back) YES NO   **28.** TOTAL CHARGE $ **29.** AMOUNT PAID $ **30.** Rsvd for NUCC Use

31. SIGNATURE OF PHYSICIAN OR SUPPLIER INCLUDING DEGREES OR CREDENTIALS (I certify that the statements on the reverse apply to this bill and are made a part thereof.) SIGNED DATE   **32.** SERVICE FACILITY LOCATION INFORMATION a. NPI b.   **33.** BILLING PROVIDER INFO & PH # ( ) a. NPI b.

NUCC Instruction Manual available at: www.nucc.org   PLEASE PRINT OR TYPE

FIGURE 7-4b Blank CMS-1500 form for case study exercise (use ICD-9 coding).

Rindy Rain, M.D.
0072 Route 79 • Brick, NJ 08724 • (732) 999-9999
Tax ID# 11-9436799
NPI# 0001112223

Case Study

PATIENT INFORMATION:

Name:	Jack Frost
Social Security #:	222-00-0002
Address:	0070 Birch Blvd
City:	Toms River
State:	NJ
Zip Code:	08755
Home Telephone:	(732) 555-5555
Date of Birth:	12-25-1925
Gender:	Male
Occupation:	Retired
Employer:	
Employer Telephone:	
Spouse:	
Spouse's Social Security #:	
Spouse's Employer:	
Spouse's Date of Birth:	

INSURANCE INFORMATION:

Patient Number:	Froja000
Place of Service:	In-patient hospital
Primary Insurance Plan:	Medicare
Primary Insurance Plan ID #:	222-00-0002A
Group #:	
Primary Policyholder:	Jack Frost
Policyholder Date of Birth:	12-25-1925
Relationship to Patient:	Self
Secondary Insurance Plan:	Blue Cross/Blue Shield
Secondary Insurance Plan ID #:	BB 1238976
Secondary Policyholder:	Jack Frost

Patient Status   ☐ Married   ☐ Divorced   ☒ Single   ☐ Student   ☐ Other

DIAGNOSIS INFORMATION

Diagnosis	Code	Diagnosis	Code
1. Respiratory failure	J96.90	5.	
2.		6.	
3.		7.	
4.		8.	

PROCEDURE INFORMATION

Description of Procedure or Service	Date	Code	Charge
1. Initial In-patient hospital care - level 3	12-31-YY	99223	$175.00
2. Critical Care Services (30-74 minutes)	12-31-YY	99291	$275.00
3. Critical Care Services (ea add'l 30 minutes)	12-31-YY	99292	$250.00
4.			
5.			
6.			

SPECIAL NOTES: Physician Rindy Rain, M.D. spent a total of one and one half hours devoted to
KENDRALL HOSPITAL   the Critical Care Service of patient on 12-31-YY
0930 ROUTE 10
LAKEWOOD, NJ 08701
FACILITY NPI# 0202020211

FIGURE 7-5a Case study form for critical care services provided by the admitting physician (using ICD-10 coding).

HEALTH INSURANCE CLAIM FORM

APPROVED BY NATIONAL UNIFORM CLAIM COMMITTEE (NUCC) 02/12

| | PICA | | | | | | | | | PICA | |

1. MEDICARE (Medicare#) **MEDICAID** (Medicaid#) **TRICARE** (ID#/DoD#) **CHAMPVA** (Member ID#) **GROUP HEALTH PLAN** (ID#) **FECA BLK LUNG** (ID#) **OTHER** (ID#)   **1a. INSURED'S I.D. NUMBER**   (For Program in Item 1)

2. PATIENT'S NAME (Last Name, First Name, Middle Initial)

3. PATIENT'S BIRTH DATE MM DD YY   **SEX** M F

4. INSURED'S NAME (Last Name, First Name, Middle Initial)

5. PATIENT'S ADDRESS (No., Street)

6. PATIENT RELATIONSHIP TO INSURED Self Spouse Child Other

7. INSURED'S ADDRESS (No., Street)

CITY   STATE

8. RESERVED FOR NUCC USE

CITY   STATE

ZIP CODE   TELEPHONE (Include Area Code) ( )

ZIP CODE   TELEPHONE (Include Area Code) ( )

9. OTHER INSURED'S NAME (Last Name, First Name, Middle Initial)

10. IS PATIENT'S CONDITION RELATED TO:

11. INSURED'S POLICY GROUP OR FECA NUMBER

a. OTHER INSURED'S POLICY OR GROUP NUMBER

a. EMPLOYMENT? (Current or Previous) YES NO

a. INSURED'S DATE OF BIRTH MM DD YY **SEX** M F

b. RESERVED FOR NUCC USE

b. AUTO ACCIDENT? YES NO PLACE (State)

b. OTHER CLAIM ID (Designated by NUCC)

c. RESERVED FOR NUCC USE

c. OTHER ACCIDENT? YES NO

c. INSURANCE PLAN NAME OR PROGRAM NAME

d. INSURANCE PLAN NAME OR PROGRAM NAME

10d. CLAIM CODES (Designated by NUCC)

d. IS THERE ANOTHER HEALTH BENEFIT PLAN? YES NO *If yes*, complete items 9, 9a, and 9d.

READ BACK OF FORM BEFORE COMPLETING & SIGNING THIS FORM.

12. PATIENT'S OR AUTHORIZED PERSON'S SIGNATURE I authorize the release of any medical or other information necessary to process this claim. I also request payment of government benefits either to myself or to the party who accepts assignment below.

SIGNED _____ DATE _____

13. INSURED'S OR AUTHORIZED PERSON'S SIGNATURE I authorize payment of medical benefits to the undersigned physician or supplier for services described below.

SIGNED _____

14. DATE OF CURRENT ILLNESS, INJURY, or PREGNANCY (LMP) MM DD YY   QUAL.

15. OTHER DATE QUAL. MM DD YY

16. DATES PATIENT UNABLE TO WORK IN CURRENT OCCUPATION MM DD YY FROM   MM DD YY TO

17. NAME OF REFERRING PROVIDER OR OTHER SOURCE   17a.   17b. NPI

18. HOSPITALIZATION DATES RELATED TO CURRENT SERVICES MM DD YY FROM   MM DD YY TO

19. ADDITIONAL CLAIM INFORMATION (Designated by NUCC)

20. OUTSIDE LAB? YES NO $ CHARGES

21. DIAGNOSIS OR NATURE OF ILLNESS OR INJURY Relate A-L to service line below (24E)   ICD Ind.

A. ____ B. ____ C. ____ D. ____
E. ____ F. ____ G. ____ H. ____
I. ____ J. ____ K. ____ L. ____

22. RESUBMISSION CODE   ORIGINAL REF. NO.

23. PRIOR AUTHORIZATION NUMBER

24. A. DATE(S) OF SERVICE						B. PLACE OF SERVICE	C. EMG	D. PROCEDURES, SERVICES, OR SUPPLIES (Explain Unusual Circumstances)		E. DIAGNOSIS POINTER	F. $ CHARGES	G. DAYS OR UNITS	H. EPSDT Family Plan	I. ID. QUAL.	J. RENDERING PROVIDER ID. #
From MM	DD	YY	To MM	DD	YY			CPT/HCPCS	MODIFIER						
1														NPI	
2														NPI	
3														NPI	
4														NPI	
5														NPI	
6														NPI	

25. FEDERAL TAX I.D. NUMBER SSN EIN

26. PATIENT'S ACCOUNT NO.

27. ACCEPT ASSIGNMENT? (For govt. claims, see back) YES NO

28. TOTAL CHARGE $

29. AMOUNT PAID $

30. Rsvd for NUCC Use

31. SIGNATURE OF PHYSICIAN OR SUPPLIER INCLUDING DEGREES OR CREDENTIALS (I certify that the statements on the reverse apply to this bill and are made a part thereof.)

SIGNED _____ DATE _____

32. SERVICE FACILITY LOCATION INFORMATION

a. NPI   b.

33. BILLING PROVIDER INFO & PH # ( )

a. NPI   b.

NUCC Instruction Manual available at: www.nucc.org   *PLEASE PRINT OR TYPE*

FIGURE 7-5b   Blank CMS-1500 form for case study exercise (use ICD-10 coding).

Case Study

Autumn Anderson, M.D.

0873 Route 10 • Lakewood, NJ 08701 • (732) 888-8888
Tax ID# 11-1122999
NPI# 5522998877

PATIENT INFORMATION:

Name:	Serena Summers
Social Security #:	772-77-2222
Address:	0099 Peach Lane
City:	Wall
State:	NJ
Zip Code:	07719
Home Telephone:	(732) 666-6666
Date of Birth:	08-08-1908
Gender:	Female
Occupation:	Retired
Employer:	
Employer Telephone:	
Spouse:	
Spouse's Social Security #:	
Spouse's Employer:	
Spouse's Date of Birth:	

INSURANCE INFORMATION:

Patient Number:	Sumse000
Place of Service:	Nursing facility
Primary Insurance Plan:	Medicare
Primary Insurance Plan ID #:	772-77-2222A
Group #:	
Primary Policyholder:	Serena Summers
Policyholder Date of Birth:	08-08-1908
Relationship to Patient:	Self
Secondary Insurance Plan:	
Secondary Insurance Plan ID #:	
Secondary Policyholder:	

Patient Status ☐ Married ☐ Divorced ☒ Single ☐ Student ☐ Other

DIAGNOSIS INFORMATION

Diagnosis	Code	Diagnosis	Code
1. Dementia	F03.90	5.	
2.		6.	
3.		7.	
4.		8.	

PROCEDURE INFORMATION

Description of Procedure or Service	Date	Code	Charge
1. Initial nursing facility care - level 1	03-27-YY	99304	$125.00
2. Subsequent + nursing facility care - level 1	03-28-YY	99307	$115.00
3.			
4.			
5.			
6.			

SPECIAL NOTES:

Sunnyvale Senior Home
0090 County Creek Road
Lakewood, NJ 08701
Facility NPI# 9988776655

FIGURE 7-6a Case study form for services provided in a nursing facility (using ICD-10 coding).

HEALTH INSURANCE CLAIM FORM

APPROVED BY NATIONAL UNIFORM CLAIM COMMITTEE (NUCC) 02/12

| | PICA | | | | | | PICA | |

CARRIER

| 1. MEDICARE MEDICAID TRICARE CHAMPVA GROUP HEALTH PLAN FECA BLK LUNG OTHER | 1a. INSURED'S I.D. NUMBER (For Program in Item 1) |
| (Medicare#) (Medicaid#) (ID#/DoD#) (Member ID#) (ID#) (ID#) (ID#) | |

| 2. PATIENT'S NAME (Last Name, First Name, Middle Initial) | 3. PATIENT'S BIRTH DATE MM DD YY SEX M F | 4. INSURED'S NAME (Last Name, First Name, Middle Initial) |

5. PATIENT'S ADDRESS (No., Street)	6. PATIENT RELATIONSHIP TO INSURED Self Spouse Child Other	7. INSURED'S ADDRESS (No., Street)
CITY STATE	8. RESERVED FOR NUCC USE	CITY STATE
ZIP CODE TELEPHONE (Include Area Code) ( )		ZIP CODE TELEPHONE (Include Area Code) ( )

9. OTHER INSURED'S NAME (Last Name, First Name, Middle Initial)	10. IS PATIENT'S CONDITION RELATED TO:	11. INSURED'S POLICY GROUP OR FECA NUMBER
a. OTHER INSURED'S POLICY OR GROUP NUMBER	a. EMPLOYMENT? (Current or Previous) YES NO	a. INSURED'S DATE OF BIRTH MM DD YY SEX M F
b. RESERVED FOR NUCC USE	b. AUTO ACCIDENT? YES NO PLACE (State)	b. OTHER CLAIM ID (Designated by NUCC)
c. RESERVED FOR NUCC USE	c. OTHER ACCIDENT? YES NO	c. INSURANCE PLAN NAME OR PROGRAM NAME
d. INSURANCE PLAN NAME OR PROGRAM NAME	10d. CLAIM CODES (Designated by NUCC)	d. IS THERE ANOTHER HEALTH BENEFIT PLAN? YES NO If yes, complete items 9, 9a, and 9d.

PATIENT AND INSURED INFORMATION

READ BACK OF FORM BEFORE COMPLETING & SIGNING THIS FORM.

| 12. PATIENT'S OR AUTHORIZED PERSON'S SIGNATURE I authorize the release of any medical or other information necessary to process this claim. I also request payment of government benefits either to myself or to the party who accepts assignment below. SIGNED_____ DATE_____ | 13. INSURED'S OR AUTHORIZED PERSON'S SIGNATURE I authorize payment of medical benefits to the undersigned physician or supplier for services described below. SIGNED_____ |

14. DATE OF CURRENT ILLNESS, INJURY, or PREGNANCY (LMP) MM DD YY QUAL.	15. OTHER DATE MM DD YY QUAL.	16. DATES PATIENT UNABLE TO WORK IN CURRENT OCCUPATION MM DD YY MM DD YY FROM TO
17. NAME OF REFERRING PROVIDER OR OTHER SOURCE	17a. 17b. NPI	18. HOSPITALIZATION DATES RELATED TO CURRENT SERVICES MM DD YY MM DD YY FROM TO
19. ADDITIONAL CLAIM INFORMATION (Designated by NUCC)		20. OUTSIDE LAB? YES NO $ CHARGES

| 21. DIAGNOSIS OR NATURE OF ILLNESS OR INJURY Relate A-L to service line below (24E) ICD Ind. A. B. C. D. E. F. G. H. I. J. K. L. | 22. RESUBMISSION CODE ORIGINAL REF. NO. |
| | 23. PRIOR AUTHORIZATION NUMBER |

24. A. DATE(S) OF SERVICE From To MM DD YY MM DD YY	B. PLACE OF SERVICE	C. EMG	D. PROCEDURES, SERVICES, OR SUPPLIES (Explain Unusual Circumstances) CPT/HCPCS MODIFIER	E. DIAGNOSIS POINTER	F. $ CHARGES	G. DAYS OR UNITS	H. EPSDT Family Plan	I. ID. QUAL.	J. RENDERING PROVIDER ID. #
1									NPI
2									NPI
3									NPI
4									NPI
5									NPI
6									NPI

PHYSICIAN OR SUPPLIER INFORMATION

| 25. FEDERAL TAX I.D. NUMBER SSN EIN | 26. PATIENT'S ACCOUNT NO. | 27. ACCEPT ASSIGNMENT? (For govt. claims, see back) YES NO | 28. TOTAL CHARGE $ | 29. AMOUNT PAID $ | 30. Rsvd for NUCC Use |
| 31. SIGNATURE OF PHYSICIAN OR SUPPLIER INCLUDING DEGREES OR CREDENTIALS (I certify that the statements on the reverse apply to this bill and are made a part thereof.) SIGNED DATE | 32. SERVICE FACILITY LOCATION INFORMATION a. NPI b. | 33. BILLING PROVIDER INFO & PH # ( ) a. NPI b. |

NUCC Instruction Manual available at: www.nucc.org   *PLEASE PRINT OR TYPE*

From www.cms.gov

FIGURE 7-6b   Blank CMS-1500 form for case study exercise (use ICD-10 coding).

Chapter 8

Electronic Claims Submissions and Clearinghouses

Learning Objectives

Upon completion of this chapter, the student should be able to:

- Describe the difference between manual claims billing and electronic claims billing.
- Describe the role of a clearinghouse.
- Describe the significance of ANSI X12N.
- Explain the advantages of electronic claims submission.
- Define key terms.

Key Terms

ANSI X12	Electronically	Encrypted	Manual Claims
Batch	Electronic Claims	File	Submission
Claim Attachment	Submission	Online-based	Scrubbing
Clean	Electronic Data	Medical Billing	
Clearinghouse	Interchange (EDI)		

Billing via "Snail Mail"

Manual claims submission

the process of submitting health insurance claims via mail. The claim may be either handwritten or printed from the computer.

In today's advanced technological age, the probability of manual claims submission by medical establishments is low. Nevertheless, there are a few instances in which a biller might need to submit a claim manually. These include:

- Billing a secondary insurance company with the primary's explanation of benefits (EOB) or Remittance Advice (RA) attached.

- Billing critical care codes with the provider's progress notes from the patient's hospital medical record.
- Billing an initial motor vehicle or workers' compensation claim with a personal injury protection (PIP) or a first report of injury form, respectively, attached.

In these instances, each claim submitted must have a claim attachment in order for the claim to be considered for payment.

Claim attachment

additional information submitted with the health insurance claim (e.g., progress notes).

Electronic Claims Submission

Because of advances in computer and communications technology in the twenty-first century, it has become possible to submit health insurance claims electronically. After the medical biller has completed a billing session, all the claims in that batch are then sent to a file. Two common formats for electronic claims submission are NSF and ANSI.

Electronically

via a computer modem.

Batch

a set of claims.

File

an element of data storage.

Electronic claims submission

the process of submitting health insurance claims via computer modem.

National Standard Format (NSF)

When seen on a computer screen, the National Standard Format (NSF) claim format looks exactly like an actual completed CMS-1500 form, but without any lines. The NSF was created by the Health Care Financing Administration, which is now known as the Center for Medicare Services, or CMS. NSF contained a plethora of information on anything related to a medical practice, including patient and provider information. NSF was not widely accepted in the industry. Many companies made modifications to the NSF format in order for it to work for their practice. Most recently, HIPAA managed to replace NSF with a new standard called ANSI-X12N.

ANSI-X12

standardized encryption of patient and provider information completed on a CMS-1500 form.

American National Standards Institute (ANSI)

The American National Standards Institute (ANSI) is an organization that is responsible for approving U.S. standards involving computers and communications utilizing ANSI-X12N. The ANSI claim format contains all the patient and provider information that a completed CMS-1500 form has; however, the information is encrypted (see Figure 8-1). Most claims are now being sent this way to ensure security and confidentiality of patient information.

Encrypted

information that is converted into code for security purposes.

The Role of a Clearinghouse

A clearinghouse acts as a middleman between the biller and the insurance company. Before electronic claims reach their final destination, which is the insurance company, the batch is first sent to a clearinghouse. The clearinghouse reviews the claims for errors or missing information. This process is called scrubbing. If the claim is clean, the clearinghouse will forward it to the appropriate insurance company (see Figure 8-2). If the claim is not clean, it will be sent back to the biller for corrections (see Figure 8-3).

Clearinghouse

an entity that forwards claims to insurance payers electronically.

Scrubbing

reviewing a claim for errors or missing information.

Clean

describes a claim with no errors.

FIGURE 8-1 Sample of encrypted data.

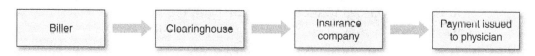

FIGURE 8-2 Flowchart for the cycle of a clean claim.

FIGURE 8-3 Flowchart for the cycle of a claim with errors.

Electronic Data Interchange (EDI)

Electronic Data
Interchange (EDI)

a mutual exchange of data via
computer modem.

The process of the biller sending claims electronically to the clearinghouse and the clearinghouse reporting back with the status of the claims is called electronic data interchange (EDI). The reports received from the clearinghouse will also inform the biller of the following:

- Report of all payers included in the batch
- Total amount of claims and dollar amount forwarded to each payer
- Claims that were forwarded manually to a specific payer (not all payers accept claims electronically)

Benefits of Electronic Claims Submission

There are several reasons why offices still submitting claims manually to insurance companies should strongly consider switching to electronic claims submission:

- Faster reimbursement
- Reduced error rate
- No excuses or delays from insurance carriers stating "claim never received"

Medical Billing via the World Wide Web

Online-based medical
billing

the process of submitting health
claims through a website on the
Internet.

A new and growing trend in the submission of health insurance claims is online-based medical billing. This type of billing is not done on software in the provider's office. Instead, the biller (in the medical office or a medical billing company) uses a login identification (ID) and password to the website of a company that offers this service. Once the biller has logged onto the website, the page used to perform the medical billing function is similar to that produced by software used in providers' offices.

When a provider or medical billing company signs a contract with a company offering this service, there is no software to purchase or install. There is typically a start-up fee and a subsequent monthly fee (for the subscription or maintenance) to pay.

This service may seem enticing to the new provider who is just starting a practice, or to the newly opened medical billing company, but there are several things to consider before choosing this option. Consider the following:

- How long has the company providing the service been in business?
- Can the company provide references from existing clients?
- How secure is the patient's private health information?
- What would happen to the data if the company were to shut down tomorrow?

Summary

Most medical offices and medical billing companies today submit claims electronically rather than manually. The numerous advantages of electronic claims processing include quicker payment turnaround, reduced error rate, and avoidance of claim-receipt problems and excuses from insurance companies.

Clearinghouses act as liaisons between the medical biller and the insurance company. A clearinghouse will review a claim for inaccuracies, but will not fix it. Within hours of electronic submission of claims, the medical biller can retrieve reports sent by the clearinghouse. These reports will detail the total batch that was submitted and note if there were any claims in need of correction. If there are any rejections, the biller can quickly fix and resubmit the claim. This mutual exchange of information is known as electronic data interchange.

Although Internet-based medical billing may seem intriguing, it is important to carefully investigate the company with which the medical practice is considering entering into a contract.

REVIEW QUESTIONS

1. The process of submitting claims through the mail is called _____.

2. Progress notes are an example of a _____.

3. When claims are submitted via a computer modem, this is called _____.

4. A set of claims is referred to as a:
   a. file
   b. batch
   c. folder
   d. subdirectory

5. An element of data storage is a:
   a. folder
   b. bin
   c. file
   d. directory

6. The term used to describe information that has been converted into a code for security precautions is ___.

7. Which format looks like a CMS-1500 form without lines?
   a. ANSI
   b. EDI
   c. NSF
   d. MRA

8. Explain why the ANSI format is considered more desirable from a patient's point of view.

9. What is the role of a clearinghouse?

10. A claim with no errors is a ___ claim.

11. Within ___, the medical biller can retrieve a report on the computer from the clearinghouse.
    a. seconds
    b. minutes
    c. hours
    d. weeks

12. ANSI is an organization that is responsible for approving U.S. standards involving computers and communications utilizing a format known as: _____

13. List three benefits of submitting claims electronically.

14. Medical billing done through a company's website is called _____.

15. List three things to consider before choosing to submit claims through an Internet-based company.

Chapter 9
EOBs and Payments

Learning Objectives

Upon completion of this chapter, the student should be able to:

- Decipher the EOB.
- Describe the concept of insurance adjustments.
- Explain the importance of accurate posting of payments and insurance adjustments.
- Discuss the benefits of EFT.
- Define key terms.

Key Terms

Adjustment	Electronic Funds	Explanation of	Turnaround Time
Clean Claim	Transfer (EFT)	Benefits (EOB)	
Decipher		Posting	

Filing a Clean Medical Claim

Turnaround time

the time it takes for the insurance carrier to process a claim.

The medical biller will gather all pertinent patient information, complete, and send out the CMS-1500, which lists all the care the provider has given the patient for insurance reimbursement. It saves a lot of time fixing billing errors of a rejected claim if the necessary data review happens before the claim leaves the facility for payment. The provider's office will enjoy a continuing cash flow if the turnaround time (the time it takes for the insurance carrier to process a claim) falls within a reasonable period, which is different depending on the payer. Follow these easy steps to make sure your claim gets paid the first time:

- Obtain correct and complete patient information
- Verify insurance benefits
- Obtain all signatures, including assignment of benefits and release of information
- Completely prepare the encounter form
- Accurately enter all charges and diagnoses in the computer
- Submit your clean claim

Payment of the Claim

Payment from the insurance companies can be sent by check in the mail, but that is not as likely in this paperless society. Most facilities will use electronic fund transfer (EFT), which deposits the funds directly into the provider's bank account. The bank your provider uses will require a signed authorization form to allow the transfer of funds. See Figure 9-1 for a sample authorization form for EFT.

Deciphering the Explanation of Benefits

When the claim has been processed, the insurance company will send an explanation of benefits letter to the patient and the provider. The explanation of benefits (EOB) is a notification that states the status of the claim, whether it has been paid, rejected, or denied. See Figure 9-2 for an example of an EOB. The EOB lists such things as:

- Patient's name
- Policyholder's name
- Patient's account number
- Health insurance identification number
- Health insurance group/plan name or number
- Date of service
- CPT, ICD-9 or ICD-10 codes, and any modifiers
- Allowed and disallowed amounts for procedures/services billed
- Amount applied to patient's deductible
- Patient's co-insurance or co-payment amount due
- Remark codes with explanation as to why claim was denied
- Payment amount to provider

The explanation of benefits letter sent from each insurance company can be set up in different formats depending on the type of service your facility provides, for example, cardiology or physical therapy. Some payers have other names for the assignment of benefits, including

- Remittance advice
- Standard paper remittance
- Medicare remittance notice (used by Medicare; see Figure 9-3)
- Explanation of payment report
- Provider voucher
- Provider claim summary

Clean claim

is a claim that has no data errors when submitted to the insurance company.

Electronic Funds Transfer (EFT)

payment method in which funds are deposited directly into the provider's bank account.

Explanation of Benefits (EOB)

the form sent to a provider or patient detailing benefits paid or denied by the insurance company.

DEPARTMENT OF HEALTH AND HUMAN SERVICES
CENTERS FOR MEDICARE & MEDICAID SERVICES

Form Approved
OMB No. 0938-0626

ELECTRONIC FUNDS TRANSFER (EFT) AUTHORIZATION AGREEMENT

PART I – REASON FOR SUBMISSION

Reason for Submission:
- ❑ New EFT Authorization
- ❑ Revision to Current Authorization (e.g. account or bank changes)

Chain Home Office:
Organization
- ❑ Check here if EFT payment is being made to the Home Office of Chain
(Attach letter authorizing EFT payment to Chain Home Office)

PART II – PROVIDER OR SUPPLIER INFORMATION

Name _____

Provider/Supplier Legal Business Name _____

Chain Organization Name_____

Home Office Legal Business Name (if different from Chain Organization Name) _____

Tax Identification Number: (Designate SSN ❑ or EIN ❑)___ ___ ___ ___ ___ ___ ___ ___ ___

Medicare Identification Number (if issued) _____

National Provider Identifier (NPI) _____

PART III – DEPOSITORY INFORMATION (Financial Institution)

Depository Name_____

Street Address_____

City _____ State _____ Zip Code _____

Depository Telephone Number _____

Depository Contact Person _____

Depository Routing Transit Number (nine digit) ___ ___ ___ ___ ___ ___ ___ ___ ___

Depositor Account Number _____

Type of Account (check one) ❑ Checking Account ❑ Savings Account

Please include a voided check or deposit slip or confirmation of account information on bank letterhead. When submitting the documentation, it should contain the name on the account, electronic routing transit number, account number and type, and the bank officer's name signature. This information will be used to verify your account number.

PART IV – CONTACT PERSON

First Name	Middle Initial	Last Name

Telephone Number	Fax Number (if applicable)

Address Line 1 (Street Name and Number)

Address Line 2 (Suite, Room, etc.)

City/Town	State	ZIP Code + 4

E-mail Address

FORM CMS-588 (08/06) EF 09/2006

FIGURE 9-1 Example of an EFT authorization form from CMS. (*Continues*).

PART V – AUTHORIZATION

I hereby authorize the Centers for Medicare & Medicaid Services fee-for-service contractor, _____ _____, hereinafter called the CONTRACTOR, to initiate credit entries, and in accordance with 31 CFR part 210.6(f) initiate adjustments for any credit entries made in error to the account indicated above. I hereby authorize the financial institution/bank named above, hereinafter called the DEPOSITORY, to credit and/or debit the same to such account.

If payment is being made to an account controlled by a Chain Home Office, the Provider of Services hereby acknowledges that payment to the Chain Office under these circumstances is still considered payment to the Provider, and the Provider authorizes the forwarding of Medicare payments to the Chain Home Office.

If the account is drawn in the Physician's or Individual Practitioner's Name, or the Legal Business Name of the Provider/ Supplier, the said Provider or Supplier certifies that he/she has sole control of the account referenced above, and certifies that all arrangements between the DEPOSITORY and the said Provider or Supplier are in accordance with all applicable Medicare regulations and instructions.

This authorization agreement is effective as of the signature date below and is to remain in full force and effect until the CONTRACTOR has received written notification from me of its termination in such time and such manner as to afford the CONTRACTOR and the DEPOSITORY a reasonable opportunity to act on it. The CONTRACTOR will continue to send the direct deposit to the DEPOSITORY indicated above until notified by me that I wish to change the DEPOSITORY receiving the direct deposit. If my DEPOSITORY information changes, I agree to submit to the CONTRACTOR an updated EFT Authorization Agreement.

Signature Line

Authorized/Delegated Official Name (Print) _____

Authorized/Delegated Official Title _____

Authorized/Delegated Official Signature _____ Date _____

PRIVACY ACT ADVISORY STATEMENT

Sections 1842, 1862(b) and 1874 of title XVIII of the Social Security Act authorize the collection of this information. The purpose of collecting this information is to authorize electronic funds transfers.

Under 31 U.S.C. 3332(f)(1), all Federal payments, including Medicare payments to providers and suppliers, shall be made by electronic funds transfer.

The information collected will be entered into system No. 09-70-0501, titled "Carrier Medicare Claims Records," and No. 09-70-0503, titled "Intermediary Medicare Claims Records" published in the Federal Register Privacy Act Issuances, 1991 Comp. Vol. 1, pages 419 and 424, or as updated and republished. Disclosures of information from this system can be found in this notice.

You should be aware that P.L. 100-503, the Computer Matching and Privacy Protection Act of 1988, permits the government, under certain circumstances, to verify the information you provide by way of computer matches.

FORM CMS-588 (08/06) EF 09/2006

FIGURE 9-1 (*Continued*).

From www.cms.gov

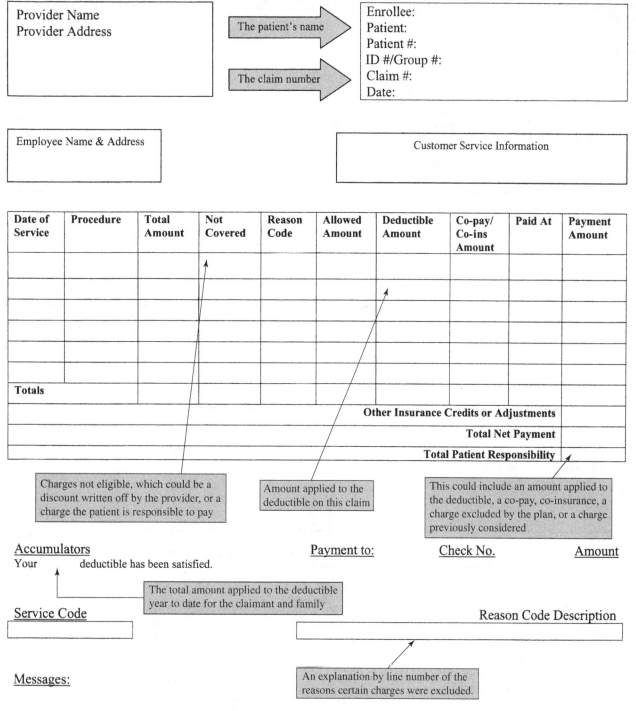

| Provider Name Provider Address | | The patient's name → | | Enrollee: Patient: Patient #: ID #/Group #: Claim #: Date: | | | |

| Employee Name & Address | | | Customer Service Information | |

Date of Service	Procedure	Total Amount	Not Covered	Reason Code	Allowed Amount	Deductible Amount	Co-pay/ Co-ins Amount	Paid At	Payment Amount
Totals									
							Other Insurance Credits or Adjustments		
							Total Net Payment		
							Total Patient Responsibility		

Charges not eligible, which could be a discount written off by the provider, or a charge the patient is responsible to pay

Amount applied to the deductible on this claim

This could include an amount applied to the deductible, a co-pay, co-insurance, a charge excluded by the plan, or a charge previously considered

Accumulators   Payment to: Check No.   Amount
Your   deductible has been satisfied.

The total amount applied to the deductible year to date for the claimant and family

Service Code   Reason Code Description

Messages:

An explanation by line number of the reasons certain charges were excluded.

FIGURE 9-2 Example of how to read an explanation of benefits (EOB).

Medicare Services
1 Insurance Avenue
Anycity, NY 12345
888-123-4567

Medicare Remittance Notice

Barbara Brown, MD
234 Physicians Way
Anytown, NY 13579

If patient has a supplemental insurance on file, Medicare will forward claim

ASG-Y or N for accepts assignment

NPI # 7722228888
Page 1 of 1
Date: 07/01/20YY
Check/ EFT # 103471897

Patient's Medicare health insurance claim number

Perf Prov	Serv Date	POS	NOS	Proc	Mods	Billed	Allowed	Deduct	Co-Ins	Grp/RC Amt	Prov Paid
Alden, Lisa		HIC 1124589XXA		ACNT Aldili00		ICN 020012459874		ASG-Y			
7722228888	6/01/YY	11	1	99214		125.00	84.01	0.00	16.80 CO-42	40.99	67.21
PT RESP 16.80				Claim totals		125.00	84.01	0.00	16.80	40.99	67.21 NET
Claim info forwarded to AARP											
Bart, Frank		HIC 1549856XXA		ACNT Barfr000		ICN 054125896525		ASG-Y			
7722228888	6/04/YY	21	1	99202		175.00	0.00	0.00	0.00	175.00 –ZZ01	0.00
PT RESP 0.00				Claim totals		175.00	0.00	0.00	0.00	175.00	0.00 NET
Class, Mary		HIC 1276325XXB		ACNT Clama000		ICN 041257896523		ASG-Y			
7722228888	6/05/YY	11	1	99213		75.00	63.20	63.20	0.00	11.80	0.00
PT RESP 63.20				Claim totals		75.00	63.20	63.20	0.00	11.80	0.00 NET
Davis, Louise		HIC 1748249XXHA		ACNT Davio000		ICN 092265489653		ASG-Y			
7722228888	6/02/YY	11	1	99245		225.00	0.00	0.00	0.00	225.00-MA130	0.00
PT RESP 0.00				Claim totals		225.00	0.00	0.00	0.00	225.00	0.00 NET
Engle, Diane		HIC 2234476XX		ACNT Eagdi000		ICN 021458974562		ASG-Y			
7722228888	6/03/YY	11	1	99214		110.00	0.00	0.00	0.00	110.00-MA104	0.00
PT RESP 0.00				Claim totals		110.00	0.00	0.00	0.00	110.00	0.00 NET
Totals						Billed	Allowed	Deduct	Co-Ins	Grp/RC Amt	Prov Paid
						710.00	147.21	63.20	16.80	562.79	67.21

The internal control number of claim — assigned by Medicare

Remark Codes:

MA104   HIC number does not match our files
CO-42   Contractual obligation
OA01   Other primary insurance
ZZ01   POS does not match CPT code
MA130   Refer phys NPI missing

Explanation of Column Headings:
Perf Prov — NPI # of performing provider
Serv Date — Date service was performed
POS — Place of service
NOS — Number or units of services
Proc — Procedure code of service
Mods — Modifier
Billed — The billed dollar amount
Allowed — The allowed amount of procedure
Deduct — Deductible
Co-Ins — Co-insurance due
Grp/RC Amt — The amount to be written off
Prov Paid — The amount provider paid for

FIGURE 9-3 Sample Medicare remittance notice.

Decipher

to interpret the meaning of.

The medical biller must have the ability to decipher the EOB so that payments and insurance adjustments can be properly posted to the patient's accounts. This is a critical skill for any medical biller!

Adjustments to Patient Accounts

Adjustment

the dollar amount adjusted off the patient's account reflecting the difference between the fee for services billed and the allowed amount determined by the insurance company.

An adjustment is a positive or negative change to the patient's account balance. An adjustment can be a correction, a change, or a write-off. When the EOB is received, compare it with the copy of the claim filed. Check to see that all the data are correct, including all math calculations. Review the EOB carefully to see if a balance is due from the patient or a refund needs to be made. For example, if a patient paid for a service in advance, leading to an overpayment on the account, then a refund needs to be sent back to the patient.

Here is another example of an insurance adjustment.

Provider fee for procedure 99203 is:	$100.00
Insurance company allowed amount for procedure	$ 80.00
Amount of the insurance adjustment is:	$ 20.00

The patient's account would be adjusted by subtracting the $20 difference between the billed fee and the allowed amount.

Posting

the act of making an entry in the patient's account.

Insurance adjustments are done at the same time the biller is posting the insurance company's payment to the patient's account. It is imperative for the biller to accurately post insurance adjustments when necessary, because failure to do so directly affects the provider's accounts receivable balance. The patient can also be affected by inaccurate posting if you mail them a balance-due statement when no payment is actually due. It is not in the best interest of the facility to receive a phone call from an irate patient. Do it right the first time.

Many times a patient will be confused by the EOB and cannot understand why there is still a balance due after the insurance has paid. It is important to understand all the information presented on the EOB, so you can explain it to the patient in an easy-to-understand manner. It is your part of patient care.

Summary

The medical biller must know how to read the EOB so that payments and insurance adjustments can be accurately posted to patients' accounts.

Although each insurance company may use a different name or format for the EOB, the purpose of the document is the same. Accurate posting of payments and insurance adjustments from the EOB is crucial so that patient-due statements will reflect the correct balance and the provider's accounts receivable balance will be correct.

REVIEW QUESTIONS

1. Define key terms:

   a. What does EOB stand for and what does it mean?

   _____

   b. What does EFT stand for and what does it mean?

   _____

   c. insurance adjustment

   _____

   d. posting

   _____

   e. clean claim

   _____

2. Explain the importance of accurate posting of payments and insurance adjustments. Give an example of a problem you might have if it is not done correctly.

   _____

   _____

   _____

Refer to Figure 9-4 to answer the following.

3. Who is the policyholder of the insurance?

   _____

4. What is the CPT code of the procedure billed?

   _____

5. What is the reason for the not-covered amount?

   _____

6. The payment of $47.60 is ___ percent of ___.

7. What dollar amount will the biller adjust on this claim, presuming that the provider is a participating provider?

   _____

Refer to Figure 9-5 to answer the following.

8. Where were services performed for this patient?

   _____

9. Why was no payment made for procedure code 99223?

   _____

Provider Name
Provider Address

Michael Moe, M.D.
0009 Brick Blvd
Brick, NJ 08724
NPI# 9922375892

Policyholder: Mary Doe
Patient: John Doe
Patient #: Doejo 111
ID #/Group #: 00327569/9937
Claim #: 72-4937JD
Date: 05-01-YYYY

Employee Name & Address

Mary Doe
002 Apple La
Brick, NJ 08724

Customer Service Information

(800) 999-8888

Date of Service	Procedure	Total Amount	Not Covered	Reason Code	Allowed Amount	Deductible Amount	Co-pay/ Co-ins Amount	Paid At	Payment Amount
04-01-YY	99214	$80.00	$20.50	03	$59.50		$11.90	80%	$47.60
Totals		$80.00	$20.50		$59.50		$11.90		$47.60
Other Insurance Credits or Adjustments									
Total Net Payment									$47.60
Total Patient Responsibility									$11.90

Accumulators
Your YYYY deductible has been satisfied.

Payment to: Check No.   Amount
Michael Moe, M.D.   201197 $47.60

Service Code

Medical

Reason Code Description

03- Exceeds fee schedule

Messages:

FIGURE 9-4 Sample explanation of benefits for John Doe.

10. What is the patient's health insurance group number?

_____

11. Is the $50.00 in the "Not Covered" column part of the "Total Patient Responsibility" amount that the patient must pay? If not, how was the $200.00 decided as the patient's responsibility?

_____

Provider Name
Provider Address

Charlie Chintz, DO
0020 Hooper Ave
Toms River, NJ 08755

Employee Name & Address

Sally Sunrise
999 Sunny Lane
Brick, NJ 08723

Policyholder: Sally Sunrise
Patient: Sally Sunrise
Patient #: Salsu 000
ID #/Group #: 197Q42A/2799
Claim #: 622-590ss
Date: 03-07-YYYY

Customer Service Information

(800) 999-1111

Date of Service	Procedure	Total Amount	Not Covered	Reason Code	Allowed Amount	Deductible Amount	Co-pay/ Co-ins Amount	Paid At	Payment Amount
02-01-YY	99223	$175.00	$25.00	03	$150.00	$150.00			$0.00
02-02-YY	99232	$150.00	$15.00	03	$135.00		$27.00	80%	$108.00
02-03-YY	99238	$125.00	$10.00	03	$115.00		$23.00	80%	$92.00
Totals		$450.00	$50.00		$400.00	$150.00	$50.00		$200.00
				Other Insurance Credits or Adjustments					
				Total Net Payment					$200.00
				Total Patient Responsibility					$200.00

Accumulators
Your YYYY deductible has been satisfied.

Payment to: Check No.

Charlie Chintz, DO   79963

Amount

$200.00

Service Code

Hospital

Reason Code Description

03- Exceeds fee schedule

Messages:

FIGURE 9-5 Sample explanation of benefits for Sally Sunrise.

Refer to Figure 9-6 to answer the following.

12. Do any patients have supplemental insurance? If so, who?

   _____

   _____

13. Were any of the patients' claims applied to their deductible? If so, whose?

   _____

   _____

14. Which two claims were clean claims?

   _____

   _____

15. Why was Frank Bart's claim denied? What does the biller need to do before resubmitting this claim?

   _____

   _____

16. Why was Louise Davis's claim denied? What does the biller need to do before resubmitting this claim?

   _____

   _____

17. Why was Diane Engle's claim denied? What does the biller need to do before resubmitting this claim?

   _____

   _____

18. What is the total dollar amount the biller will adjust on this remittance notice?

   _____

   _____

Medicare Services
1 Insurance Avenue
Anycity, NY 12345
888-123-4567

Medicare Remittance Notice

Barbara Brown, MD
234 Physicians Way
Anytown, NY 13579

NPI # 7722228888
Page 1 of 1
Date: 07/01/20YY
Check/ EFT # 103471897

Perf Prov	Serv Date	POS	NOS	Proc	Mods	Billed	Allowed	Deduct	Co-Ins	Grp/RC Amt	Prov Paid
Alden, Lisa		HIC 1124589XXA		ACNT Aldili00		ICN 020012459874		ASG-Y			
7722228888	061520YY	11	1	99214		125.00	84.01	0.00	16.80 CO-42	40.99	67.21
PT RESP 16.80				Claim totals		125.00	84.01	0.00	16.80	40.99	67.21 NET
Claim info forwarded to AARP											
Bart, Frank		HIC 1549856XXA		ACNT Barfr000		ICN 054125896525		ASG-Y			
7722228888	022220YY	21	1	99202		175.00	0.00	0.00	0.00	175.00 –ZZ01	0.00
PT RESP 0.00				Claim totals		175.00	0.00	0.00	0.00	175.00	0.00 NET
Class, Mary		HIC 1276325XXB		ACNT Clama000		ICN 041257896523		ASG-Y			
7722228888	013020YY	11	1	99213		75.00	63.20	63.20	0.00	11.80	0.00
PT RESP 63.20				Claim totals		75.00	63.20	63.20	0.00	11.80	0.00 NET
Davis, Louise		HIC 1748249XXHA		ACNT Davio000		ICN 092265489653		ASG-Y			
7722228888	061220YY	11	1	99245		225.00	0.00	0.00	0.00	225.00-MA130	0.00
PT RESP 0.00				Claim totals		225.00	0.00	0.00	0.00	225.00	0.00 NET
Engle, Diane		HIC 2234476XX		ACNT Eagdi000		ICN 021458974562		ASG-Y			
7722228888	061320YY	11	1	99214		110.00	0.00	0.00	0.00	110.00-MA104	0.00
PT RESP 0.00				Claim totals		110.00	0.00	0.00	0.00	110.00	0.00 NET
Totals						**Billed**	**Allowed**	**Deduct**	**Co-Ins**	**Grp/RC Amt**	**Prov Paid**
						710.00	**147.21**	**63.20**	**16.80**	**562.79**	**67.21**

Remark Codes:
MA104   HIC number does not match our files
CO-42   Contractual obligation
OA01   Other primary insurance
ZZ01   POS does not match CPT code
MA130   Refer phys NPI missing

FIGURE 9-6   Sample Medicare remittance notice for Barbara Brown, MD.

Chapter 10

Denials and Appeals

Learning Objectives

Upon completion of this chapter, the student should be able to:

- Explain the difference between a rejected claim and a denied claim.
- Comprehend the reasons for claim denial.
- Discuss the necessary actions to be taken following denial of a claim.
- List important things to remember when filing an appeal.
- Define key terms.

Key Terms

Adjudication	Denied Claim	Paper Trail	Unauthorized
Appeal	Noncovered	Rejected Claim	

The Rejected Claim

Rejected claim

refused to accept due to a technical issue.

A **rejected claim** does not mean the facility will not get paid for services given to a patient. Claims that have been rejected by a clearinghouse, as discussed in Chapter 8, are not forwarded to the intended payer due to technical errors. They are returned to the submitter for correction.

Reasons for claim rejection include, but are not limited to:

- Missing patient information
- Missing provider information
- Incomplete ICD-9 or CPT codes
- Place-of-service code does not match procedure code

- Required box items not checked
- Blocks or boxes requiring a signature or "SOF" notation are left blank
- Typographical errors (e.g., date of service listed on claim is in the future)

See Figure 10-1 for a sample CMS-1500 form that contains errors.

Once the errors that caused rejection of the claim have been corrected, the claim is considered clean and can be resubmitted to the clearinghouse for processing.

The Denied Claim

Adjudication

the actual processing of the claim by the insurance carrier.

Denied claim

refused to grant payment due to an insurance coverage issue.

The acceptance of a clean claim by the clearinghouse does not guarantee payment to the provider by the insurance carrier. The actual processing of the claim by the insurance carrier is called adjudication. The carrier will evaluate the claim, deciding which services should be paid and how much they will pay for each. A denied claim is a claim not reimbursed by the payer due to an insurance coverage issue. The contract the patient has with the insurance company determines the services, procedures, and ancillary charges that will be reimbursed for that patient. The patient should have some knowledge about his or her policy, but that is not always the case. The medical biller may need to educate the patient about what their policy does or does not cover

Reasons for denials can include, but are not limited to:

- Insurance coverage not yet effective
- Insurance coverage terminated prior to the date of service
- Insured's name does not match insurance company's database
- Incorrect health insurance identification number
- Other primary insurance on file
- Diagnosis code does not support the procedure or service
- Procedure or service is considered a noncovered benefit
- Procedure or service is unauthorized
- Maximum benefits reached for this procedure or service
- Submission of claim exceeds payer's claim filing deadline

Noncovered

service or procedure not listed as a covered benefit in the payer's master benefit list.

Unauthorized

authorization or approval for services was not obtained from the payer prior to treatment.

When a claim has been denied, the insurance carrier informs both the provider and the patient of the reimbursement status of the claim by sending out an EOB. If the complete claim or any portion of the claim has been denied, the EOB will list the reason or reasons for the denial. See Figure 10-2. Denied codes are used on the EOB to communicate between the biller, the insured, and the payer the specific reason the procedure or service was denied.

Responding to the Denied Claim

Appeal

a formal way of asking the insurance carrier to reconsider the decision regarding the payment of a claim.

Once a reason for the claim denial has been determined, the claim balance must be transferred to the patient's account as the patient's responsibility. The patient can then choose to call her insurance company if she feels the denial was made in error, or call the provider's office with corrected information. Some denial codes can be addressed by the biller and the claim resubmitted for reimbursement. The following table lists reasons for denials and suggested actions to reverse or appeal the denial.

HEALTH INSURANCE CLAIM FORM

APPROVED BY NATIONAL UNIFORM CLAIM COMMITTEE (NUCC) 02/12

ABC INS COMPANY
100 RAIL ROAD
VEIL NJ 00003

CARRIER →

| | | PICA | | | | | PICA | | |

1. MEDICARE ☐ (Medicare#) MEDICAID ☐ (Medicaid#) TRICARE ☐ (ID#/DoD#) CHAMPVA ☐ (Member ID#) GROUP HEALTH PLAN ☒ (ID#) FECA BLK LUNG ☐ (ID#) OTHER ☐ (ID#)

1a. INSURED'S I.D. NUMBER   (For Program in Item 1)
QR7239603

2. PATIENT'S NAME (Last Name, First Name, Middle Initial)
FIELDS, FRAN

3. PATIENT'S BIRTH DATE MM ｜ DD ｜ YY   SEX   M ☐ F ☒

4. INSURED'S NAME (Last Name, First Name, Middle Initial)
Same

5. PATIENT'S ADDRESS (No., Street)
0039 FRAN ROAD

6. PATIENT RELATIONSHIP TO INSURED
Self ☒ Spouse ☐ Child ☐ Other ☐

7. INSURED'S ADDRESS (No., Street)

CITY
FRANKLIN   STATE NJ

8. RESERVED FOR NUCC USE

CITY   STATE

ZIP CODE
00007   TELEPHONE (Include Area Code) (908)

ZIP CODE   TELEPHONE (Include Area Code) ( )

9. OTHER INSURED'S NAME (Last Name, First Name, Middle Initial)

10. IS PATIENT'S CONDITION RELATED TO:

11. INSURED'S POLICY GROUP OR FECA NUMBER

a. OTHER INSURED'S POLICY OR GROUP NUMBER

a. EMPLOYMENT? (Current or Previous) ☐ YES ☒ NO

a. INSURED'S DATE OF BIRTH MM ｜ DD ｜ YY   SEX M ☐ F ☐

b. RESERVED FOR NUCC USE

b. AUTO ACCIDENT? ☐ YES ☐ NO   PLACE (State)

b. OTHER CLAIM ID (Designated by NUCC)

c. RESERVED FOR NUCC USE

c. OTHER ACCIDENT? ☐ YES ☒ NO

c. INSURANCE PLAN NAME OR PROGRAM NAME

d. INSURANCE PLAN NAME OR PROGRAM NAME

10d. CLAIM CODES (Designated by NUCC)

d. IS THERE ANOTHER HEALTH BENEFIT PLAN? ☐ YES ☒ NO   *If yes*, complete items 9, 9a, and 9d.

READ BACK OF FORM BEFORE COMPLETING & SIGNING THIS FORM.

12. PATIENT'S OR AUTHORIZED PERSON'S SIGNATURE I authorize the release of any medical or other information necessary to process this claim. I also request payment of government benefits either to myself or to the party who accepts assignment below.
SIGNED _SOF_   DATE _0504YY_

13. INSURED'S OR AUTHORIZED PERSON'S SIGNATURE I authorize payment of medical benefits to the undersigned physician or supplier for services described below.
SIGNED _SOF_

14. DATE OF CURRENT ILLNESS, INJURY, or PREGNANCY (LMP) MM ｜ DD ｜ YY   QUAL.

15. OTHER DATE QUAL.   MM ｜ DD ｜ YY

16. DATES PATIENT UNABLE TO WORK IN CURRENT OCCUPATION MM ｜ DD ｜ YY   FROM   TO   MM ｜ DD ｜ YY

17. NAME OF REFERRING PROVIDER OR OTHER SOURCE
LUKE LUCAS MD

17a.
17b. NPI

18. HOSPITALIZATION DATES RELATED TO CURRENT SERVICES MM ｜ DD ｜ YY   FROM   TO   MM ｜ DD ｜ YY

19. ADDITIONAL CLAIM INFORMATION (Designated by NUCC)

20. OUTSIDE LAB? ☐ YES ☒ NO $ CHARGES

21. DIAGNOSIS OR NATURE OF ILLNESS OR INJURY Relate A-L to service line below (24E)   ICD Ind.

A. 784.0   B.   C.   D.
E.   F.   G.   H.
I.   J.   K.   L.

22. RESUBMISSION CODE   ORIGINAL REF. NO.

23. PRIOR AUTHORIZATION NUMBER

24. A. DATE(S) OF SERVICE From MM DD YY — To MM DD YY	**B.** PLACE OF SERVICE	**C.** EMG	**D.** PROCEDURES, SERVICES, OR SUPPLIES (Explain Unusual Circumstances) CPT/HCPCS ｜ MODIFIER	**E.** DIAGNOSIS POINTER	**F.** $ CHARGES	**G.** DAYS OR UNITS	**H.** EPSDT Family Plan	**I.** ID. QUAL.	**J.** RENDERING PROVIDER ID. #
1 05 04 YY 05 04 YY	21		99244		175			NPI	
2								NPI	
3								NPI	
4								NPI	
5								NPI	
6								NPI	

25. FEDERAL TAX I.D. NUMBER   SSN ☐ EIN ☒

26. PATIENT'S ACCOUNT NO.
FIEFA000

27. ACCEPT ASSIGNMENT? (For govt. claims, see back) ☒ YES ☐ NO

28. TOTAL CHARGE
$ 175｜00

29. AMOUNT PAID
$ 0｜00

30. Rsvd for NUCC Use
175｜00

31. SIGNATURE OF PHYSICIAN OR SUPPLIER INCLUDING DEGREES OR CREDENTIALS (I certify that the statements on the reverse apply to this bill and are made a part thereof.)
DINA DIAMOND MD 0510YY
SIGNED   DATE

32. SERVICE FACILITY LOCATION INFORMATION
DINA DIAMOND MD
050 ROUTE 27
EDISON NJ 00099
a. NPI   b.

33. BILLING PROVIDER INFO & PH # (732)
DINA DIAMOND MD
050 ROUTE 27
EDISON NJ 00099
a. NPI   b.

NUCC Instruction Manual available at: www.nucc.org   *PLEASE PRINT OR TYPE*

PATIENT AND INSURED INFORMATION → PHYSICIAN OR SUPPLIER INFORMATION →

From www.cms.gov

FIGURE 10-1 Sample CMS-1500 form with errors.

Denial Reason	Suggested Action
Insurance coverage not yet effective	Patient should contact the physician's office with correct insurance information.
Insurance coverage terminated	Patient should contact the physician's office with correct insurance information.
Other primary insurance on file	Patient should contact the physician's office with correct insurance information.
Insured's name does not match payer's database	Biller should check copy of ID card to see if name mismatch was a result of a typographical error.
Incorrect health insurance identification number	Biller should check copy of ID card to see if incorrect number was a result of a typographical error.
Diagnosis code does not meet requirements for procedure or service	If not a billing error, file an appeal with the insurance company.
Procedure or service is considered a noncovered benefit	An appeal may be attempted. If appeal is denied, the balance is the patient's responsibility.
Procedure or service is unauthorized	If the physician's office had the responsibility to obtain authorization, the physician decides whether to write off the claim balance. If the responsibility to obtain authorization was the patient's, the patient is responsible for paying the claim balance.
Maximum benefits reached for this service	Attempt an appeal. If denied, responsibility for paying the claim balance is the patient's.
Submission of claim exceeds payer's filing deadline	Biller may attempt an appeal with explanation for late filing. If denied, the physician must approve a write-off of the claim balance.

Appealing the Denied Claim

Once a decision has been made to appeal the denied claim, it is essential to gather all the important documents to support the request for a claim review. The medical biller must accurately maintain a paper trail of all aspects of current appeals, in order to understand where each claim is in the process. The insurance carrier will need all the documents listed below to review the claim for resubmission:

Paper trail

written or printed evidence of someone's activities

- Write down the date, the name of the person contacted, and details of all telephone conversations and/or correspondence relating to the denied claim in question.
- Keep original documents in the physician's office and send photocopies to the insurance company, including a letter outlining why the claim should be covered.
- Include copies of the patient's records (progress notes, lab results, diagnostic testing results) to assist when appealing for reasons of medical necessity.

- Adhere to the payer's appeal filing deadlines.
- Request a written reply.

See Figures 10-3 through 10-6 for sample inquiry and appeal forms and letters.

If all efforts to appeal fail, the physician may decide to hire an attorney skilled in health insurance company matters to sue the insurance company.

Provider Name
Provider Address

Winston Wagner, DO
00330 Spring Lake Rd
Spring Lake, NJ 00004
NPI# 0000260000

Employee Name & Address

Vera Vonable
0030 Oakhurst Rd
Oakhurst, NJ 00007

Policyholder: Vera Vonable
Patient: Victor Vonable
Patient #: Vonvi 000
ID #/Group #: 339ZQ4372/996644
Claim #: 26-QRZ549
Date: 02-27-YY

Customer Service Information

(800) 555-5555

Date of Service	Procedure	Total Amount	Not Covered	Reason Code	Allowed Amount	Deductible Amount	Co-pay/ Co-ins Amount	Paid At	Payment Amount
02-01-YY	99203	$100.00	$100.00	02					$0.00
Totals		$100.00	$100.00						$0.00
Other Insurance Credits or Adjustments									
Total Net Payment									$0.00
Total Patient Responsibility									$100.00

Accumulators
Your   deductible has been satisfied.

Payment to: Check No.   Amount
$0.00

Service Code

Office visit

Reason Code Description

02- Coverage terminated prior to date of service

Messages:

FIGURE 10-2 Sample EOB for a denied claim.

MEDICARE PART B CLAIM INQUIRY/APPEAL REQUEST FORM
Fields marked with an * are REQUIRED for an Appeal Request

This form may be used for one or more claims concerning the same issue. If your request involves multiple claims, you may attach a copy of your Standard Paper Remittance (SPR) to this form and highlight the services you want reviewed.

Please mail this form and pertinent documentation (Certificate of Medical Necessity, operative notes, test results, etc.) to:

New Jersey Providers Mail to:
Empire Medicare Services
P.O. Box 69202
Harrisburg, PA 17106-9202

New York Providers Mail to:
Empire Medicare Services
P.O. Box 2280
Peekskill, NY 10566-2280

| Date of Request: |
| / / |

CLAIM INFORMATION

PROVIDER NUMBER:	*PATIENT HEALTH INSURANCE CLAIM NUMBER (HIC):
*PROVIDER NAME & ADDRESS:	*PATIENT NAME & ADDRESS:
*INTERNAL CONTROL NUMBER(S):	*PROCEDURE CODE(S):
*DATES OF SERVICE:	BILLED AMOUNT:

*REQUEST FOR: APPEAL: [ ]   **INQUIRY:** [ ]

The date of the Standard Paper Remittance (SPR) for the claim in question:

If the appeal concerns Medicare Secondary Payment, please indicate if you participate with the

Primary insurance company _____ participate _____ do not participate

| *SPR DATE: |
| / / |

*REASON FOR APPEAL/INQUIRY (AND LATE FILING EXPLANATION IF APPLICABLE):
_____
_____
_____
_____
_____

* If your request has <u>exceeded the time limit</u> for an appeal, please include the <u>reason</u> for late filing with your request.

* If requesting an appeal of an unassigned claim, as the patient's representative, complete the Appointment of Representative Form (CMS 1696-U4). Otherwise, requests on behalf of the patient can be made through this form or any written statement; however, the outcome of the appeal will only be disclosed to the patient.

| *REQUESTER'S NAME & TITLE: | TELEPHONE NUMBER: |
| *REQUESTER'S SIGNATURE: | DATE SIGNED: |

A PHOTOCOPY OF THIS FORM IS ACCEPTABLE

SMC3123 Rev. 01/11/2005

From www.cms.gov

FIGURE 10-3 Sample Medicare Part B claim inquiry/appeal request form.

Insurance Company
Address

Date

Dear Mr. _____:

We have received the explanation of benefits for the patient, Mr. Robert Crawford. However, we believe the charges, totaling **$480.00** for February 25, 20XX through March 14, 20XX, have been considered incorrectly.

The EOB states that the March 15th charge of **$80.00** is not a medical necessity. When I spoke to you at the claims center earlier this week, your explanation of the denial was because the patient is not homebound; the insurance company believes the visit was for patient convenience and not medically necessary.

In reviewing the nurse's notes for each skilled nursing visit, medical necessity appears to have been established. The March 15th visit should not have been denied. A new infusion therapy was started on that date and the patient required instruction on drug administration.

Skilled nursing visits are a medical necessity to follow up on how well the patient is learning; in this instance, errors in the patient's technique were in fact discovered. Throughout the therapy the patient was fatigued, weak, and felt sick. The patient also felt overwhelmed with the therapies, requiring further instruction and reinforcement. The results of not having skilled nursing visits could lead to further complications, such as the patient not following the drug schedule or performing inaccurate drug administration.

It appears that a review of the nurse's notes would support the medical necessity of the nursing charges. Please reconsider the denied portion of the charges and issue a payment to Valu Home Care in the amount of **$80.00**.

Sincerely,

_____ _____

Collections Manager, Valu Home Care

FIGURE 10-4   Sample appeal letter for "not medically necessary" denial of charges.

Insurance Company
Address

Date

Dear Ms. _____:

I am writing to you in regards to a claim submitted by White Oaks Hospital for my daughter, [name]. The charges were rendered on August 30, 20XX, and totaled $23,716.91. ABC Insurance Company has considered the charges and made a payment of $18,269.86, but this was after a penalty of $1,500.00 was deducted from the payment.

My daughter was involved in a serious car accident. We were unaware of a required preauthorization procedure and, under the circumstances, didn't think to investigate the policy booklet about preauthorizing inpatient hospital stays. The policy booklet does state that the preauthorization hotline must be called within three days of the patient's admittance to the hospital for emergency situations. However, both the hospital and attending physician were preferred providers. I called the PPO agency and they advised me that it is the medical provider's responsibility, if they are preferred providers, to initiate the preauthorization. [Name] from [name] PPO network, at (800) 555-1234, extension 567, was my contact for this information. Because of this, I believe the benefit penalty was applied in error.

Please reconsider the charges and issue the additional payment to the hospital. Thank you.

Sincerely,

[insured's name]

FIGURE 10-5   Sample appeal letter concerning reduction of payment for failure to preauthorize treatment.

Insurance Company
Address

Date

Dear Claims Review Department:

I am writing to you in regards to a claim submitted by Home Health Agency [medical provider] for [patient]. The charges were rendered on [date] and totaled [claim dollar total]. [Health plan] has denied payment for this procedure, stating that the home health agency was not licensed.

The State of Kentucky does not require a home health agency to be a licensed provider. The current condition requires that the services of a home health agency be obtained. Home health agency visits are a covered expense under my plan. I am requesting that you reconsider your denial of the claim for this service and immediately authorize payment. I am including, with this appeal letter, documentation that supports this statement.

As a member of [health plan], I am requesting your reconsideration of this denial and that you extend the coverage for me. If there is any additional information I could provide to you that would expedite this matter, please feel free to contact me. Thank you for your time and assistance in this matter.

Sincerely,

[insured's name]

Enclosures:

_____

_____

FIGURE 10-6   Sample appeal letter for "place of service" denial.

Summary

A rejected claim and a denied claim are not the same. A rejected claim is sent back to the physician's office via a clearinghouse report with a list of technical errors, which may be corrected and the claim resubmitted. A denied claim was processed by the clearinghouse and presented to a payer but has insurance coverage issues that denied the claim.

Appeals may be initiated by either the physician or the patient/insured. An appeal should include a list of reasons why the physician or patient feels the claim should be reconsidered for payment. It is important to maintain a paper trail for each claim to understand how the reimbursement of the claim is progressing.

An excess number of rejected or denied claims results in delay of payment to the physician and additional work for the medical biller.

REVIEW QUESTIONS

1. See Figure 10-7 and circle errors that would cause the claim to be rejected.

2. See Figure 10-8 and give an explanation for claim denial and suggest a course of action.

3. Define key terms:
   a. rejected

   _____

   b. denied

   _____

   c. noncovered

   _____

   d. unauthorized

   _____

   e. appeal

   _____

4. Explain the difference between a rejected claim and a denied claim.

   _____

   _____

5. List three reasons why a claim may be rejected:

   _____

   _____

   _____

6. List five reasons for denial of a claim and suggested actions to take thereafter:

   _____

   _____

   _____

   _____

   _____

7. What can a physician do if appeal requests have failed?

   _____

   _____

HEALTH INSURANCE CLAIM FORM

APPROVED BY NATIONAL UNIFORM CLAIM COMMITTEE (NUCC) 02/12

LOCAL 00970
0055 ROUTE 22
GREENFIELD NJ 00399

CARRIER →

	PICA								PICA	

1. MEDICARE (Medicare#)	MEDICAID (Medicaid#)	TRICARE (ID#/DoD#)	CHAMPVA (Member ID#)	GROUP HEALTH PLAN (ID#)	FECA BLK LUNG (ID#)	OTHER (ID#)	1a. INSURED'S I.D. NUMBER (For Program in Item 1)
							729P46R292

2. PATIENT'S NAME (Last Name, First Name, Middle Initial)
KITE, KYLE

3. PATIENT'S BIRTH DATE — MM 02 DD 28 YY 92 — SEX M ☐ F ☐

4. INSURED'S NAME (Last Name, First Name, Middle Initial)
KITE KAREN

5. PATIENT'S ADDRESS (No., Street)
055 NECTAR LANE

6. PATIENT RELATIONSHIP TO INSURED
Self ☐ Spouse ☐ Child ☒ Other ☐

7. INSURED'S ADDRESS (No., Street)
055 NECTOR LANE

CITY TOMS RIVER — STATE NJ

8. RESERVED FOR NUCC USE

CITY TOMS RIVER — STATE NJ

ZIP CODE 08753 — TELEPHONE (Include Area Code) (732)0552995

ZIP CODE 08753 — TELEPHONE (Include Area Code) (732)0552995

9. OTHER INSURED'S NAME (Last Name, First Name, Middle Initial)

10. IS PATIENT'S CONDITION RELATED TO:

11. INSURED'S POLICY GROUP OR FECA NUMBER
639976

a. OTHER INSURED'S POLICY OR GROUP NUMBER

a. EMPLOYMENT? (Current or Previous) YES ☐ NO ☒

a. INSURED'S DATE OF BIRTH MM DD YY — SEX M ☐ F ☒

b. RESERVED FOR NUCC USE

b. AUTO ACCIDENT? YES ☐ NO ☒ PLACE (State)

b. OTHER CLAIM ID (Designated by NUCC)

c. RESERVED FOR NUCC USE

c. OTHER ACCIDENT? YES ☐ NO ☒

c. INSURANCE PLAN NAME OR PROGRAM NAME
IRON WORKERS UNION

d. INSURANCE PLAN NAME OR PROGRAM NAME

10d. CLAIM CODES (Designated by NUCC)

d. IS THERE ANOTHER HEALTH BENEFIT PLAN?
YES ☐ NO ☒ *If yes, complete items 9, 9a, and 9d.*

READ BACK OF FORM BEFORE COMPLETING & SIGNING THIS FORM.
12. PATIENT'S OR AUTHORIZED PERSON'S SIGNATURE I authorize the release of any medical or other information necessary to process this claim. I also request payment of government benefits either to myself or to the party who accepts assignment below.

SIGNED SOF — DATE

13. INSURED'S OR AUTHORIZED PERSON'S SIGNATURE I authorize payment of medical benefits to the undersigned physician or supplier for services described below.

SIGNED SOF

14. DATE OF CURRENT ILLNESS, INJURY, or PREGNANCY (LMP) MM DD YY — QUAL.

15. OTHER DATE QUAL. — MM DD YY

16. DATES PATIENT UNABLE TO WORK IN CURRENT OCCUPATION — FROM MM DD YY — TO MM DD YY

17. NAME OF REFERRING PROVIDER OR OTHER SOURCE
17a.
17b. NPI

18. HOSPITALIZATION DATES RELATED TO CURRENT SERVICES — FROM MM DD YY — TO MM DD YY

19. ADDITIONAL CLAIM INFORMATION (Designated by NUCC)

20. OUTSIDE LAB? YES ☐ NO ☒ — $ CHARGES

21. DIAGNOSIS OR NATURE OF ILLNESS OR INJURY Relate A-L to service line below (24E) — ICD Ind.
A. 477.9   B.   C.   D.
E.   F.   G.   H.
I.   J.   K.   L.

22. RESUBMISSION CODE — ORIGINAL REF. NO.

23. PRIOR AUTHORIZATION NUMBER

24. A. DATE(S) OF SERVICE From MM DD YY To MM DD YY	B. PLACE OF SERVICE	C. EMG	D. PROCEDURES, SERVICES, OR SUPPLIES (Explain Unusual Circumstances) CPT/HCPCS | MODIFIER	E. DIAGNOSIS POINTER	F. $ CHARGES	G. DAYS OR UNITS	H. EPSDT Family Plan	I. ID. QUAL.	J. RENDERING PROVIDER ID. #
1	04 29 YY 04 29 YY			99213		65 00			NPI	
2									NPI	
3									NPI	
4									NPI	
5									NPI	
6									NPI	

25. FEDERAL TAX I.D. NUMBER SSN ☐ EIN ☐
119956788

26. PATIENT'S ACCOUNT NO.
KITKY000

27. ACCEPT ASSIGNMENT? (For govt. claims, see back) YES ☐ NO ☐

28. TOTAL CHARGE $ 65 00

29. AMOUNT PAID $ 0 00

30. Rsvd for NUCC Use 65 00

31. SIGNATURE OF PHYSICIAN OR SUPPLIER INCLUDING DEGREES OR CREDENTIALS (I certify that the statements on the reverse apply to this bill and are made a part thereof.)
SIGNED 0507YY DATE

32. SERVICE FACILITY LOCATION INFORMATION
HARRY HINES MD
011 HOOPER AVENUE
BRICK NJ 08724
a. NPI   b.

33. BILLING PROVIDER INFO & PH # (732)010 1110
HARRY HINES MD
011 HOOPER AVENUE
BRICK NJ 08724
a. 1111000099   b.

NUCC Instruction Manual available at: www.nucc.org — *PLEASE PRINT OR TYPE*

PATIENT AND INSURED INFORMATION — PHYSICIAN OR SUPPLIER INFORMATION

From www.cms.gov

FIGURE 10-7 Sample CMS-1500 form with errors for patient Kyle Kite.

Provider Name
Provider Address

Ben Foe, M.D.
002 Rainy Road
Neptune, NJ 00022
NPI# 0000777799

Employee Name & Address

John Doe
111 Fawn Road
Brick, NJ 08724

Policyholder: John Doe
Patient: Jane Doe
Patient #: Dojan 000
ID #/Group #: QRS2794Y33/694331
Claim #: 99-2278
Date: 04-15-YY

Customer Service Information

(800) 000-2222

Date of Service	Procedure	Total Amount	Not Covered	Reason Code	Allowed Amount	Deductible Amount	Co-pay/ Co-ins Amount	Paid At	Payment Amount
03-01-YY	58301	$500.00	$500.00	07					$0.00
Totals		$500.00	$500.00						$0.00
							Other Insurance Credits or Adjustments		
							Total Net Payment		$0.00
							Total Patient Responsibility		$500.00

Accumulators
Your YYYY deductible has been satisfied.

Payment to: Check No.   Amount
                                    $0.00

Service Code

Surgery

Reason Code Description

07- POS not required for this procedure

Messages:

Procedure code 58301 (removal of intrauterine device)
Does not meet guidelines for care in an out-patient hospital setting. Procedure could
have been performed in physician's office.

FIGURE 10-8   Sample EOB denial for patient Jane Doe.

Chapter 11

Maintaining Accounts Receivable, Aging Reports, and Rebilling

Learning Objectives

Upon completion of this chapter, the student should be able to:

- Describe the function of rebilling.
- Explain the importance of claim follow-up.
- Decipher patient aging and insurance aging reports.
- Comprehend the significance of maintaining the office's accounts receivable.
- Define key terms.

Key Terms

Cash Flow
Follow-up
Insurance Aging Report

Overhead
Patient Aging Report

Maintaining the Accounts Receivable

Cash flow

a stream of cash (income) used for disbursements.

Overhead

costs such as rent, utilities, malpractice insurance, and salaries; a business expense.

In a perfect world, all the payments are collected from the patient at the time the health care services are rendered; but this is not a perfect world. The patient has many options for payment, including credit cards and payment plans. Accounts receivable is monies owed to a provider for services, as stated in Chapter 1. Maintaining an accurate accounts receivable is a very large part of the medical biller's job responsibility. Unpaid claims will decrease the amount of actual cash or cash flow available to the medical practice at any given time. The provider's practice cannot function at full capacity if all monies are spent on overhead costs (such as rent, utilities, malpractice insurance, and salaries) and not enough coming into the office.

The Aging Process

Once a claim has been submitted, either electronically or via mail, it begins to age. The dollar amount submitted on this claim becomes part of the provider's accounts receivable. The age of an unpaid claim needs to be controlled by follow-up with the insurance company and the patient. The older a claim gets, the more direct effect it has on the provider's monthly accounts receivable.

Offices vary on the protocol of claim follow-up. Some providers will rebill a claim after 30 days if no payment or a denial has been received. Other providers will require the medical biller to call the insurance company first to find out the reason for the delay in payment. The medical biller must track all denied and rejected claims, or many would not be paid. A tickler file, also called a suspense or follow-up file, can be set up to track all the correspondences a biller has made on any pending or resubmitted insurance claims.

Each month, the medical biller should print an insurance aging report and a patient aging report as part of working with the provider's accounts receivable.

Insurance Aging Report

The insurance aging report is a list of outstanding claims for each insurance company that owes the provider money. Depending on the software used in the office, an insurance aging report can be printed for only one specific insurance company, or for a summary of all companies (usually listed alphabetically). The report is broken into increments of 30 days per column. These columns indicate how many days old a claim is (see Figure 11-1). Other information on this report includes:

- Patient's name and account number
- Date of service
- Procedure or service rendered
- Total balance for each amount
- Telephone number of the insurance company

A claim should be processed and reimbursed within 30 days. One goal of the medical biller is to reduce the dollar amount listed in any column after 60 days. When a claim gets to the 120+ column of this report, it becomes harder to collect the money due on that claim.

Note: *The insurance aging report shown in this text is only an example. Software programs and capabilities vary among offices, so the format of the insurance aging report will vary also. Some reports have as few as three columns, reflecting claims that are 90 days old; other reports may extend beyond the 120+ column.*

Patient Aging Report

The patient aging report is an alphabetical list of all the patients of the practice who owe the provider money. Monies due on this list may include balances after the primary insurance has paid, balances after both the primary and supplemental insurances have paid, and balances for patients who have no insurance. Like the insurance aging report, it is sectioned into three columns (see Figure 11-2). The monies shown in each column represent the age of patient claims that have a balance due after the

---

Follow-up

the process of checking the status of a claim.

Insurance aging report

shows monies owed to the provider from insurance companies.

Patient aging report

shows monies owed to the provider from patients (patient balances due).

Date of Service	Procedure	0–30	31–60	61–90	91–120	120+	Total Balance
Aetna						Aetna Total	$175.00
Aplsu 000							
Apples, Susan							
06-01-20XX	99214	$75.00					$75.00
Attal 000	99203		$100.00				$100.00
Atty, Alice						BC/BS Total	$205.00
Barbe 000							
Barnes, Belinda							
04-07-20XX	99204			$125.00			$125.00
Beeba 000							
Beeker, Barney							
01-17-20XX	69210					$80.00	$80.00
Cigna						Cigna Total	$155.00
Janja 000	81002				$20.00		
Jones, Janet	87070				$30.00		
02-27-20XX	99211				$40.00		$90.00
Scosa 000							
Scott, Sarah							
04-01-20XX	99213			$65.00			$65.00
Healthnet						Healthnet Total	$225.00
Mapmi 000							
Maples, Michelle							
01-22-20XX	99223					$175.00	$175.00
Truta 000							
Trucker, Tammy							
06-07-20XX	93000	$50.00					$50.00
Medicare						Medicare Total	$220.00
Vasre 000							
Vasquez, Vern							
05-02-20XX	99205		$150.00				$150.00
Zipze 000							
Zippo, Zenny							
02-28-20XX	99212				$70.00		$70.00

FIGURE 11-1   Sample insurance aging report.

insurance carriers has paid their portion. The age of monies listed for patients without insurance reflects back to the date of service. Methods of collecting balances due from patients are explored in Chapter 12.

Note: *Like the insurance aging report, the patient aging report shown in this textbook is an example only. Report formats will vary from office to office.*

Account #	Name	0–30	31–60	61–90	91+	Total Balance
adamad01	Adam Adams	$10.60				$10.60
cohebe01	Betty Cohen			$150.00		$150.00
doejan01	Jane Doe	$7.80		$22.20		$30.00
flocfr03	Freda Flock		$14.60			$14.60
martma01	Martin Martinson	$11.20	$6.80		$16.50	$34.50
smitja10	John Jacob J. Smith		$12.30			$12.30
thomto02	Tom Thomas			$16.40		$16.40
westwa01	Wayne West	$4.80				$4.80

FIGURE 11-2   Sample patient aging report.

Rebilling

Rebilling means to resubmit an unpaid claim electronically or mail another printed claim to the insurance company. A claim is rebilled when there has been no response from the insurance company regarding the claim. In other words, the claim has neither been paid nor denied. The time guidelines for rebilling of claims will vary according to office policy. One office may perform a rebilling of all claims if, after 30 days, the insurance company has not responded; other offices may wait 60 days before rebilling. The medical biller should be aware of each provider's claim turn-around time before rebilling to avoid duplicate claims being sent.

Follow-Up

Another duty of the medical biller is to follow up on claims. This is done by printing an insurance aging report, calling each insurance company listed on the report, and checking the status of each claim submitted to that insurance company. Responses from insurance companies as to why the claim has not yet been responded to may include:

- Claim never received; the claim can be resubmitted and will be handled like a first-time submission.
- Claim received and is in process (this means the claim should be processed soon, with payment or denial following shortly thereafter).
- Claim has been processed and was denied on [date]. (Let the claims processor know that the denial was never received, and request the company to please send a replacement EOB.)
- Claim has been processed and a check was sent to the patient. (If benefits were assigned to the provider, request a replacement check, or call the patient to verify that the check was received and ask that the patient please forward it to the office.)

Once follow-up is done, if an insurance company insists that the claim has not been received, the medical biller will then have to rebill the claim.

Summary

The task of maintaining the practice's accounts receivable is of great importance. This task, which should be done in accordance to the provider office policy, includes:

- Printing insurance and patient aging reports
- Rebilling
- Following up on claims

  If the provider sees a decrease, month after month, in the practice's accounts receivable (with no decrease in patient encounters), this signifies the medical biller is working diligently to get claims paid in a timely fashion. A medical biller who can accomplish that will not only be a highly valued employee, but will also be one of the office's greatest assets!

REVIEW QUESTIONS

1. Monies due the provider for services rendered are called _____.

2. Two reports that total the provider's accounts receivable are the _____ and _____ reports.

3. To resubmit a claim that has neither been paid nor denied is called _____.

4. Calling an insurance company to check the status of a claim listed on an insurance aging report is known as _____.

5. Claims not yet paid are called _____.

6. Explain the importance of maintaining the provider's accounts receivable. Discuss cash flow.

   _____

   _____

   _____

Refer to Figure 11-3 to answer the following questions.

7. Which insurance company shows the highest accounts receivable?

   _____

8. Which patients' claims are current and do not yet need to be followed up?

   _____

   _____

9. Which patients' claims should be considered for rebilling? ___

   _____

   _____

Date of Service	Procedure	0–30	31–60	61–90	91–120	120+	Total Balance
Aetna						Aetna Total	$175.00
Ablal 000 Ables, Allison 06-01-20XX	99214	$75.00					$75.00
Andag 000 Anders, Agnes 03-05-20XX	99203			$100.00			$100.00
Blue Cross Blue Shield						BC/BS Total	$280.00
Bonbe 000 Bones, Betty 01-03-20XX	99213 81002					$50.00 $25.00	$75.00
Bulbo 000 Bully, Bonnie 05-10-20XX	99204 69210		$125.00 $80.00				$205.00
Cigna						Cigna Total	$175.00
Culco 000 Cullen, Colleen 06-05-20XX	99215	$100.00					$100.00
Czeca 000 Czey, Cathy 05-11-20XX	99202		$75.00				$75.00
Healthnet						Healthnet Total	$210.00
Harhe 000 Harvey, Henry 12-15-20XX	99205					$150.00	$150.00
Hulho 000 Hulk, Howard 04-27-20XX	36415 81002		$35.00 $25.00				$60.00
Medicare						Medicare Total	$245.00
Meama 000 Mears, Marvin 03-07-20XX	99212				$45.00		$45.00
Mulma 000 Muller, Mary 04-01-20XX	20610			$200.00			$200.00

FIGURE 11-3 Sample insurance aging report for exercise.

10. Will all insurance aging forms look like the ones in this textbook? If not, how are other forms formatted?

_____

_____

11. Which patients' claims are more than four months old?

_____

_____

12. Which patient has the oldest claim on this report?

_____

Refer to Figure 11-4 to answer the following questions.

13. Which patients have balances reflecting that an insurance payment has been made in the last 15 days?

_____

_____

14. Which patient either has no insurance or has had the insurance company deny the claim?

_____

15. Assuming that patient due statements are sent monthly, which patients have not been paying on the account?

_____

16. Which patients will be hard to collect money from?

_____

_____

17. Which column from this report shows the highest balance due?

_____

Account #	Name	0–30	31–60	61–90	91+	Total Balance
adamad01	Adam Adams	$20.70				$20.70
cohebe01	Betty Cohen				$175.00	$175.00
doejan01	Jane Doe	$7.40		$11.20		$18.60
flocfr03	Freda Flock		$21.60			$21.60
martma01	Martin Martinson		$7.20	$11.20	$6.80	$25.20
smitja10	John Jacob J. Smith	$11.20				$11.20
thomto02	Tom Thomas		$12.30			$12.30
westwa01	Wayne West	$5.60				$5.60

FIGURE 11-4   Sample patient aging report for exercise.

Chapter 12

Collections and the State Insurance Commissioner

Learning Objectives

Upon completion of this chapter, the student should be able to:

- Describe the different approaches to collections.
- Comprehend the importance of collecting monies due up front.
- Explain the role of the state insurance commissioner in getting claims paid.
- Define key terms.

Key Terms

Check Forgery	Department of	Soft Collections	Write Off
Collection	Insurance	State Insurance	
Agency	Post-dated Check	Commissioner	

The Need to Collect

The medical practice wants to provide the best treatment for each of its patients, and that treatment costs money. The collection of money for services rendered is the responsibility of the medical biller. It is good to have in place consistent policies about collecting payment, so that everyone, the provider's workers and the patient, can know what is expected after each visit. Patients will come to know this policy does not discriminate or change so they will be better able to abide by it.

Get the Money Up Front

Some patients visit the office frequently (once per month or more), and it is common for the front-desk personnel to have a friendly rapport with these patients. Asking patients to pay their past-due balances or their share of the cost responsibility for the current visit can be a difficult task for some front-desk personnel. They may know the patient is having a rough time financially, due to the illness treated or other personal information a patient might have shared in previous visits. Some patients are very adept at making the staff feel sorry for them. Some explanations or excuses for not paying include:

- "I don't have any cash on me."
- "I left my checkbook or credit card at home."
- "Can I just pay next time?"
- "I'll send it in."

A biller must remember to look directly at the patient expecting payment after the request is made. Do not let the patient give multiple rationalizations about why they cannot pay their bill or co-pay today. Services have been rendered, and the provider deserves to be paid.

Each office should have a "time-of-treatment collection" script posted at the front desk where the patient cannot see it. This can be a constant reminder to *not* let patients leave without paying. Notice the emphasis on the word *today* in the sample script in Figure 12-1. Some providers post a sign at the registration desk or patient lobby that reminds patients of the payment policy.

Co-Insurance Amount Due List

To assist the front-desk staff in their collection efforts, it is imperative that each office post a list of patients' co-insurance amounts due for the insurance companies with which the practice participates. This can be done for indemnity plans and Medicare, as the patients' cost-share responsibility is 20 percent of the insurance company's allowed amount, according to the company's fee schedule. This 20 percent will remain constant throughout the year and will not increase unless and until the insurance company increases the dollar amounts on its fee schedule. See Figure 12-2.

The medical biller can create a list of co-insurance amounts due by taking a blank superbill in the office and entering the 20 percent of the allowed dollar amount next to each CPT and HCPCS national level II code listed on the superbill. See Figure 12-3.

Collecting the 20 percent co-insurance amounts due from Medicare patients who have no supplemental insurance *before* these patients leave the office is a surefire way of maintaining cash flow and reducing the practice's accounts receivable.

Paying by Credit or Debit Card

Learn to identify payment cards by familiarizing yourself with a legitimate card. Visit the websites of the major credit card companies, like Visa or MasterCard. Verify the cardholder by asking for photo identification such as a driver's license. Be sure to only

> "Okay, Mrs. Jones, the fee for today's services is $200. You can pay that by cash, check or credit card, whichever works best for you today."

FIGURE 12-1   Sample time-of-treatment collection script.

NOTE	PROCEDURE CODE	MOD	PAR AMOUNT	NON-PAR AMOUNT	LIMITING CHARGE
	G0008		20.23	20.23	N/A
	G0009		20.23	20.23	N/A
	G0010		20.23	20.23	N/A
#	10021		76.79	72.95	83.89
	10021		145.49	138.22	158.95
#	10022		70.96	67.41	77.52
	10022		161.29	153.23	176.21
#	10040		81.99	77.89	89.57
	10040		91.32	86.75	99.76
#	10060		90.11	85.60	98.44
	10060		101.98	96.88	111.41
#	10061		168.06	159.66	183.61
	10061		182.06	172.96	198.90
#	10080		97.37	92.50	106.38
	10080		182.19	173.08	199.04
#	10081		169.30	160.84	184.97
	10081		278.71	264.77	304.49
#	10120		93.78	89.09	102.45
	10120		145.10	137.85	158.53
#	10121		194.41	184.69	212.39
	10121		267.77	254.38	292.54
#	10140		122.19	116.08	133.49
	10140		142.97	135.82	156.19
#	10160		98.39	93.47	107.49
	10160		120.45	114.43	131.59
#	10180		186.23	176.92	203.46
	10180		228.64	217.21	249.79
#	11000		35.63	33.85	38.93
	11000		50.89	48.35	55.60
#	11001		18.00	17.10	19.67
	11001		23.09	21.94	25.23
	11004		598.04	568.14	653.36
	11005		815.53	774.75	890.96
	11006		751.74	714.15	821.27
	11008		306.22	290.91	334.55
#	11010		301.49	286.42	329.38
	11010		482.14	458.03	526.73
#	11011		322.21	306.10	352.02
	11011		569.44	540.97	622.12
#	11012		477.59	453.71	521.77
	11012		829.15	787.69	905.84
#	11042		67.72	64.33	73.98
	11042		90.20	85.69	98.54
#	11043		216.13	205.32	236.12

\# - These amounts apply when service is performed in a facility setting. Limiting charge applies to unassigned claims by nonparticipating providers.

All Current Procedural Terminology (CPT) codes and descriptors copyrighted by the American Medical Association.

FIGURE 12-2 Sample Medicare fee schedule.

Office Codes

New Pt	Established Pt	Consult
$7^{93} 99201	$4^{73} 99211	$ 108^{86}99241
$14^{03}99202	$8^{36} 99212	$ 19^{76}99242
$20^{84}99203	$11^{37}99213	$26^{35} 99243
$29^{42}99204	$17^{80}99214	$37^{10} 99244
$37^{30}99205	$25^{78}99215	$47^{92} 99245

$5^{89} 93000 EKG

$0   36415 Venipuncture

$4^{05} 71010 Chest ray, single view

$10^{53}69210 Cerumen removal

$0   99000 Specimen handling

.71   81002 Urinalysis

.91   85014 Hemocult

.17   J3420 Vitamin B-12 injection

$1^{05} J1030 Depo-Medrol

$2^{41} 87070 Throat culture

$4^{05} 90471 Immunization admin

$15^{20}11200 Skin tag removal

ICD-9 Codes

_____789.00 Abdominal pain	_____V70.0 Routine visit
_____477.9 Allergies	_____784.0 Headache
_____285.9 Anemia	_____401.1 Hypertension
_____427.9 Arrhythmia	_____458.9 Hypotension
_____466.0 Bronchitis, acute	_____272.4 Hyperlipidemia
_____436 Cardiovascular accident	_____410.91 Myocardial infarction
_____414.00 Coronary artery disease	_____382.90 Otitis media
_____250.00 DM-controlled	_____462 Pharyngitis
_____782.3 Edema	_____482 Pneumonia
_____780.79 Fatigue	_____461.9 Sinusitis
_____530.81 GERD	_____599.0 Urinary tract infection

Name _____ Date _____

Prim ins _____ Sec ins _____

Self-pay _____ Co-pay _____ Pd-ck _____ CHG _____ Cash _____

FIGURE 12-3   Sample "Co-insurance Amounts Due" list for Medicare.

take a credit card from the person whose name is on the card. Check the expiration date and signature on the back. Verify the signature with the one given by the patient at the time of payment.

Debit cards allow a withdrawal from a patient's account for the amount due on a bill without the risk of nonsufficient funds as with a personal check. This is the way of payment for most people. Protect your facility by establishing a procedure to handle potentially fraudulent transactions, including who to notify if there is a need to report the transaction.

Payment by Check

When you do accept a check as payment, be sure to verify the patient's information, including their driver's license, and request one other form of identification. Check forgery is a false writing or alteration of a document. Check to see if the back of the check matches the name on the front. Be sure the patient signed the check; if not, the medical biller will have to contact the patient and have them come back into the office to sign the check. Get it right the first time!

Check forgery

is a false writing or alternation of a document.

Post-Dated Checks

If the patient cannot pay a current balance in full, accept a partial payment at the time of service and request that the patient post-date a check or checks (depending on the balance) for the remainder due. Keep post-dated checks in a secure location, and be sure *not* to deposit them until the date written on the check.

Note: *Although it is legal in all states to post-date checks, be sure to have patients contact their banks for policies and procedures regarding postdated checks.*

Soft Collections

Soft collections

mailing patient-due statements or calling patients to remind them of their past-due balances.

The soft collections are the normal billing by statement and all calls reminding patients of past due accounts. Calls placed to the patient are intentionally kept non-threatening and nonharassing in nature. The "patient-due" statements (invoices for the amounts due from the patient) are usually printed and sent out on a monthly basis. See Figure 12-4.

Remember these helpful hints when sending out patient-due statements:

- If writing anything on the statement, use red ink.
- If affixing collection labels to the statement, include insignia of credit cards the office accepts and a place for the credit-card account number, card expiration date, and the cardholder's signature.
- Enclose a self-addressed, stamped envelope (so the patient will not have to pay postage).
- Print "Do Not Fold" across the front of the envelope (this indicates to patients that it is an important document so they will not throw it away).
- Include the practice's return address *only*. Omit the doctor's name.

Write It Off

Write off

to adjust the dollar amount due from the patient or insurance company to reflect a zero balance due on the claim in question, or sometimes the patient's entire balance. The amount adjusted is called a *write-off*.

There are instances in every medical office when the provider may instruct the biller to write off the balance due on an account. There should be a policy in place about the types of situations that constitute a write-off. These situations may include:

- The patient is deceased
- The patient has skipped town (or the state)
- The biller did not submit the claim in a timely fashion
- The patient is financially indigent (has no income)

When write-offs are performed, the provider has essentially lost money on the services or procedures performed.

Time for Help

Collection agency

an agency retained by the practice for the purpose of collecting debts.

When soft collection efforts have failed, some providers will turn to an outside collection agency in an attempt to collect balances due from patients.

Most collection agencies do not charge an up-front fee to the provider. The usual arrangement is for the agency to get paid only if it is successful in collecting on an account. These agencies usually charge the provider a percentage on money collected for each account (for example, 10 percent. If the agency collected $100 on a patient-due statement, the agency would be paid $10 on that account.).

David Operatomy, MD
123 Shady Lane
Anycity, USA 12345

ADDRESS SERVICE REQUESTED

ANY QUESTIONS PLEASE CALL 999-999-9999
TAX ID: 123456789
PATIENT: PATIENT, JOHN Q

JOHN Q. PATIENT
202 MAIN STREET
ANYTOWN, USA 12345-0000

HEALTHCARE, USA
1234 MAIN STREET
ANYTOWN, USA 12345-0000

11048574500000100000000000000000090123119950000008⁹003   235352*OW5QA0000000000

☐ Please check box if your address is incorrect or insurance information has changed, please indicate change(s) on reverse side.   **STATEMENT**   PLEASE DETACH AND RETUN TOP PORTION WITH YOUR PAYMENT

DATE	PATIENT	CPT	DESCRIPTION OF SERVICE	CHARGE	RECEIPT	ADJUSTMENT	LINE ITEM BALANCE
00/00/00	STEVE	99212	EST. PATIENT LEVEL 2	50.00	0.00	0.00	50.00
00/00/00	STEVE	99213	EST. PATIENT LEVEL 3	75.00	0.00	0.00	75.00
00/00/00	STEVE	99211	EST. PATIENT LEVEL 1	40.00	0.00	0.00	40.00

ACCOUNT NO.	CURRENT	30 DAYS	60 DAYS	90 DAYS	120 DAYS	TOTAL ACCOUNT BALANCE
031284 82	165.00	0.00	0.00	0.00	0.00	$165.00

PLEASE PAY THIS AMOUNT ▶▶▶ $165.00

FIGURE 12-4 Sample patient-due statement.

Some collection agencies will have the patients send their money directly to the provider's office. At the end of the month, the provider will tally the total dollar amount collected specifically through the agency's efforts and send the agency a check for the agreed-upon percentage amount. Other agencies require that patients pay the agency directly. In this latter scenario, the agency tallies the total amount collected on the provider's account and deducts its percentage fee amount before forwarding a check for the remainder to the provider. See Figures 12-5, 12-6, and 12-7.

Insurance Companies Beware

Chapter 11 explained the need for claim follow-up with insurance companies and the excuses these companies may give to the medical biller who calls to check on the status of claims. Unfortunately, many provider offices are not aware of state laws and regulations regarding the timely payment of claims. See Table 12-1 for a state-by-state listing of these laws. For the exact text of your state's statute (and the legal citation of the statute section or number), and to be sure that you have the most up-to-date information, check the website of your state government or state insurance commissioner.

It is imperative that the medical biller inform the insurance companies of their legal obligation to obey these prompt-payment statutes, and stress that their failure to do so may result in financial penalties and the need for the practice to contact a higher authority.

The State Insurance Commissioner

If all normal attempts to obtain reimbursement of a claim have failed, the medical biller has the right to ask for intervention from the state government. Each state has an Insurance Commissioner, whose job it is to be the liaison between the provider, carrier, and patient. The commissioner will work with any of the three parties who feel they have been treated unfairly. The insurance commissioner works under the Department of Insurance, which controls and regulates insurance companies.

A complaint for lack of payment could result in a financial penalty—or worse—for the insurance company. If enough complaints are filed against an individual company, that company could lose its license to practice insurance in that state. It is important to always check each states law for prompt payment before submitting a claim with the state commissioner. See Figure 12-8.

Doctor-Initiated Complaint

When a complaint is filed with the state insurance commissioner, the complaint should include the following:

- Letter to the insurance commissioner
- Copy of claim in question
- Printout from patient's account of all documented inquiries to and correspondence with the insurance company in question

A copy of the complaint should be sent to the insurance company in question. See Figure 12-9.

State insurance commissioner

the appointed official in charge of each state's Department of Insurance.

Department of Insurance

the governmental agency in charge of controlling and regulating insurance companies.

ABC Credit Services LLC
P.O. Box 12345
City, ST 67890

Date: April 21, 20YY

To: First Name Last Name   RE: Your account with:
       Debtor Company   Creditor
       Address   Address
       City, State, ZIP   City, State, ZIP

                                                      For the amount of $Amount
                                                      Phone: xxx-xxx-xxxx
                                                      Account ID: 1234567890

                     * * * * COURTESY NOTICE * * * *

The above client has requested that we contact you regarding the above referenced account. We realize that this amount due could be an oversight on your part and not a willful disregard of an apparent obligation.

Unless you notify this office within 30 days after receiving this notice that you dispute the validity of this debt or any portion thereof, this office will assume this debt is valid. If you notify this office in writing within 30 days from receiving this notice that you dispute the validity of this debt or any portion thereof, this office will obtain verification of the debt or obtain a copy of a judgment and mail you a copy of such judgment or verification. If you request this office in writing within 30 days after receiving this notice this office will provide you with the name and address of the original creditor, if different from the current creditor.

This communication is from a debt collector. **ABC Credit Services, LLC** is a collection agency attempting to collect a debt and any information obtained will be used for that purpose. Send correspondence, other than PAYMENTS, to this collection agency at P.O. Box 767095, City, ST 67890.

                     SEE REVERSE SIDE FOR IMPORTANT INFORMATION

***************************Detach and return with payment to*****************************

Date: April 21, 20YY

Make check payable to: Creditor   Account ID: 1234567890

                                             Amount Paid:_____
Mail payment to:
                                             Home Phone: _____

       Creditor
       CreditorAddress
       CreditorCity, State, ZIP

             Please make any address corrections: Debtor First Name Debtor Last Name
                                                      Debtor Address
                                                      Debtor City, State, ZIP

FIGURE 12-5   Sample courtesy notice letter from collection agency.

ABC Credit Services LLC
P.O. Box 767095
City, ST 67890

Date: April 21, 20YY

To: First Name Last Name   RE: Your account with:
      DebtorCompany   Creditor
      Address   Address
      City, State, ZIP   City, State, ZIP

                                          For the amount of $Amount
                                          Phone: xxx-xxx-xxxx
                                          Account ID: 1234567890

* * * * 2nd PAST DUE NOTICE * * * *

Our client, **CREDITOR NAME**,
continues to show a past due balance on your account.

We are attempting to resolve this matter amicably; however, unless you forward payment to our client listed above, we will have no choice but to continue collection attempts.

This communication is from a debt collector. **ABC Credit Services, LLC** is a collection agency attempting to collect a debt and any information obtained will be used for that purpose. Send correspondence, other than PAYMENTS, to this collection agency at P.O. Box 767095, City, ST 67890.

SEE REVERSE SIDE FOR IMPORTANT INFORMATION

*****************************Detach and return with payment to*****************************

Make check payable to: Creditor   Account ID: 1234567890

                                         Amount Paid: _____

Mail payment to: Home Phone: _____

   Creditor   Please make any address corrections:
   Address   Debtor First name Debtor Last name
   City, State, ZIP   Debtor Address
                                         Debtor City, State, ZIP

FIGURE 12-6   Sample second past-due notice letter from collection agency.

ABC Credit Services LLC
P.O. Box 12345
City, ST

Date: April 21, 20YY

To: First Name Last Name
DebtorCompany
Address
City, State, ZIP

RE: Your account with:
Creditor
Address
City, State, ZIP

For the amount of $Amount
Phone: xxx-xxx-xxxx
Account ID: 1234567890

＊＊＊＊FINAL NOTICE＊＊＊＊

The statutory dispute period has expired. We are now permitted under Federal law to assume that this debt to **CREDITOR NAME** is valid.

Please make further collection efforts unnecessary by resolving this matter immediately.

This communication is from a debt collector. **ABC Credit Services, LLC** is a collection agency attempting to collect a debt and any information obtained will be used for that purpose. Send correspondence, other than PAYMENTS, to this collection agency at P.O. Box 767095, City, ST 67890.

SEE REVERSE SIDE FOR IMPORTANT INFORMATION

*****************************Detach and return with payment to*****************************

Make check payable to: Creditor

Account ID: 1234567890

Amount Paid: _____

Mail payment to:

Home Phone: _____

Creditor
Address
City, State, ZIP

Please make any address corrections:
Debtor First Name Last Name
Debtor Address
Debtor City, State, ZIP

FIGURE 12-7 Sample final-notice letter from collection agency.

TABLE 12-1	State Laws on Insurance Claim Payment Timing
State	**Status/Terms of Law**
Alabama	Clean claims must be paid within 30 days electronic or 45 working days if written. Penalty 1.5% prorated daily.
Alaska	Clean claims must be paid within 30 working days. Penalty 15% annually.
Arizona	Clean claims must be paid within 30 days. Penalty 10% annually.
Arkansas	Clean, electronic claims must be paid or denied within 30 calendar days, 45 days for written claims. Penalty 12% annually.
California	Claims must be paid within 30 working days. Interest accrues at 10% per annum.
Colorado	Claims must be paid within 30 calendar days if submitted electronically, or 45 days if submitted on paper. 10% annual interest penalty.
Connecticut	Claims must be paid within 45 days. Interest accrues at 15% per annum.
Delaware	Clean claims must be paid within 30 days. Penalty 1% per month.
District of Columbia	Clean claims will be paid within 30 days. Interest payable at 1.5% for days 31–60, 2% for days 61–120, and 2.5% after 120 days.
Florida	Clean claims will be paid within 45 days. Penalty 10% annually.
Georgia	Claims must be paid within 15 working days if submitted electronically, 30 days if written. Interest accrues at 15% per annum.
Hawaii	Clean paper claims must be paid within 30 days; electronic claims within 15 days. Interest accrues at 15% per annum.
Idaho	Paper claims settled within 30 days. Penalty is 12% annually.
Illinois	Clean claims must be paid within 60 days. Interest accrues at 9% per annum.
Indiana	Paper claims must be paid within 45 days; electronic claims must be paid within 30 days.
Iowa	Payment to be made within 30 days. Penalty is 10% per annum.
Kansas	Claims will be paid within 30 days. Interest accrues at a rate of 1% per month.
Kentucky	Claims must be paid or denied within 30 calendar days. Interest accrues at 1–3 days 12% annually. Days 31–60 at 18%. Days 60 and over 21%.
Louisiana	Claims submitted electronically must be paid within 45 days. Penalty 12% annually.
Maine	Clean claims must be paid within 30 days. Interest accrues at 1.5% per month.
Maryland	Clean claims must be paid within 30 days. Interest accrues at monthly rates of 1.5% (31–60 days late), 2% (61–120 days late), or 2.5% (121 or more days late) respectively.

Continues

TABLE 12-1 State Laws on Insurance Claim Payment Timing (Continues)

State	Status/Terms of Law
Massachusetts	Claims must be paid within 45 days. Penalty 1.5% monthly. No more than 18%.
Michigan	A clean claim submitted to an insurance company with all the correct information shall be paid within 45 days. Penalty is 12%.
Minnesota	Clean claims must be paid within 30 days. Interest accrues at 1.5% per month if not paid or denied.
Mississippi	Clean claims must be paid within 25 days, if electronic, 35 days if written. Interest accrues at 1.5% per month.
Missouri	Claims must be within 30 days. Penalty is 1% monthly.
Montana	Clean claims must be paid within 30 days. Interest accrues at 10% per annum.
Nebraska	Claims must be paid or denied within 30 days electronic or 45 days written. Penalty 12% annually.
Nevada	Claims must be paid within 30 days. Interest equal to the prime rate at the largest bank in Nevada.
New Hampshire	Clean paper claims must be paid within 30 days, electronic claims within 15 days; 1.5% monthly interest penalty.
New Jersey	Clean electronic claims must be paid within 30 days, paper claims within 40 days. Penalty 10% annually.
New Mexico	Clean claims must be paid within 30 days if electronic, 45 days if paper. Interest accrues at 1.5% per month.
New York	Claims must be paid within 30 days electronic or 45 days written. Interest accrues at greater of 12% per year or corporate tax rate determined by commissioner.
North Carolina	Claims must be paid or denied within 30 days. Annual interest penalty of 18%.
North Dakota	Claims must be paid within 15 days.
Ohio	Payer must notify provider within 30 days of receipt. Penalty 18% annually.
Oklahoma	Clean claims must be paid within 45 days. Penalty of 10% of claim as interest for late claims payment.
Oregon	Clean claims must be paid within 30 days; 12% interest penalty applies.
Pennsylvania	Clean claims must be paid within 45 days. Penalty is 10% annually.
Rhode Island	Written claims to be paid within 40 calendar days, electronic claims within 30 days. Penalty is 12% annually.
South Carolina	Written claims to be paid within 40 days, electronic claims within 20 days. Penalty is 8.75% annually.

Continues

TABLE 12-1	State Laws on Insurance Claim Payment Timing (Continues)	
State	**Status/Terms of Law**	
South Dakota	Electronic claims must be paid within 30 days, paper claims within 45 days.	
Tennessee	Clean, commercial claims sent electronically must be paid within 21 days, paper claims within 30 days. Interest accrues at 1% per month.	
Texas	Clean claims within 30 days if electronic, 45 days if written. Penalty is 18% plus attorney fees.	
Utah	Claims must be paid or denied within 30 days.	
Vermont	Claims must be paid or denied within 30 days. Interest penalty is 12% per annum.	
Virginia	Clean claims must be paid within 40 days. Penalty is the legal rate of interest.	
Washington	95% of the monthly volume of clean claims shall be paid within 30 days. 95% of the monthly volume of all claims shall be paid or denied within 60 days. Penalty is 1% month beginning on the 62nd day.	
West Virginia	Claims must be paid within 30 days if electronic, 40 days if paper. Interest and fines may apply. Interest penalty of 10% per annum.	
Wisconsin	If clean claims are not paid within 30 days, the insurance company is subject to a penalty interest rate of 12% per year.	
Wyoming	Claims must be paid within 45 days. Penalty of 10% plus attorney fees.	

Federal Ruling

A quote from Judge Rafeedie in the federal court case of: Kanne v. Connecticut General Ins. Co., 607 F. Supp. 899 (1985) on upholding $750,000 in additional damages for unreasonable delay in payment of medical claims:

"Repeated requests for payment of the bills were made to the claims representative, and copies of the bills were in the Insurance Company's possession. Under these circumstances, it is not proper for the insurer to sit back and delay payment claims, under the pretextual theory that the Doctors have not dotted all the i's and crossed all the t's. On the contrary, the insurer has the duty to see to it that the promised protection is delivered when needed. It must act to facilitate the claims instead of searching for reasons not to do so."

FIGURE 12-8   Example of a federal ruling against insurance company.

Patient-Initiated Complaint

A patient-initiated complaint is similar to that from a provider. A patient complaint can be used to:

* Support the provider's decision to file a complaint
* Express the patient's anger to the insurance company (some practices may turn over the claim balance to the patient if the insurance company does not respond to a claim in a timely fashion). See Figure 12-10.

The complaint letters shown in Figures 12-10 are particularly helpful in claims for treatment of injuries suffered in motor vehicle accidents or covered by workers' compensation.

Practice Name _____   Date _____

Address _____

City, State, Zip _____

Phone _____

We filed the attached claim form with the _(insert name of company)_ Insurance Company on _(insert date)_____. It has not been paid or denied.

Please accept this letter as a formal written complaint against the _(insert name of company)_ Insurance Company.

FIGURE 12-9   Sample doctor-initiated complaint to a state insurance commissioner.

Practice Name _____

Address _____

City, State, Zip _____

Phone _____   Date _____

(practice name) filed the attached claim form with the _(insert name of company)_ Insurance Company on____(insert date)_____. It has not been paid or denied.

Benefits were assigned to____(insert practice name)____and, as of today's date, payment has not been received. I am now responsible for payment of this bill.

Please accept this letter as a formal written complaint against the _(insert name of company)_ Insurance Company.

Patient's Signature _____

FIGURE 12-10   Sample patient-initiated complaint to a state insurance commissioner.

Summary

The task of collecting monies is an ongoing process for the medical biller in any given practice. To ease this process, it is strongly advised that the front-desk staff keep available a list of co-insurance amounts due from the insurance companies with which the provider participates, especially Medicare.

The provider's office will have great success obtaining reimbursement for the services it provides if all members of the office team do their part to adhere to the written policies of collection. Soft collections are the normal billing by statement and all calls reminding patients of past due accounts which is done within the office setting. When these efforts have failed, the provider may choose to turn collection efforts over to an outside collection agency.

When claim inquiries and follow-up have failed, the office should proceed to file a complaint with the state insurance commissioner. The complaint may be initiated by the provider, the patient, or both. Such complaints could result in:

- Payment of the claim in question

- Financial penalties for the insurance company

- Insurance company's loss of its license to practice insurance (in that state)

REVIEW QUESTIONS

1. List three excuses given by patients for failure to pay at the time services are rendered.

   _____

   _____

   _____

2. Explain the function and importance of a co-insurance amount due list.

   _____

   _____

3. Collection efforts done in the office are called _____ collections.

4. List three helpful hints when sending out patient-due statements.

   _____

   _____

   _____

5. Practices may turn to a _____ when soft collection efforts have failed.

6. Name the agency in charge of controlling and regulating insurance companies.

   _____

7. Name two types of complaints that can be filed against an insurance company.

_____

_____

8. List three possible results of filing a complaint against an insurance company.

_____

_____

9. Define the following key terms.

    a. post-dated check

_____

    b. soft collections

_____

    c. write off

_____

    d. collection agency

_____

    e. Department of Insurance

_____

    f. state insurance commissioner

_____

Appendix I

Case Studies for the CMS-1500 Form

STEVEN SPRING, M.D.

0909 Route 68 • Point Pleasant, NJ 08742 • (732) 004-0090
Tax ID# 11-9923989
NPI# 0101010101

Case Study

PATIENT INFORMATION:

Name:	Marcus Marks
Social Security #:	000-01-0011
Address:	0762 Apricot Lane
City:	Point Pleasant
State:	NJ
Zip Code:	08742
Home Telephone:	(732) 003-0976
Date of Birth:	07-12-1979
Gender:	Male
Occupation:	Welder
Employer:	XYZ Welding Inc
Employer Telephone:	(732) 004-2791
Spouse:	Mary Marks
Spouse's Social Security #:	000-02-2222
Spouse's Employer:	Dal-Mart
Spouse's Date of Birth:	08-22-1970

INSURANCE INFORMATION:

Patient Number:	Marma000
Place of Service:	Office
Primary Insurance Plan:	Prudential
Primary Insurance Plan ID #:	XYZ2790017
Group #:	6642
Primary Policyholder:	Marcus Marks
Policyholder Date of Birth:	07-12-1979
Relationship to Patient:	Self
Secondary Insurance Plan:	
Secondary Insurance Plan ID #:	
Secondary Policyholder:	

Patient Status ☒ Married ☐ Divorced ☐ Single ☐ Student ☐ Other

DIAGNOSIS INFORMATION

Diagnosis	Code	Diagnosis	Code
1. Hyperlipidemia	272.4	5.	
2.		6.	
3.		7.	
4.		8.	

PROCEDURE INFORMATION

Description of Procedure or Service	Date	Code	Charge
1. Level 3 office visit - est patient	04-11-YYYY	99213	$65.00
2.			
3.			
4.			
5.			
6.			

SPECIAL NOTES:

Case Study 1-1 (ICD-9)

STEVEN SPRING, M.D.
0909 Route 68 • Point Pleasant, NJ 08742 • (732) 004-0090

Tax ID# 11-9923989

NPI# 0101010101

Case Study

PATIENT INFORMATION:		INSURANCE INFORMATION:	
Name:	Marcus Marks	Patient Number:	Marma000
Social Security #:	000-01-0011	Place of Service:	Office
Address:	0762 Apricot Lane		
City:	Point Pleasant	Primary Insurance Plan:	Prudential
State:	NJ	Primary Insurance Plan ID #:	XYZ2790017
Zip Code:	08742		
Home Telephone:	(732) 003-0976	Group #:	6642
Date of Birth:	07-12-1979	Primary Policyholder:	Marcus Marks
Gender:	Male		
Occupation:	Welder	Policyholder Date of Birth:	07-12-1979
Employer:	XYZ Welding Inc	Relationship to Patient:	Self
Employer Telephone:	(732) 004-2791		
Spouse:	Mary Marks	Secondary Insurance Plan:	
Spouse's Social Security #:	000-02-2222	Secondary Insurance Plan ID #:	
Spouse's Employer:	Dal-Mart		
Spouse's Date of Birth:	08-22-1970	Secondary Policyholder:	

Patient Status	☒ Married	☐ Divorced	☐ Single	☐ Student	☐ Other

DIAGNOSIS INFORMATION

	Diagnosis	Code		Diagnosis	Code
1.	Hyperlipidemia	E78.5	5.		
2.			6.		
3.			7.		
4.			8.		

PROCEDURE INFORMATION

	Description of Procedure or Service	Date	Code	Charge
1.	Level 3 office visit - est patient	04-11-YYYY	99213	$65.00
2.				
3.				
4.				
5.				
6.				

SPECIAL NOTES:

Case Study 1-2 (ICD-10)

STEVEN SPRING, M.D.

0909 Route 68 • Point Pleasant, NJ 08742 • (732) 004-0090

Tax ID# 11-9923989

NPI# 0101010101

Case Study

PATIENT INFORMATION:

Name:	Melissa Marks
Social Security #:	111-11-2222
Address:	0762 Apricot Lane
City:	Point Pleasant
State:	NJ
Zip Code:	08742
Home Telephone:	(732) 003-0976
Date of Birth:	01-16-2000
Gender:	Female
Occupation:	Student
Employer:	
Employer Telephone:	
Spouse:	
Spouse's Social Security #:	
Spouse's Employer:	
Spouse's Date of Birth:	

INSURANCE INFORMATION:

Patient Number:	Marme000
Place of Service:	Office
Primary Insurance Plan:	Prudential
Primary Insurance Plan ID #:	XYZ2790017
Group #:	6642
Primary Policyholder:	Marcus Marks
Policyholder Date of Birth:	07-12-1979
Relationship to Patient:	Parent
Secondary Insurance Plan:	
Secondary Insurance Plan ID #:	
Secondary Policyholder:	

Patient Status   ☐ Married   ☐ Divorced   ☒ Single   ☒ Student   ☐ Other

DIAGNOSIS INFORMATION

Diagnosis	Code	Diagnosis	Code
1. Acne	706.1	5.	
2.		6.	
3.		7.	
4.		8.	

PROCEDURE INFORMATION

Description of Procedure or Service	Date	Code	Charge
1. Level 2 office visit - new patient	05-02-YYYY	99202	$85.00
2.			
3.			
4.			
5.			
6.			

SPECIAL NOTES:

Pt was referred to dermatologist Claire Clearing, M.D.

Case Study 2-1 (ICD-9)

STEVEN SPRING, M.D.

0909 Route 68 • Point Pleasant, NJ 08742 • (732) 004-0090

Tax ID# 11-9923989

NPI# 0101010101

Case Study

PATIENT INFORMATION:

Name:	Melissa Marks
Social Security #:	111-11-2222
Address:	0762 Apricot Lane
City:	Point Pleasant
State:	NJ
Zip Code:	08742
Home Telephone:	(732) 003-0976
Date of Birth:	01-16-2000
Gender:	Female
Occupation:	Student
Employer:	
Employer Telephone:	
Spouse:	
Spouse's Social Security #:	
Spouse's Employer:	
Spouse's Date of Birth:	

INSURANCE INFORMATION:

Patient Number:	Marme000
Place of Service:	Office
Primary Insurance Plan:	Prudential
Primary Insurance Plan ID #:	XYZ2790017
Group #:	6642
Primary Policyholder:	Marcus Marks
Policyholder Date of Birth:	07-12-1979
Relationship to Patient:	Parent
Secondary Insurance Plan:	
Secondary Insurance Plan ID #:	
Secondary Policyholder:	

Patient Status   ☐ Married   ☐ Divorced   ☒ Single   ☒ Student   ☐ Other

---

DIAGNOSIS INFORMATION

Diagnosis	Code	Diagnosis	Code
1. Acne	L70.9	5.	
2.		6.	
3.		7.	
4.		8.	

PROCEDURE INFORMATION

Description of Procedure or Service	Date	Code	Charge
1. Level 2 office visit - new patient	05-02-YYYY	99202	$85.00
2.			
3.			
4.			
5.			
6.			

SPECIAL NOTES:

Pt was referred to dermatologist Claire Clearing, M.D.

Case Study 2-2 (ICD-10)

CLAIRE CLEARING, M.D.
0579 Bridge Ave • Point Pleasant, NJ 08742 • (732) 009-5555
Tax ID# 11-8256989
NPI# 0044002299

Case Study

PATIENT INFORMATION:		INSURANCE INFORMATION:	
Name:	Melissa Marks	Patient Number:	Marme000
Social Security #:	111-11-2222	Place of Service:	Office
Address:	0762 Apricot Lane	Primary Insurance Plan:	Prudential
City:	Point Pleasant	Primary Insurance Plan ID #:	XYZ2790017
State:	NJ	Group #:	6642
Zip Code:	08742	Primary Policyholder:	Marcus Marks
Home Telephone:	(732) 003-0976	Policyholder Date of Birth:	07-12-1979
Date of Birth:	01-16-2000	Relationship to Patient:	Parent
Gender:	Female	Secondary Insurance Plan:	
Occupation:	Student	Secondary Insurance Plan ID #:	
Employer:		Secondary Policyholder:	
Employer Telephone:			
Spouse:			
Spouse's Social Security #:			
Spouse's Employer:			
Spouse's Date of Birth:			

Patient Status ☐ Married ☐ Divorced ☒ Single ☒ Student ☐ Other

DIAGNOSIS INFORMATION

	Diagnosis	Code		Diagnosis	Code
1.	Acne	706.1	5.		
2.			6.		
3.			7.		
4.			8.		

PROCEDURE INFORMATION

	Description of Procedure or Service	Date	Code	Charge
1.	Level 2 office consultation	05-12-YYYY	99242	$125.00
2.				
3.				
4.				
5.				
6.				

SPECIAL NOTES:
Referred by Steven Spring, M.D., NPI# 0101010101.

Case Study 3-1 (ICD-9)

CLAIRE CLEARING, M.D.

0579 Bridge Ave • Point Pleasant, NJ 08742 • (732) 009-5555

Tax ID# 11-8256989

NPI# 0044002299

Case Study

PATIENT INFORMATION:

Name:	Melissa Marks
Social Security #:	111-11-2222
Address:	0762 Apricot Lane
City:	Point Pleasant
State:	NJ
Zip Code:	08742
Home Telephone:	(732) 003-0976
Date of Birth:	01-16-2000
Gender:	Female
Occupation:	Student
Employer:	
Employer Telephone:	
Spouse:	
Spouse's Social Security #:	
Spouse's Employer:	
Spouse's Date of Birth:	

INSURANCE INFORMATION:

Patient Number:	Marme000
Place of Service:	Office
Primary Insurance Plan:	Prudential
Primary Insurance Plan ID #:	XYZ2790017
Group #:	6642
Primary Policyholder:	Marcus Marks
Policyholder Date of Birth:	07-12-1979
Relationship to Patient:	Parent
Secondary Insurance Plan:	
Secondary Insurance Plan ID #:	
Secondary Policyholder:	

Patient Status ☐ Married ☐ Divorced ☒ Single ☒ Student ☐ Other

DIAGNOSIS INFORMATION

Diagnosis	Code	Diagnosis	Code
1. Acne	L70.9	5.	
2.		6.	
3.		7.	
4.		8.	

PROCEDURE INFORMATION

Description of Procedure or Service	Date	Code	Charge
1. Level 2 office consultation	05-12-YYYY	99242	$125.00
2.			
3.			
4.			
5.			
6.			

SPECIAL NOTES:

Referred by Steven Spring, M.D., NPI# 0101010101.

GARY GRAY, M.D.
0222 Route 70 • Brick, NJ 08723 • (732) 555-0000
Tax ID# 11-4311999
NPI# 9988001122

Case Study

PATIENT INFORMATION:

Name:	Yvonne Yager
Social Security #:	500-00-0000
Address:	030 Mango Court
City:	Brick
State:	NJ
Zip Code:	08724
Home Telephone:	(732) 008-8401
Date of Birth:	04-18-1940
Gender:	Female
Occupation:	Retired
Employer:	
Employer Telephone:	
Spouse:	
Spouse's Social Security #:	
Spouse's Employer:	
Spouse's Date of Birth:	

INSURANCE INFORMATION:

Patient Number:	Yagyv000
Place of Service:	Office
Primary Insurance Plan:	Medicare
Primary Insurance Plan ID #:	500-50-0000A
Group #:	
Primary Policyholder:	Yvonne Yager
Policyholder Date of Birth:	04-18-1940
Relationship to Patient:	Self
Secondary Insurance Plan:	AARP
Secondary Insurance Plan ID #:	114Z2397G
Secondary Policyholder:	Yvonne Yager

Patient Status ☐ Married ☐ Divorced ☒ Single ☐ Student ☐ Other

DIAGNOSIS INFORMATION

Diagnosis	Code	Diagnosis	Code
1. Fatigue	780.79	5.	
2. Anemia	285.9	6.	
3.		7.	
4.		8.	

PROCEDURE INFORMATION

Description of Procedure or Service	Date	Code	Charge
1. Level 3 office visit - est patient	03-01-YYYY	99213	$65.00
2. Urinalysis	03-01-YYYY	81002	$20.00
3. Vitamin B-12 injection	03-01-YYYY	J3420	$15.00
4. Injection	03-01-YYYY	96372	$10.00
5.			
6.			

SPECIAL NOTES:
Vitamin B-12 - up to 1000mcg.

Case Study 4-1 (ICD-9)

GARY GRAY, M.D.
0222 Route 70 • Brick, NJ 08723 • (732) 555-0000
Tax ID# 11-4311999
NPI# 9988001122

Case Study

PATIENT INFORMATION:

Name:	Yvonne Yager
Social Security #:	500-00-0000
Address:	030 Mango Court
City:	Brick
State:	NJ
Zip Code:	08724
Home Telephone:	(732) 008-8401
Date of Birth:	04-18-1940
Gender:	Female
Occupation:	Retired
Employer:	
Employer Telephone:	
Spouse:	
Spouse's Social Security #:	
Spouse's Employer:	
Spouse's Date of Birth:	

INSURANCE INFORMATION:

Patient Number:	Yagyv000
Place of Service:	Office
Primary Insurance Plan:	Medicare
Primary Insurance Plan ID #:	500-50-0000A
Group #:	
Primary Policyholder:	Yvonne Yager
Policyholder Date of Birth:	04-18-1940
Relationship to Patient:	Self
Secondary Insurance Plan:	AARP
Secondary Insurance Plan ID #:	114Z2397G
Secondary Policyholder:	Yvonne Yager

Patient Status   ☐ Married   ☐ Divorced   ☒ Single   ☐ Student   ☐ Other

DIAGNOSIS INFORMATION

Diagnosis	Code		Diagnosis	Code
1. Fatigue	R53.83	5.		
2. Anemia	D64.9	6.		
3.		7.		
4.		8.		

PROCEDURE INFORMATION

Description of Procedure or Service	Date	Code	Charge
1. Level 3 office visit - est patient	03-01-YYYY	99213	$65.00
2. Urinalysis	03-01-YYYY	81002	$20.00
3. Vitamin B-12 injection	03-01-YYYY	J3420	$15.00
4. Injection	03-01-YYYY	96372	$10.00
5.			
6.			

SPECIAL NOTES:
Vitamin B-12 - up to 1000mcg.

Case Study 4-2 (ICD-10)

JUNEY JONES, M.D.
0995 Hooper Ave • Toms River, NJ 08755 • (732) 999-5555
Tax ID# 11-99556789
NPI# 0077660055

Case Study

PATIENT INFORMATION:

Name:	Sierra Shrewd
Social Security #:	999-00-8899
Address:	0512 Mango Road
City:	Asbury Park
State:	NJ
Zip Code:	00040
Home Telephone:	(732) 999-1111
Date of Birth:	05-17-1976
Gender:	Female
Occupation:	Teacher
Employer:	St. Anne's
Employer Telephone:	(732) 888-0000
Spouse:	
Spouse's Social Security #:	
Spouse's Employer:	
Spouse's Date of Birth:	

INSURANCE INFORMATION:

Patient Number:	Shrsi000
Place of Service:	Office
Primary Insurance Plan:	Oxford
Primary Insurance Plan ID #:	4497601
Group #:	P6239
Primary Policyholder:	Sierra Shrewd
Policyholder Date of Birth:	05-17-1976
Relationship to Patient:	Self
Secondary Insurance Plan:	
Secondary Insurance Plan ID #:	
Secondary Policyholder:	

Patient Status ☐ Married ☒ Divorced ☐ Single ☐ Student ☐ Other

DIAGNOSIS INFORMATION

Diagnosis	Code	Diagnosis	Code
1. Irregular periods	626.4	5.	
2. Fatigue	780.79	6.	
3. Hyperlipidemia	272.4	7.	
4.		8.	

PROCEDURE INFORMATION

Description of Procedure or Service	Date	Code	Charge
1. Level 4 office visit - est patient	04-11-YYYY	99214	$75.00
2. Venipuncture	04-11-YYYY	36415	$30.00
3.			
4.			
5.			
6.			

SPECIAL NOTES:
Juney Jones, M.D., is part of: Hooper Medical Group, NPI# 0606010188,
Tax ID# 22-9988779. Pt referred to Hooper OB/GYN.

Case Study 5-1 (ICD-9)

JUNEY JONES, M.D.
0995 Hooper Ave • Toms River, NJ 08755 • (732) 999-5555
Tax ID# 11-99556789
NPI# 0077660055

Case Study

PATIENT INFORMATION:
Name:	Sierra Shrewd
Social Security #:	999-00-8899
Address:	0512 Mango Road
City:	Asbury Park
State:	NJ
Zip Code:	00040
Home Telephone:	(732) 999-1111
Date of Birth:	05-17-1976
Gender:	Female
Occupation:	Teacher
Employer:	St. Anne's
Employer Telephone:	(732) 888-0000
Spouse:	
Spouse's Social Security #:	
Spouse's Employer:	
Spouse's Date of Birth:	

INSURANCE INFORMATION:
Patient Number:	Shrsi000
Place of Service:	Office
Primary Insurance Plan:	Oxford
Primary Insurance Plan ID #:	4497601
Group #:	P6239
Primary Policyholder:	Sierra Shrewd
Policyholder Date of Birth:	05-17-1976
Relationship to Patient:	Self
Secondary Insurance Plan:	
Secondary Insurance Plan ID #:	
Secondary Policyholder:	

Patient Status   ☐ Married   ☒ Divorced   ☐ Single   ☐ Student   ☐ Other

DIAGNOSIS INFORMATION
#	Diagnosis	Code	#	Diagnosis	Code
1.	Irregular periods	N92.6	5.		
2.	Fatigue	R53.83	6.		
3.	Hyperlipidemia	E78.5	7.		
4.			8.		

PROCEDURE INFORMATION
	Description of Procedure or Service	Date	Code	Charge
1.	Level 4 office visit - est patient	04-11-YYYY	99214	$75.00
2.	Venipuncture	04-11-YYYY	36415	$30.00
3.				
4.				
5.				
6.				

SPECIAL NOTES:
Juney Jones, M.D., is part of: Hooper Medical Group, NPI# 0606010188,
Tax ID# 22-9988779. Pt referred to Hooper OB/GYN.

Case Study 5-2 (ICD-10)

HOOPER OB/GYN

0401 Hooper Ave • Toms River, NJ 08755 • (732) 000-2200

Tax ID# 22-0011289

NPI# 1000290001

Case Study

PATIENT INFORMATION:

Name:	Sierra Shrewd
Social Security #:	999-00-8899
Address:	0512 Mango Road
City:	Asbury Park
State:	NJ
Zip Code:	00040
Home Telephone:	(732) 999-1111
Date of Birth:	05-17-1976
Gender:	Female
Occupation:	Teacher
Employer:	St. Anne's
Employer Telephone:	(732) 888-0000
Spouse:	
Spouse's Social Security #:	
Spouse's Employer:	
Spouse's Date of Birth:	

INSURANCE INFORMATION:

Patient Number:	Shrsi000
Place of Service:	Office
Primary Insurance Plan:	Oxford
Primary Insurance Plan ID #:	4497601
Group #:	P6239
Primary Policyholder:	Sierra Shrewd
Policyholder Date of Birth:	05-17-1976
Relationship to Patient:	Self
Secondary Insurance Plan:	
Secondary Insurance Plan ID #:	
Secondary Policyholder:	

Patient Status ☐ Married ☒ Divorced ☐ Single ☐ Student ☐ Other

DIAGNOSIS INFORMATION

Diagnosis	Code		Diagnosis	Code
1. Irregular periods	626.4	5.		
2.		6.		
3.		7.		
4.		8.		

PROCEDURE INFORMATION

Description of Procedure or Service	Date	Code	Charge
1. Level 3 office consultation	04-19-YYYY	99243	$150.00
2.			
3.			
4.			
5.			
6.			

SPECIAL NOTES:

Pt was seen by Mindy Mable, M.D., NPI# 0707566500. Referred by Dr. Juney Jones, NPI# 0077660055

HOOPER OB/GYN
0401 Hooper Ave • Toms River, NJ 08755 • (732) 000-2200
Tax ID# 22-0011289
NPI# 1000290001

Case Study

PATIENT INFORMATION:

Name:	Sierra Shrewd
Social Security #:	999-00-8899
Address:	0512 Mango Road
City:	Asbury Park
State:	NJ
Zip Code:	00040
Home Telephone:	(732) 999-1111
Date of Birth:	05-17-1976
Gender:	Female
Occupation:	Teacher
Employer:	St. Anne's
Employer Telephone:	(732) 888-0000
Spouse:	
Spouse's Social Security #:	
Spouse's Employer:	
Spouse's Date of Birth:	

INSURANCE INFORMATION:

Patient Number:	Shrsi000
Place of Service:	Office
Primary Insurance Plan:	Oxford
Primary Insurance Plan ID #:	4497601
Group #:	P6239
Primary Policyholder:	Sierra Shrewd
Policyholder Date of Birth:	05-17-1976
Relationship to Patient:	Self
Secondary Insurance Plan:	
Secondary Insurance Plan ID #:	
Secondary Policyholder:	

Patient Status   ☐ Married   ☒ Divorced   ☐ Single   ☐ Student   ☐ Other

DIAGNOSIS INFORMATION

Diagnosis	Code		Diagnosis	Code
1. Irregular periods	N92.6	5.		
2.		6.		
3.		7.		
4.		8.		

PROCEDURE INFORMATION

Description of Procedure or Service	Date	Code	Charge
1. Level 3 office consultation	04-19-YYYY	99243	$150.00
2.			
3.			
4.			
5.			
6.			

SPECIAL NOTES:

Pt was seen by Mindy Mable, M.D., NPI# 0707566500. Referred by Dr. Juney Jones, NPI# 0077660055

Case Study 6-2 (ICD-10)

HOOPER OB/GYN

0401 Hooper Ave • Toms River, NJ 08755 • (732) 000-2200
Tax ID# 22-0011289
NPI# 1000290001

Case Study

PATIENT INFORMATION:

Name:	Sierra Shrewd
Social Security #:	999-00-8899
Address:	0512 Mango Road
City:	Asbury Park
State:	NJ
Zip Code:	00040
Home Telephone:	(732) 999-1111
Date of Birth:	05-17-1976
Gender:	Female
Occupation:	Teacher
Employer:	St. Anne's
Employer Telephone:	(732) 888-0000
Spouse:	
Spouse's Social Security #:	
Spouse's Employer:	
Spouse's Date of Birth:	

INSURANCE INFORMATION:

Patient Number:	Shrsi000
Place of Service:	Out-patient hospital
Primary Insurance Plan:	Oxford
Primary Insurance Plan ID #:	4497601
Group #:	P6239
Primary Policyholder:	Sierra Shrewd
Policyholder Date of Birth:	05-17-1976
Relationship to Patient:	Self
Secondary Insurance Plan:	
Secondary Insurance Plan ID #:	
Secondary Policyholder:	

Patient Status   ☐ Married   ☒ Divorced   ☐ Single   ☐ Student   ☐ Other

DIAGNOSIS INFORMATION

Diagnosis	Code	Diagnosis	Code
1. Irregular periods	626.4	5.	
2.		6.	
3.		7.	
4.		8.	

PROCEDURE INFORMATION

Description of Procedure or Service	Date	Code	Charge
1. Dilation and curettage	04-26-YYYY	58120	$750.00
2.			
3.			
4.			
5.			
6.			

SPECIAL NOTES:

Performing physician Mindy Mable, M.D., NPI# 0707566500,
Hooper Medical Center, 011 Hospital Drive, Toms River, NJ 08755,
Facility NPI# 9900000011.

Case Study 7-1 (ICD-9)

HOOPER OB/GYN

0401 Hooper Ave • Toms River, NJ 08755 • (732) 000-2200

Tax ID# 22-0011289

NPI# 1000290001

Case Study

PATIENT INFORMATION:

Name:	Sierra Shrewd
Social Security #:	999-00-8899
Address:	0512 Mango Road
City:	Asbury Park
State:	NJ
Zip Code:	00040
Home Telephone:	(732) 999-1111
Date of Birth:	05-17-1976
Gender:	Female
Occupation:	Teacher
Employer:	St. Anne's
Employer Telephone:	(732) 888-0000
Spouse:	
Spouse's Social Security #:	
Spouse's Employer:	
Spouse's Date of Birth:	

INSURANCE INFORMATION:

Patient Number:	Shrsi000
Place of Service:	Out-patient hospital
Primary Insurance Plan:	Oxford
Primary Insurance Plan ID #:	4497601
Group #:	P6239
Primary Policyholder:	Sierra Shrewd
Policyholder Date of Birth:	05-17-1976
Relationship to Patient:	Self
Secondary Insurance Plan:	
Secondary Insurance Plan ID #:	
Secondary Policyholder:	

Patient Status   ☐ Married   ☒ Divorced   ☐ Single   ☐ Student   ☐ Other

DIAGNOSIS INFORMATION

	Diagnosis	Code		Diagnosis	Code
1.	Irregular periods	N92.6	5.		
2.			6.		
3.			7.		
4.			8.		

PROCEDURE INFORMATION

	Description of Procedure or Service	Date	Code	Charge
1.	Dilation and curettage	04-26-YYYY	58120	$750.00
2.				
3.				
4.				
5.				
6.				

SPECIAL NOTES:

Performing physician Mindy Mable, M.D., NPI# 0707566500,
Hooper Medical Center, 011 Hospital Drive, Toms River, NJ 08755,
Facility NPI# 9900000011.

Case Study 7-2 (ICD-10)

CATHY CRANE, M.D.
0626 Route 88 • Point Pleasant, NJ 08742 • (732) 001-6793
Tax ID# 11-4455798
NPI# 8007006000

Case Study

PATIENT INFORMATION:

Name:	Diane Dells
Social Security #:	000-47-0000
Address:	032 Ridge Trail
City:	Brick
State:	NJ
Zip Code:	08723
Home Telephone:	(732) 050-9927
Date of Birth:	03-24-1973
Gender:	Female
Occupation:	Secretary
Employer:	The Office Place
Employer Telephone:	(732) 090-2299
Spouse:	David Dells
Spouse's Social Security #:	000-66-0066
Spouse's Employer:	Telecom
Spouse's Date of Birth:	07-01-1961

INSURANCE INFORMATION:

Patient Number:	Deldi000
Place of Service:	Office
Primary Insurance Plan:	Connecticut General
Primary Insurance Plan ID #:	279322XZ27
Group #:	930001
Primary Policyholder:	Diane Dells
Policyholder Date of Birth:	03-24-1973
Relationship to Patient:	Self
Secondary Insurance Plan:	Aetna
Secondary Insurance Plan ID #:	273BA9264
Secondary Policyholder:	David Dells

Patient Status   ☒ Married   ☐ Divorced   ☐ Single   ☐ Student   ☐ Other

DIAGNOSIS INFORMATION

Diagnosis	Code	Diagnosis	Code
1. Mass, breast	611.72	5.	
2.		6.	
3.		7.	
4.		8.	

PROCEDURE INFORMATION

Description of Procedure or Service	Date	Code	Charge
1. Level 3 office visit - new patient	03-16-YYYY	99203	$100.00
2.			
3.			
4.			
5.			
6.			

SPECIAL NOTES:
Pt referred to Dr. Lisa Lane who is part of XYZ Medical Group.

Case Study 8-1 (ICD-9)

CATHY CRANE, M.D.
0626 Route 88 • Point Pleasant, NJ 08742 • (732) 001-6793
Tax ID# 11-4455798
NPI# 8007006000

Case Study

PATIENT INFORMATION:

Name:	Diane Dells
Social Security #:	000-47-0000
Address:	032 Ridge Trail
City:	Brick
State:	NJ
Zip Code:	08723
Home Telephone:	(732) 050-9927
Date of Birth:	03-24-1973
Gender:	Female
Occupation:	Secretary
Employer:	The Office Place
Employer Telephone:	(732) 090-2299
Spouse:	David Dells
Spouse's Social Security #:	000-66-0066
Spouse's Employer:	Telecom
Spouse's Date of Birth:	07-01-1961

INSURANCE INFORMATION:

Patient Number:	Deldi000
Place of Service:	Office
Primary Insurance Plan:	Connecticut General
Primary Insurance Plan ID #:	279322XZ27
Group #:	930001
Primary Policyholder:	Diane Dells
Policyholder Date of Birth:	03-24-1973
Relationship to Patient:	Self
Secondary Insurance Plan:	Aetna
Secondary Insurance Plan ID #:	273BA9264
Secondary Policyholder:	David Dells

Patient Status   ☒ Married   ☐ Divorced   ☐ Single   ☐ Student   ☐ Other

DIAGNOSIS INFORMATION

Diagnosis	Code	Diagnosis	Code
1. Mass, breast	N63	5.	
2.		6.	
3.		7.	
4.		8.	

PROCEDURE INFORMATION

Description of Procedure or Service	Date	Code	Charge
1. Level 3 office visit - new patient	03-16-YYYY	99203	$100.00
2.			
3.			
4.			
5.			
6.			

SPECIAL NOTES:
Pt referred to Dr. Lisa Lane who is part of XYZ Medical Group.

LISA LANE, M.D.
0797 Route 88 • Point Pleasant, NJ 08742 • (732) 000-1792
Tax ID# 11-9955333
NPI# 6005004001

Case Study

PATIENT INFORMATION:

Name:	Diane Dells
Social Security #:	000-47-0000
Address:	032 Ridge Trail
City:	Brick
State:	NJ
Zip Code:	08723
Home Telephone:	(732) 050-9927
Date of Birth:	03-24-1973
Gender:	Female
Occupation:	Secretary
Employer:	The Office Place
Employer Telephone:	(732) 090-2299
Spouse:	David Dells
Spouse's Social Security #:	000-66-0066
Spouse's Employer:	Telecom
Spouse's Date of Birth:	07-01-1961

INSURANCE INFORMATION:

Patient Number:	Deldi000
Place of Service:	Office
Primary Insurance Plan:	Connecticut General
Primary Insurance Plan ID #:	279322XZ27
Group #:	930001
Primary Policyholder:	Diane Dells
Policyholder Date of Birth:	03-24-1973
Relationship to Patient:	Self
Secondary Insurance Plan:	Aetna
Secondary Insurance Plan ID #:	273BA9264
Secondary Policyholder:	David Dells

Patient Status ☒ Married ☐ Divorced ☐ Single ☐ Student ☐ Other

DIAGNOSIS INFORMATION

Diagnosis	Code	Diagnosis	Code
1. Mass, breast	611.72	5.	
2.		6.	
3.		7.	
4.		8.	

PROCEDURE INFORMATION

Description of Procedure or Service	Date	Code	Charge
1. Level 4 office consultation	03-29-YYYY	99244	$175.00
2.			
3.			
4.			
5.			
6.			

SPECIAL NOTES:

Physician is part of: XYZ Medical Group, Tax ID# 22-9346789, NPI# 0004400330.
Pt referred by: Cathy Crane, M.D., NPI# 8007006000.

Case Study 9-1 (ICD-9)

LISA LANE, M.D.
0797 Route 88 • Point Pleasant, NJ 08742 • (732) 000-1792
Tax ID# 11-9955333
NPI# 6005004001

Case Study

PATIENT INFORMATION:

Name:	Diane Dells
Social Security #:	000-47-0000
Address:	032 Ridge Trail
City:	Brick
State:	NJ
Zip Code:	08723
Home Telephone:	(732) 050-9927
Date of Birth:	03-24-1973
Gender:	Female
Occupation:	Secretary
Employer:	The Office Place
Employer Telephone:	(732) 090-2299
Spouse:	David Dells
Spouse's Social Security #:	000-66-0066
Spouse's Employer:	Telecom
Spouse's Date of Birth:	07-01-1961

INSURANCE INFORMATION:

Patient Number:	Deldi000
Place of Service:	Office
Primary Insurance Plan:	Connecticut General
Primary Insurance Plan ID #:	279322XZ27
Group #:	930001
Primary Policyholder:	Diane Dells
Policyholder Date of Birth:	03-24-1973
Relationship to Patient:	Self
Secondary Insurance Plan:	Aetna
Secondary Insurance Plan ID #:	273BA9264
Secondary Policyholder:	David Dells

Patient Status ☒ Married ☐ Divorced ☐ Single ☐ Student ☐ Other

DIAGNOSIS INFORMATION

Diagnosis	Code		Diagnosis	Code
1. Mass, breast	N63	5.		
2.		6.		
3.		7.		
4.		8.		

PROCEDURE INFORMATION

Description of Procedure or Service	Date	Code	Charge
1. Level 4 office consultation	03-29-YYYY	99244	$175.00
2.			
3.			
4.			
5.			
6.			

SPECIAL NOTES:
Physician is part of: XYZ Medical Group, Tax ID# 22-9346789, NPI# 0004400330.
Pt referred by: Cathy Crane, M.D., NPI# 8007006000.

LINDA LEGGY, M.D.

0424 Route 88 • Brick, NJ 08724 • (732) 000-0977

Tax ID# 11-8844697

NPI# 0411021100

Case Study

PATIENT INFORMATION:

Name:	Fiona Flags
Social Security #:	010-10-0110
Address:	030 Maple Drive
City:	West Long Branch
State:	NJ
Zip Code:	07764
Home Telephone:	(732) 090-0120
Date of Birth:	07-12-1948
Gender:	Female
Occupation:	Retired
Employer:	
Employer Telephone:	
Spouse:	
Spouse's Social Security #:	
Spouse's Employer:	
Spouse's Date of Birth:	

INSURANCE INFORMATION:

Patient Number:	Fiofl000
Place of Service:	In-patient hospital
Primary Insurance Plan:	Medicare
Primary Insurance Plan ID #:	010-10-0110A
Group #:	
Primary Policyholder:	Fiona Flags
Policyholder Date of Birth:	07-12-1948
Relationship to Patient:	Self
Secondary Insurance Plan:	
Secondary Insurance Plan ID #:	
Secondary Policyholder:	

Patient Status ☐ Married ☐ Divorced ☒ Single ☐ Student ☐ Other

DIAGNOSIS INFORMATION

Diagnosis	Code		Diagnosis	Code
1. Pneumonia	486	5.		
2.		6.		
3.		7.		
4.		8.		

PROCEDURE INFORMATION

Description of Procedure or Service	Date	Code	Charge
1. Initial hospital care - level 3	03-15-YYYY	99223	$175.00
2. Subsequent hospital care - level 2	03-16-YYYY	99232	$115.00
3.			
4.			
5.			
6.			

SPECIAL NOTES:

Linda Leggy, M.D., requests a consult from Peggy Peters, M.D., Community Central Hospital, 0599 Third Avenue, Howell, NJ 07701, Facility NPI# 0009207777.

Case Study 10-1 (ICD-9)

LINDA LEGGY, M.D.
0424 Route 88 • Brick, NJ 08724 • (732) 000-0977
Tax ID# 11-8844697
NPI# 0411021100

Case Study

PATIENT INFORMATION:

Name:	Fiona Flags
Social Security #:	010-10-0110
Address:	030 Maple Drive
City:	West Long Branch
State:	NJ
Zip Code:	07764
Home Telephone:	(732) 090-0120
Date of Birth:	07-12-1948
Gender:	Female
Occupation:	Retired
Employer:	
Employer Telephone:	
Spouse:	
Spouse's Social Security #:	
Spouse's Employer:	
Spouse's Date of Birth:	

INSURANCE INFORMATION:

Patient Number:	Fiof1000
Place of Service:	In-patient hospital
Primary Insurance Plan:	Medicare
Primary Insurance Plan ID #:	010-10-0110A
Group #:	
Primary Policyholder:	Fiona Flags
Policyholder Date of Birth:	07-12-1948
Relationship to Patient:	Self
Secondary Insurance Plan:	
Secondary Insurance Plan ID #:	
Secondary Policyholder:	

Patient Status ☐ Married ☐ Divorced ☒ Single ☐ Student ☐ Other

DIAGNOSIS INFORMATION

Diagnosis	Code	Diagnosis	Code
1. Pneumonia	J18.9	5.	
2.		6.	
3.		7.	
4.		8.	

PROCEDURE INFORMATION

Description of Procedure or Service	Date	Code	Charge
1. Initial hospital care - level 3	03-15-YYYY	99223	$175.00
2. Subsequent hospital care - level 2	03-16-YYYY	99232	$115.00
3.			
4.			
5.			
6.			

SPECIAL NOTES:

Linda Leggy, M.D., requests a consult from Peggy Peters, M.D., Community Central Hospital, 0599 Third Avenue, Howell, NJ 07701, Facility NPI# 0009207777.

Case Study 10-2 (ICD-10)

PEGGY PETERS, M.D.
0799 Broadway Ave • Long Branch, NJ 07740 • (732) 333-5555
Tax ID# 11-3344555
NPI# 0411332200

Case Study

PATIENT INFORMATION:		INSURANCE INFORMATION:	
Name:	Fiona Flags	Patient Number:	Fiofl000
Social Security #:	010-10-0110	Place of Service:	In-patient hospital
Address:	030 Maple Drive	Primary Insurance Plan:	Medicare
City:	West Long Branch	Primary Insurance Plan ID #:	010-10-0110A
State:	NJ		
Zip Code:	07764	Group #:	
Home Telephone:	(732) 090-0120		
Date of Birth:	07-12-1948	Primary Policyholder:	Fiona Flags
Gender:	Female	Policyholder Date of Birth:	07-12-1948
Occupation:	Retired	Relationship to Patient:	Self
Employer:			
Employer Telephone:		Secondary Insurance Plan:	
Spouse:		Secondary Insurance Plan ID #:	
Spouse's Social Security #:			
Spouse's Employer:		Secondary Policyholder:	
Spouse's Date of Birth:			

Patient Status	☐ Married	☐ Divorced	☒ Single	☐ Student	☐ Other

DIAGNOSIS INFORMATION

Diagnosis	Code	Diagnosis	Code
1. Pneumonia	486	5.	
2.		6.	
3.		7.	
4.		8.	

PROCEDURE INFORMATION

Description of Procedure or Service	Date	Code	Charge
1. Initial in-patient consultation - level 3	03-15-YYYY	99253	$225.00
2. Pneumocentesis, puncture of lung for aspiration	03-16-YYYY	32405	$675.00
3.			
4.			
5.			
6.			

SPECIAL NOTES:

Referring physician: Linda Leggy, M.D., NPI# 0411021100.
Community Central Hospital, 0599 Third Avenue, Howell, NJ 07701,
Facility NPI# 0009207777.

Case Study 11-1 (ICD-9)

PEGGY PETERS, M.D.
0799 Broadway Ave • Long Branch, NJ 07740 • (732) 333-5555
Tax ID# 11-3344555
NPI# 0411332200

Case Study

PATIENT INFORMATION:

Name:	Fiona Flags
Social Security #:	010-10-0110
Address:	030 Maple Drive
City:	West Long Branch
State:	NJ
Zip Code:	07764
Home Telephone:	(732) 090-0120
Date of Birth:	07-12-1948
Gender:	Female
Occupation:	Retired
Employer:	
Employer Telephone:	
Spouse:	
Spouse's Social Security #:	
Spouse's Employer:	
Spouse's Date of Birth:	

INSURANCE INFORMATION:

Patient Number:	Fiof1000
Place of Service:	In-patient hospital
Primary Insurance Plan:	Medicare
Primary Insurance Plan ID #:	010-10-0110A
Group #:	
Primary Policyholder:	Fiona Flags
Policyholder Date of Birth:	07-12-1948
Relationship to Patient:	Self
Secondary Insurance Plan:	
Secondary Insurance Plan ID #:	
Secondary Policyholder:	

Patient Status   ☐ Married   ☐ Divorced   ☒ Single   ☐ Student   ☐ Other

DIAGNOSIS INFORMATION

Diagnosis	Code	Diagnosis	Code
1. Pneumonia	J18.9	5.	
2.		6.	
3.		7.	
4.		8.	

PROCEDURE INFORMATION

Description of Procedure or Service	Date	Code	Charge
1. Initial in-patient consultation - level 3	03-15-YYYY	99253	$225.00
2. Pneumocentesis, puncture of lung for aspiration	03-16-YYYY	32405	$675.00
3.			
4.			
5.			
6.			

SPECIAL NOTES:
Referring physician: Linda Leggy, M.D., NPI# 0411021100.
Community Central Hospital, 0599 Third Avenue, Howell, NJ 07701,
Facility NPI# 0009207777.

Case Study 11-2 (ICD-10)

ELLEN EMBERS, D.O.

076 Lakeridge Road • Manchester, NJ 00034 • (732) 111-4710
Tax ID# 11-9811223
NPI# 0132130000

Case Study

PATIENT INFORMATION:

Name:	Julie Jasper
Social Security #:	000-88-0008
Address:	0411 Haskill Road
City:	Manchester
State:	NJ
Zip Code:	00034
Home Telephone:	(732) 555-9959
Date of Birth:	04-09-1942
Gender:	Female
Occupation:	Retired
Employer:	
Employer Telephone:	
Spouse:	
Spouse's Social Security #:	
Spouse's Employer:	
Spouse's Date of Birth:	

INSURANCE INFORMATION:

Patient Number:	Jasju000
Place of Service:	Nursing facility
Primary Insurance Plan:	CIGNA Medicare
Primary Insurance Plan ID #:	422QME0008
Group #:	CM99326
Primary Policyholder:	Julie Jasper
Policyholder Date of Birth:	04-09-1942
Relationship to Patient:	Self
Secondary Insurance Plan:	
Secondary Insurance Plan ID #:	
Secondary Policyholder:	

Patient Status ☐ Married ☐ Divorced ☒ Single ☐ Student ☐ Other

DIAGNOSIS INFORMATION

Diagnosis	Code	Diagnosis	Code
1. Alzheimer's	331.0	5.	
2.		6.	
3.		7.	
4.		8.	

PROCEDURE INFORMATION

Description of Procedure or Service	Date	Code	Charge
1. Initial nursing facility care - level 2	05-17-YYYY	99305	$150.00
2. Subsequent nursing facility care - level 2	05-18-YYYY	99308	$130.00
3.			
4.			
5.			
6.			

SPECIAL NOTES:

Ocean Senior Care Village, 066 Route 1, Lake Hurst, NJ 02222,
Facility NPI# 0210304050.

Case Study 12-1 (ICD-9)

ELLEN EMBERS, D.O.
076 Lakeridge Road • Manchester, NJ 00034 • (732) 111-4710
Tax ID# 11-9811223
NPI# 0132130000

Case Study

PATIENT INFORMATION:

Name:	Julie Jasper
Social Security #:	000-88-0008
Address:	0411 Haskill Road
City:	Manchester
State:	NJ
Zip Code:	00034
Home Telephone:	(732) 555-9959
Date of Birth:	04-09-1942
Gender:	Female
Occupation:	Retired
Employer:	
Employer Telephone:	
Spouse:	
Spouse's Social Security #:	
Spouse's Employer:	
Spouse's Date of Birth:	

INSURANCE INFORMATION:

Patient Number:	Jasju000
Place of Service:	Nursing facility
Primary Insurance Plan:	CIGNA Medicare
Primary Insurance Plan ID #:	422QME0008
Group #:	CM99326
Primary Policyholder:	Julie Jasper
Policyholder Date of Birth:	04-09-1942
Relationship to Patient:	Self
Secondary Insurance Plan:	
Secondary Insurance Plan ID #:	
Secondary Policyholder:	

Patient Status   ☐ Married   ☐ Divorced   ☒ Single   ☐ Student   ☐ Other

DIAGNOSIS INFORMATION

Diagnosis	Code		Diagnosis	Code
1. Alzheimer's dementia w/o behavioral disturbances	G30.9	5.		
2. Dementia in other diseases classified elsewhere without behavioral disturbance	F02.80	6.		
3.		7.		
4.		8.		

PROCEDURE INFORMATION

Description of Procedure or Service	Date	Code	Charge
1. Initial nursing facility care - level 2	05-17-YYYY	99305	$150.00
2. Subsequent nursing facility care - level 2	05-18-YYYY	99308	$130.00
3.			
4.			
5.			
6.			

SPECIAL NOTES:
Ocean Senior Care Village, 066 Route 1, Lake Hurst, NJ 02222,
Facility NPI# 0210304050.

Case Study 12-2 (ICD-10)

PATRICIA PLATINUM, M.D.

010 Cedar Bridge Lane • Brick, NJ 08723 • (732) 333-4444
Tax ID# 11-8181811
NPI# 1002003000

Case Study

PATIENT INFORMATION:

Name:	John Johnson
Social Security #:	009-08-0007
Address:	0418 Lucy Court
City:	Brick
State:	NJ
Zip Code:	08723
Home Telephone:	(732) 555-7777
Date of Birth:	04-01-1945
Gender:	Male
Occupation:	Retired
Employer:	
Employer Telephone:	
Spouse:	
Spouse's Social Security #:	
Spouse's Employer:	
Spouse's Date of Birth:	

INSURANCE INFORMATION:

Patient Number:	Johjo000
Place of Service:	Office
Primary Insurance Plan:	Medicare
Primary Insurance Plan ID #:	009-08-0007A
Group #:	
Primary Policyholder:	John Johnson
Policyholder Date of Birth:	04-01-1945
Relationship to Patient:	Self
Secondary Insurance Plan:	Blue Cross/Blue Shield
Secondary Insurance Plan ID #:	009-08-0007BB
Secondary Policyholder:	John Johnson

Patient Status ☐ Married ☐ Divorced ☒ Single ☐ Student ☐ Other

DIAGNOSIS INFORMATION

Diagnosis	Code	Diagnosis	Code
1. Irritable bowel syndrome w/o diarrhea	564.1	5.	
2.		6.	
3.		7.	
4.		8.	

PROCEDURE INFORMATION

Description of Procedure or Service	Date	Code	Charge
1. Level 3 office visit - est patient	02-09-YYYY	99213	$65.00
2.			
3.			
4.			
5.			
6.			

SPECIAL NOTES:

Pt referred to Gary Gold, D.O., NPI# 9008007000.

PATRICIA PLATINUM, M.D.

010 Cedar Bridge Lane • Brick, NJ 08723 • (732) 333-4444

Tax ID# 11-8181811

NPI# 1002003000

Case Study

PATIENT INFORMATION:

Name:	John Johnson
Social Security #:	009-08-0007
Address:	0418 Lucy Court
City:	Brick
State:	NJ
Zip Code:	08723
Home Telephone:	(732) 555-7777
Date of Birth:	04-01-1945
Gender:	Male
Occupation:	Retired
Employer:	
Employer Telephone:	
Spouse:	
Spouse's Social Security #:	
Spouse's Employer:	
Spouse's Date of Birth:	

INSURANCE INFORMATION:

Patient Number:	Johjo000
Place of Service:	Office
Primary Insurance Plan:	Medicare
Primary Insurance Plan ID #:	009-08-0007A
Group #:	
Primary Policyholder:	John Johnson
Policyholder Date of Birth:	04-01-1945
Relationship to Patient:	Self
Secondary Insurance Plan:	Blue Cross/Blue Shield
Secondary Insurance Plan ID #:	009-08-0007BB
Secondary Policyholder:	John Johnson

Patient Status   ☐ Married   ☐ Divorced   ☒ Single   ☐ Student   ☐ Other

DIAGNOSIS INFORMATION

Diagnosis	Code	Diagnosis	Code
1. Irritable bowel syndrome w/o diarrhea	K58.9	5.	
2.		6.	
3.		7.	
4.		8.	

PROCEDURE INFORMATION

Description of Procedure or Service	Date	Code	Charge
1. Level 3 office visit - est patient	02-09-YYYY	99213	$65.00
2.			
3.			
4.			
5.			
6.			

SPECIAL NOTES:

Pt referred to Gary Gold, D.O., NPI# 9008007000.

Case Study 13-2 (ICD-10)

GARY GOLD, D.O.
020 Chambers Rd • Brick, NJ 08724 • (732) 444-6666
Tax ID# 11-6677119
NPI# 9008007000

Case Study

PATIENT INFORMATION:

Name:	John Johnson
Social Security #:	009-08-0007
Address:	0418 Lucy Court
City:	Brick
State:	NJ
Zip Code:	08723
Home Telephone:	(732) 555-7777
Date of Birth:	04-01-1945
Gender:	Male
Occupation:	Retired
Employer:	
Employer Telephone:	
Spouse:	
Spouse's Social Security #:	
Spouse's Employer:	
Spouse's Date of Birth:	

INSURANCE INFORMATION:

Patient Number:	Johjo000
Place of Service:	Office
Primary Insurance Plan:	Medicare
Primary Insurance Plan ID #:	009-08-0007A
Group #:	
Primary Policyholder:	John Johnson
Policyholder Date of Birth:	04-01-1945
Relationship to Patient:	Self
Secondary Insurance Plan:	Blue Cross/Blue Shield
Secondary Insurance Plan ID #:	009-08-0007BB
Secondary Policyholder:	John Johnson

Patient Status   ☐ Married   ☐ Divorced   ☒ Single   ☐ Student   ☐ Other

DIAGNOSIS INFORMATION

	Diagnosis	Code		Diagnosis	Code
1.	Irritable bowel syndrome w/o diarrhea	564.1	5.		
2.			6.		
3.			7.		
4.			8.		

PROCEDURE INFORMATION

	Description of Procedure or Service	Date	Code	Charge
1.	Level 4 office consultation	02-17-YYYY	99244	$175.00
2.				
3.				
4.				
5.				
6.				

SPECIAL NOTES:
Pt referred by Patricia Platinum, M.D., NPI# 1002003000.
Pt scheduled for colonoscopy on 02-25-YYYY.

Case Study 14-1 (ICD-9)

GARY GOLD, D.O.
020 Chambers Rd • Brick, NJ 08724 • (732) 444-6666
Tax ID# 11-6677119
NPI# 9008007000

Case Study

PATIENT INFORMATION:
Name: John Johnson
Social Security #: 009-08-0007
Address: 0418 Lucy Court
City: Brick
State: NJ
Zip Code: 08723
Home Telephone: (732) 555-7777
Date of Birth: 04-01-1945
Gender: Male
Occupation: Retired
Employer:
Employer Telephone:
Spouse:
Spouse's Social Security #:
Spouse's Employer:
Spouse's Date of Birth:

INSURANCE INFORMATION:
Patient Number: Johjo000
Place of Service: Office
Primary Insurance Plan: Medicare
Primary Insurance Plan ID #: 009-08-0007A
Group #:
Primary Policyholder: John Johnson
Policyholder Date of Birth: 04-01-1945
Relationship to Patient: Self
Secondary Insurance Plan: Blue Cross/Blue Shield
Secondary Insurance Plan ID #: 009-08-0007BB
Secondary Policyholder: John Johnson

Patient Status   ☐ Married   ☐ Divorced   ☒ Single   ☐ Student   ☐ Other

DIAGNOSIS INFORMATION

Diagnosis	Code	Diagnosis	Code
1. Irritable bowel syndrome w/o diarrhea	K58.9	5.	
2.		6.	
3.		7.	
4.		8.	

PROCEDURE INFORMATION

Description of Procedure or Service	Date	Code	Charge
1. Level 4 office consultation	02-17-YYYY	99244	$175.00
2.			
3.			
4.			
5.			
6.			

SPECIAL NOTES:
Pt referred by Patricia Platinum, M.D., NPI# 1002003000.
Pt scheduled for colonoscopy on 02-25-YYYY.

Case Study 14-2 (ICD-10)

GARY GOLD, D.O.
020 Chambers Rd • Brick, NJ 08724 • (732) 444-6666
Tax ID# 11-6677119
NPI# 9008007000

Case Study

PATIENT INFORMATION:

Name:	John Johnson
Social Security #:	009-08-0007
Address:	0418 Lucy Court
City:	Brick
State:	NJ
Zip Code:	08723
Home Telephone:	(732) 555-7777
Date of Birth:	04-01-1945
Gender:	Male
Occupation:	Retired
Employer:	
Employer Telephone:	
Spouse:	
Spouse's Social Security #:	
Spouse's Employer:	
Spouse's Date of Birth:	

INSURANCE INFORMATION:

Patient Number:	Johjo000
Place of Service:	Out-patient hospital
Primary Insurance Plan:	Medicare
Primary Insurance Plan ID #:	009-08-0007A
Group #:	
Primary Policyholder:	John Johnson
Policyholder Date of Birth:	04-01-1945
Relationship to Patient:	Self
Secondary Insurance Plan:	Blue Cross/Blue Shield
Secondary Insurance Plan ID #:	009-08-0007BB
Secondary Policyholder:	John Johnson

Patient Status ☐ Married ☐ Divorced ☒ Single ☐ Student ☐ Other

DIAGNOSIS INFORMATION

	Diagnosis	Code		Diagnosis	Code
1.	IBS w/o diarrhea	564.1	5.		
2.	Polyps, colon	211.3	6.		
3.			7.		
4.			8.		

PROCEDURE INFORMATION

	Description of Procedure or Service	Date	Code	Charge
1.	Colonoscopy	02-25-YYYY	45378	$800.00
2.				
3.				
4.				
5.				
6.				

SPECIAL NOTES:

Hooper Medical Center, 011 Hospital Drive, Toms River, NJ 08755,
Facility NPI# 9900000011.

GARY GOLD, D.O.

020 Chambers Rd • Brick, NJ 08724 • (732) 444-6666
Tax ID# 11-6677119
NPI# 9008007000

Case Study

PATIENT INFORMATION:

Name:	John Johnson
Social Security #:	009-08-0007
Address:	0418 Lucy Court
City:	Brick
State:	NJ
Zip Code:	08723
Home Telephone:	(732) 555-7777
Date of Birth:	04-01-1945
Gender:	Male
Occupation:	Retired
Employer:	
Employer Telephone:	
Spouse:	
Spouse's Social Security #:	
Spouse's Employer:	
Spouse's Date of Birth:	

INSURANCE INFORMATION:

Patient Number:	Johjo000
Place of Service:	Out-patient hospital
Primary Insurance Plan:	Medicare
Primary Insurance Plan ID #:	009-08-0007A
Group #:	
Primary Policyholder:	John Johnson
Policyholder Date of Birth:	04-01-1945
Relationship to Patient:	Self
Secondary Insurance Plan:	Blue Cross/Blue Shield
Secondary Insurance Plan ID #:	009-08-0007BB
Secondary Policyholder:	John Johnson

Patient Status	☐ Married	☐ Divorced	☒ Single	☐ Student	☐ Other

DIAGNOSIS INFORMATION

	Diagnosis	Code		Diagnosis	Code
1.	IBS w/o diarrhea	K58.9	5.		
2.	Polyps, colon	K63.5	6.		
3.			7.		
4.			8.		

PROCEDURE INFORMATION

	Description of Procedure or Service	Date	Code	Charge
1.	Colonoscopy	02-25-YYYY	45378	$800.00
2.				
3.				
4.				
5.				
6.				

SPECIAL NOTES:

Hooper Medical Center, 011 Hospital Drive, Toms River, NJ 08755,
Facility NPI# 9900000011.

Case Study 15-2 (ICD-10)

JUNEY JONES, M.D.
0995 Hooper Ave • Toms River, NJ 08755 • (732) 999-5555
Tax ID# 11-99556789
NPI# 0077660055

Case Study

PATIENT INFORMATION:

Name:	Theresa Lewis
Social Security #:	944-00-0000
Address:	0490 Gary Lane
City:	Brick
State:	NJ
Zip Code:	08724
Home Telephone:	(732) 999-1111
Date of Birth:	06-08-1950
Gender:	Female
Occupation:	
Employer:	
Employer Telephone:	
Spouse:	Steve Lewis
Spouse's Social Security #:	866-00-0000
Spouse's Employer:	ABC Electronics
Spouse's Date of Birth:	05-30-1939

INSURANCE INFORMATION:

Patient Number:	Lewth000
Place of Service:	Office
Primary Insurance Plan:	Aetna
Primary Insurance Plan ID #:	729QR44731
Group #:	666426
Primary Policyholder:	Steve Lewis
Policyholder Date of Birth:	05-30-1949
Relationship to Patient:	Spouse
Secondary Insurance Plan:	
Secondary Insurance Plan ID #:	
Secondary Policyholder:	

Patient Status ☒ Married ☐ Divorced ☐ Single ☐ Student ☐ Other

DIAGNOSIS INFORMATION

Diagnosis	Code	Diagnosis	Code
1. Rash	782.1	5.	
2.		6.	
3.		7.	
4.		8.	

PROCEDURE INFORMATION

Description of Procedure or Service	Date	Code	Charge
1. Level 4 office visit - est patient	04-21-YYYY	99214	$75.00
2.			
3.			
4.			
5.			
6.			

SPECIAL NOTES:
Pt referred to dermatologist Nancy Nibbles, M.D., NPI# 8108108108.

Case Study 16-1 (ICD-9)

JUNEY JONES, M.D.
0995 Hooper Ave • Toms River, NJ 08755 • (732) 999-5555
Tax ID# 11-99556789
NPI# 0077660055

Case Study

PATIENT INFORMATION:

Name:	Theresa Lewis
Social Security #:	944-00-0000
Address:	0490 Gary Lane
City:	Brick
State:	NJ
Zip Code:	08724
Home Telephone:	(732) 999-1111
Date of Birth:	06-08-1950
Gender:	Female
Occupation:	
Employer:	
Employer Telephone:	
Spouse:	Steve Lewis
Spouse's Social Security #:	866-00-0000
Spouse's Employer:	ABC Electronics
Spouse's Date of Birth:	05-30-1939

INSURANCE INFORMATION:

Patient Number:	Lewth000
Place of Service:	Office
Primary Insurance Plan:	Aetna
Primary Insurance Plan ID #:	729QR44731
Group #:	666426
Primary Policyholder:	Steve Lewis
Policyholder Date of Birth:	05-30-1949
Relationship to Patient:	Spouse
Secondary Insurance Plan:	
Secondary Insurance Plan ID #:	
Secondary Policyholder:	

Patient Status ☒ Married ☐ Divorced ☐ Single ☐ Student ☐ Other

DIAGNOSIS INFORMATION

Diagnosis	Code	Diagnosis	Code
1. Rash	R21	5.	
2.		6.	
3.		7.	
4.		8.	

PROCEDURE INFORMATION

Description of Procedure or Service	Date	Code	Charge
1. Level 4 office visit - est patient	04-21-YYYY	99214	$75.00
2.			
3.			
4.			
5.			
6.			

SPECIAL NOTES:
Pt referred to dermatologist Nancy Nibbles, M.D., NPI# 8108108108.

NANCY NIBBLES, M.D.
04629 Brick Road • Brick, NJ 08724 • (732) 999-2299
Tax ID# 11-3434343
NPI# 8108108108

Case Study

PATIENT INFORMATION:

Name:	Theresa Lewis
Social Security #:	944-00-0000
Address:	0490 Gary Lane
City:	Brick
State:	NJ
Zip Code:	08724
Home Telephone:	(732) 999-1111
Date of Birth:	06-08-1950
Gender:	Female
Occupation:	
Employer:	
Employer Telephone:	
Spouse:	Steve Lewis
Spouse's Social Security #:	866-00-0000
Spouse's Employer:	ABC Electronics
Spouse's Date of Birth:	05-30-1939

INSURANCE INFORMATION:

Patient Number:	Lewth000
Place of Service:	Office
Primary Insurance Plan:	Aetna
Primary Insurance Plan ID #:	729QR44731
Group #:	666426
Primary Policyholder:	Steve Lewis
Policyholder Date of Birth:	05-30-1949
Relationship to Patient:	Spouse
Secondary Insurance Plan:	
Secondary Insurance Plan ID #:	
Secondary Policyholder:	

Patient Status ☒ Married   ☐ Divorced   ☐ Single   ☐ Student   ☐ Other

DIAGNOSIS INFORMATION

	Diagnosis	Code		Diagnosis	Code
1.	Rash	782.1	5.		
2.	Dermatitis	692.9	6.		
3.			7.		
4.			8.		

PROCEDURE INFORMATION

	Description of Procedure or Service	Date	Code	Charge
1.	Level 2 office consultation	05-02-YYYY	99242	$125.00
2.				
3.				
4.				
5.				
6.				

SPECIAL NOTES:
Pt was referred by Juney Jones, M.D., NPI# 0077660055.

Case Study 17-1 (ICD-9)

NANCY NIBBLES, M.D.
04629 Brick Road • Brick, NJ 08724 • (732) 999-2299
Tax ID# 11-3434343
NPI# 8108108108

Case Study

PATIENT INFORMATION:

Name:	Theresa Lewis
Social Security #:	944-00-0000
Address:	0490 Gary Lane
City:	Brick
State:	NJ
Zip Code:	08724
Home Telephone:	(732) 999-1111
Date of Birth:	06-08-1950
Gender:	Female
Occupation:	
Employer:	
Employer Telephone:	
Spouse:	Steve Lewis
Spouse's Social Security #:	866-00-0000
Spouse's Employer:	ABC Electronics
Spouse's Date of Birth:	05-30-1939

INSURANCE INFORMATION:

Patient Number:	Lewth000
Place of Service:	Office
Primary Insurance Plan:	Aetna
Primary Insurance Plan ID #:	729QR44731
Group #:	666426
Primary Policyholder:	Steve Lewis
Policyholder Date of Birth:	05-30-1949
Relationship to Patient:	Spouse
Secondary Insurance Plan:	
Secondary Insurance Plan ID #:	
Secondary Policyholder:	

Patient Status ☒ Married ☐ Divorced ☐ Single ☐ Student ☐ Other

DIAGNOSIS INFORMATION

	Diagnosis	Code		Diagnosis	Code
1.	Rash	R21	5.		
2.	Dermatitis	L30.9	6.		
3.			7.		
4.			8.		

PROCEDURE INFORMATION

	Description of Procedure or Service	Date	Code	Charge
1.	Level 2 office consultation	05-02-YYYY	99242	$125.00
2.				
3.				
4.				
5.				
6.				

SPECIAL NOTES:
Pt was referred by Juney Jones, M.D., NPI# 0077660055.

Case Study 17-2 (ICD-10)

STEVEN SPRING, M.D.

0909 Route 68 • Point Pleasant, NJ 08742 • (732) 004-0090

Tax ID# 11-9923989

NPI# 0101010101

Case Study

PATIENT INFORMATION:

Name:	Carole Cramer
Social Security #:	999-22-9992
Address:	0463 Brook Lane
City:	Brick
State:	NJ
Zip Code:	08739
Home Telephone:	(732) 444-4454
Date of Birth:	09-22-1944
Gender:	Female
Occupation:	Retired
Employer:	
Employer Telephone:	
Spouse:	
Spouse's Social Security #:	
Spouse's Employer:	
Spouse's Date of Birth:	

INSURANCE INFORMATION:

Patient Number:	Craca000
Place of Service:	Office
Primary Insurance Plan:	Medicare
Primary Insurance Plan ID #:	999-22-9992A
Group #:	
Primary Policyholder:	Carole Cramer
Policyholder Date of Birth:	09-22-1944
Relationship to Patient:	Self
Secondary Insurance Plan:	
Secondary Insurance Plan ID #:	
Secondary Policyholder:	

Patient Status ☐ Married ☒ Divorced ☐ Single ☐ Student ☐ Other

DIAGNOSIS INFORMATION

Diagnosis	Code	Diagnosis	Code
1. Asthma	493.90	5.	
2. Back pain	724.5	6.	
3.		7.	
4.		8.	

PROCEDURE INFORMATION

Description of Procedure or Service	Date	Code	Charge
1. Nebulizer treatment	04-19-YYYY	94640	$65.00
2. Level 2 office visit - est patient	04-19-YYYY	99212	$55.00
3.			
4.			
5.			
6.			

SPECIAL NOTES:

Pt comes in monthly for her asthma condition. She usually receives a nebulizer treatment on these visits. On her visit for 04-19-YYYY, she mentions a separate ailment (back pain) unrelated to her asthma.

Case Study 18-1 (ICD-9)

STEVEN SPRING, M.D.

0909 Route 68 • Point Pleasant, NJ 08742 • (732) 004-0090

Tax ID# 11-9923989

NPI# 0101010101

Case Study

PATIENT INFORMATION:

Name:	Carole Cramer
Social Security #:	999-22-9992
Address:	0463 Brook Lane
City:	Brick
State:	NJ
Zip Code:	08739
Home Telephone:	(732) 444-4454
Date of Birth:	09-22-1944
Gender:	Female
Occupation:	Retired
Employer:	
Employer Telephone:	
Spouse:	
Spouse's Social Security #:	
Spouse's Employer:	
Spouse's Date of Birth:	

INSURANCE INFORMATION:

Patient Number:	Craca000
Place of Service:	Office
Primary Insurance Plan:	Medicare
Primary Insurance Plan ID #:	999-22-9992A
Group #:	
Primary Policyholder:	Carole Cramer
Policyholder Date of Birth:	09-22-1944
Relationship to Patient:	Self
Secondary Insurance Plan:	
Secondary Insurance Plan ID #:	
Secondary Policyholder:	

Patient Status   ☐ Married   ☒ Divorced   ☐ Single   ☐ Student   ☐ Other

DIAGNOSIS INFORMATION

Diagnosis	Code	Diagnosis	Code
1. Asthma	J45.909	5.	
2. Back pain	M54.9	6.	
3.		7.	
4.		8.	

PROCEDURE INFORMATION

Description of Procedure or Service	Date	Code	Charge
1. Nebulizer treatment	04-19-YYYY	94640	$65.00
2. Level 2 office visit - est patient	04-19-YYYY	99212	$55.00
3.			
4.			
5.			
6.			

SPECIAL NOTES:

Pt comes in monthly for her asthma condition. She usually receives a nebulizer treatment on these visits. On her visit for 04-19-YYYY, she mentions a separate ailment (back pain) unrelated to her asthma.

Case Study 18-2 (ICD-10)

VICTOR VENICE, M.D.

0479 Ridge Road • Piscataway, NJ 08754 • (732) 909-9090
Tax ID# 11-3457899
NPI# 0020030049

Case Study

PATIENT INFORMATION:		INSURANCE INFORMATION:	
Name:	Megan Miles	Patient Number:	Milme000
Social Security #:	000-42-9300	Place of Service:	Office
Address:	47 Greenleaf Dr	Primary Insurance Plan:	Oxford
City:	Edison	Primary Insurance Plan ID #:	4692201
State:	NJ	Group #:	P7693
Zip Code:	08817		
Home Telephone:	(732) 400-3001	Primary Policyholder:	Michael Miles
Date of Birth:	06-28-2012	Policyholder Date of Birth:	01-28-1964
Gender:	Female	Relationship to Patient:	Parent
Occupation:			
Employer:		Secondary Insurance Plan:	
Employer Telephone:		Secondary Insurance Plan ID #:	
Spouse:			
Spouse's Social Security #:		Secondary Policyholder:	
Spouse's Employer:			
Spouse's Date of Birth:			

Patient Status	☐ Married	☐ Divorced	☒ Single	☐ Student	☐ Other

DIAGNOSIS INFORMATION

Diagnosis	Code	Diagnosis	Code
1. Pneumonia	486	5.	
2.		6.	
3.		7.	
4.		8.	

PROCEDURE INFORMATION

Description of Procedure or Service	Date	Code	Charge
1. Radiologic exam, chest, single view	01-16-YYYY	71010	$200.00
2.			
3.			
4.			
5.			
6.			

SPECIAL NOTES:
Dr. Venice is a radiologist. He is billing for reading and interpreting the patient's chest x-ray.

Case Study 19-1 (ICD-9)

VICTOR VENICE, M.D.
0479 Ridge Road • Piscataway, NJ 08754 • (732) 909-9090
Tax ID# 11-3457899
NPI# 0020030049

Case Study

PATIENT INFORMATION:

Name:	Megan Miles
Social Security #:	000-42-9300
Address:	47 Greenleaf Dr
City:	Edison
State:	NJ
Zip Code:	08817
Home Telephone:	(732) 400-3001
Date of Birth:	06-28-2012
Gender:	Female
Occupation:	
Employer:	
Employer Telephone:	
Spouse:	
Spouse's Social Security #:	
Spouse's Employer:	
Spouse's Date of Birth:	

INSURANCE INFORMATION:

Patient Number:	Milme000
Place of Service:	Office
Primary Insurance Plan:	Oxford
Primary Insurance Plan ID #:	4692201
Group #:	P7693
Primary Policyholder:	Michael Miles
Policyholder Date of Birth:	01-28-1964
Relationship to Patient:	Parent
Secondary Insurance Plan:	
Secondary Insurance Plan ID #:	
Secondary Policyholder:	

Patient Status ☐ Married ☐ Divorced ☒ Single ☐ Student ☐ Other

DIAGNOSIS INFORMATION

Diagnosis	Code	Diagnosis	Code
1. Pneumonia	J18.9	5.	
2.		6.	
3.		7.	
4.		8.	

PROCEDURE INFORMATION

Description of Procedure or Service	Date	Code	Charge
1. Radiologic exam, chest, single view	01-16-YYYY	71010	$200.00
2.			
3.			
4.			
5.			
6.			

SPECIAL NOTES:
Dr. Venice is a radiologist. He is billing for reading and interpreting the patient's chest x-ray.

Case Study 19-2 (ICD-10)

LOUISE LANCE, M.D.
092 Route 88 • Brick, NJ 08724 • (732) 555-1655
Tax ID# 11-9345789
NPI# 4040400101

Case Study

PATIENT INFORMATION:

Name:	Alyssa Allers
Social Security #:	002-00-3000
Address:	041 Cherry Rd
City:	Brick
State:	NJ
Zip Code:	08723
Home Telephone:	(732) 222-2222
Date of Birth:	05-22-1983
Gender:	Female
Occupation:	Cashier
Employer:	KBM Toys
Employer Telephone:	(732) 444-5555
Spouse:	Larry Allers
Spouse's Social Security #:	067-00-0067
Spouse's Employer:	Exxon
Spouse's Date of Birth:	04-17-1972

INSURANCE INFORMATION:

Patient Number:	Alla1000
Place of Service:	Office
Primary Insurance Plan:	Prudential
Primary Insurance Plan ID #:	P6799234802
Group #:	999367
Primary Policyholder:	Larry Allers
Policyholder Date of Birth:	04-17-1982
Relationship to Patient:	Spouse
Secondary Insurance Plan:	
Secondary Insurance Plan ID #:	
Secondary Policyholder:	

Patient Status ☒ Married ☐ Divorced ☐ Single ☐ Student ☐ Other

DIAGNOSIS INFORMATION

Diagnosis	Code	Diagnosis	Code
1. Skin tag	701.9	5.	
2.		6.	
3.		7.	
4.		8.	

PROCEDURE INFORMATION

Description of Procedure or Service	Date	Code	Charge
1. Removal of skin tags, up to 15	02-28-YYYY	11200	$75.00
2.			
3.			
4.			
5.			
6.			

SPECIAL NOTES:
Site of removal was upper left eyelid.

Case Study 20-1 (ICD-9)

LOUISE LANCE, M.D.
092 Route 88 • Brick, NJ 08724 • (732) 555-1655
Tax ID# 11-9345789
NPI# 4040400101

Case Study

PATIENT INFORMATION:

Name:	Alyssa Allers
Social Security #:	002-00-3000
Address:	041 Cherry Rd
City:	Brick
State:	NJ
Zip Code:	08723
Home Telephone:	(732) 222-2222
Date of Birth:	05-22-1983
Gender:	Female
Occupation:	Cashier
Employer:	KBM Toys
Employer Telephone:	(732) 444-5555
Spouse:	Larry Allers
Spouse's Social Security #:	067-00-0067
Spouse's Employer:	Exxon
Spouse's Date of Birth:	04-17-1972

INSURANCE INFORMATION:

Patient Number:	Allal000
Place of Service:	Office
Primary Insurance Plan:	Prudential
Primary Insurance Plan ID #:	P6799234802
Group #:	999367
Primary Policyholder:	Larry Allers
Policyholder Date of Birth:	04-17-1982
Relationship to Patient:	Spouse
Secondary Insurance Plan:	
Secondary Insurance Plan ID #:	
Secondary Policyholder:	

Patient Status   ☒ Married   ☐ Divorced   ☐ Single   ☐ Student   ☐ Other

DIAGNOSIS INFORMATION

Diagnosis	Code	Diagnosis	Code
1. Skin tag	L91.8	5.	
2.		6.	
3.		7.	
4.		8.	

PROCEDURE INFORMATION

Description of Procedure or Service	Date	Code	Charge
1. Removal of skin tags, up to 15	02-28-YYYY	11200	$75.00
2.			
3.			
4.			
5.			
6.			

SPECIAL NOTES:
Site of removal was upper left eyelid.

Case Study 20-2 (ICD-10)

BEATRICE BOWE, M.D.

091 Chambers Rd • Brick, NJ 08724 • (732) 555-7755
Tax ID# 11-2399888
NPI# 0000055555

Case Study

PATIENT INFORMATION:		INSURANCE INFORMATION:	
Name:	Steven Scally	Patient Number:	Scast000
Social Security #:	000-99-3344	Place of Service:	Office
Address:	04127 Blackhorse Lane	Primary Insurance Plan:	Medicare
City:	Point Pleasant	Primary Insurance Plan ID #:	000-99-3344A
State:	NJ	Group #:	
Zip Code:	08742		
Home Telephone:	(732) 400-5000	Primary Policyholder:	Steven Scally
Date of Birth:	01-22-1946	Policyholder Date of Birth:	01-22-1946
Gender:	Male	Relationship to Patient:	Self
Occupation:	Retired		
Employer:		Secondary Insurance Plan:	
Employer Telephone:		Secondary Insurance Plan ID #:	
Spouse:			
Spouse's Social Security #:		Secondary Policyholder:	
Spouse's Employer:			
Spouse's Date of Birth:			

Patient Status ☐ Married ☐ Divorced ☒ Single ☐ Student ☐ Other

DIAGNOSIS INFORMATION

Diagnosis	Code	Diagnosis	Code
1. Shoulder pain	719.41	5.	
2. Preventative influenza	V04.81	6.	
3.		7.	
4.		8.	

PROCEDURE INFORMATION

Description of Procedure or Service	Date	Code	Charge
1. Level 3 office visit - est patient	05-19-YYYY	99213	$65.00
2. Influenza vaccine	05-19-YYYY	90658	$30.00
3. Administration of influenza vaccine	05-19-YYYY	G0008	$25.00
4.			
5.			
6.			

SPECIAL NOTES:
Pt comes in for his annual flu vaccine. While in the exam room, patient mentions a separate ailment - he has been experiencing recent shoulder pain.

Case Study 21-1 (ICD-9)

BEATRICE BOWE, M.D.
091 Chambers Rd • Brick, NJ 08724 • (732) 555-7755
Tax ID# 11-2399888
NPI# 0000055555

Case Study

PATIENT INFORMATION:		INSURANCE INFORMATION:	
Name:	Steven Scally	Patient Number:	Scast000
Social Security #:	000-99-3344	Place of Service:	Office
Address:	04127 Blackhorse Lane		
City:	Point Pleasant	Primary Insurance Plan:	Medicare
State:	NJ	Primary Insurance Plan ID #:	000-99-3344A
Zip Code:	08742		
Home Telephone:	(732) 400-5000	Group #:	
Date of Birth:	01-22-1946	Primary Policyholder:	Steven Scally
Gender:	Male	Policyholder Date of Birth:	01-22-1946
Occupation:	Retired	Relationship to Patient:	Self
Employer:			
Employer Telephone:		Secondary Insurance Plan:	
Spouse:		Secondary Insurance Plan ID #:	
Spouse's Social Security #:			
Spouse's Employer:		Secondary Policyholder:	
Spouse's Date of Birth:			

Patient Status ☐ Married ☐ Divorced ☒ Single ☐ Student ☐ Other

DIAGNOSIS INFORMATION

Diagnosis	Code	Diagnosis	Code
1. Shoulder pain	M25.519	5.	
2. Preventative influenza	Z23	6.	
3.		7.	
4.		8.	

PROCEDURE INFORMATION

Description of Procedure or Service	Date	Code	Charge
1. Level 3 office visit - est patient	05-19-YYYY	99213	$65.00
2. Influenza vaccine	05-19-YYYY	90658	$30.00
3. Administration of influenza vaccine	05-19-YYYY	G0008	$25.00
4.			
5.			
6.			

SPECIAL NOTES:
Pt comes in for his annual flu vaccine. While in the exam room, patient mentions a separate ailment - he has been experiencing recent shoulder pain.

Case Study 21-2 (ICD-10)

GARY GRAY, M.D.

0222 Route 70 • Brick, NJ 08723 • (732) 555-0000

Tax ID# 11-4311999

NPI# 9988001122

Case Study

PATIENT INFORMATION:

Name:	Linda Lowe
Social Security #:	909-09-9090
Address:	069 Peach Blvd
City:	Toms River
State:	NJ
Zip Code:	08755
Home Telephone:	(732) 888-5555
Date of Birth:	02-13-1943
Gender:	Female
Occupation:	Retired
Employer:	
Employer Telephone:	
Spouse:	
Spouse's Social Security #:	
Spouse's Employer:	
Spouse's Date of Birth:	

INSURANCE INFORMATION:

Patient Number:	Lowli000
Place of Service:	Nursing facility
Primary Insurance Plan:	Medicare
Primary Insurance Plan ID #:	909-09-9090A
Group #:	
Primary Policyholder:	Linda Lowe
Policyholder Date of Birth:	02-13-1943
Relationship to Patient:	Self
Secondary Insurance Plan:	
Secondary Insurance Plan ID #:	
Secondary Policyholder:	

Patient Status   ☐ Married   ☐ Divorced   ☒ Single   ☐ Student   ☐ Other

DIAGNOSIS INFORMATION

Diagnosis	Code	Diagnosis	Code
1. Dementia	294.20	5.	
2.		6.	
3.		7.	
4.		8.	

PROCEDURE INFORMATION

Description of Procedure or Service	Date	Code	Charge
1. Subsequent nursing facility care - level 2	05-18-YYYY	99308	$130.00
2. Nursing facility discharge (more than 30 mins)	05-19-YYYY	99316	$110.00
3.			
4.			
5.			
6.			

SPECIAL NOTES:

Ocean City Senior Care Home, 0223 Ocean Rd, Ocean City, NJ 00204,
Facility NPI# 0201020300.
Patient was admitted on 05-15-YYYY.

Case Study 22-1 (ICD-9)

GARY GRAY, M.D.
0222 Route 70 • Brick, NJ 08723 • (732) 555-0000
Tax ID# 11-4311999
NPI# 9988001122

Case Study

PATIENT INFORMATION:

Name:	Linda Lowe
Social Security #:	909-09-9090
Address:	069 Peach Blvd
City:	Toms River
State:	NJ
Zip Code:	08755
Home Telephone:	(732) 888-5555
Date of Birth:	02-13-1943
Gender:	Female
Occupation:	Retired
Employer:	
Employer Telephone:	
Spouse:	
Spouse's Social Security #:	
Spouse's Employer:	
Spouse's Date of Birth:	

INSURANCE INFORMATION:

Patient Number:	Lowli000
Place of Service:	Nursing facility
Primary Insurance Plan:	Medicare
Primary Insurance Plan ID #:	909-09-9090A
Group #:	
Primary Policyholder:	Linda Lowe
Policyholder Date of Birth:	02-13-1943
Relationship to Patient:	Self
Secondary Insurance Plan:	
Secondary Insurance Plan ID #:	
Secondary Policyholder:	

Patient Status   ☐ Married   ☐ Divorced   ☒ Single   ☐ Student   ☐ Other

DIAGNOSIS INFORMATION

Diagnosis	Code	Diagnosis	Code
1. Dementia	F03.90	5.	
2.		6.	
3.		7.	
4.		8.	

PROCEDURE INFORMATION

Description of Procedure or Service	Date	Code	Charge
1. Subsequent nursing facility care - level 2	05-18-YYYY	99308	$130.00
2. Nursing facility discharge (more than 30 mins)	05-19-YYYY	99316	$110.00
3.			
4.			
5.			
6.			

SPECIAL NOTES:

Ocean City Senior Care Home, 0223 Ocean Rd, Ocean City, NJ 00204,
Facility NPI# 0201020300.
Patient was admitted on 05-15-YYYY.

Case Study 22-2 (ICD-10)

SAL SILVER, M.D.

00039 Route 70 • Brick, NJ 08724 • (732) 469-0009
Tax ID# 11-4239900
NPI# 6003000700

Case Study

PATIENT INFORMATION:

Name:	Chelsea Chaney
Social Security #:	090-92-0092
Address:	0437 Kitty Court
City:	Howell
State:	NJ
Zip Code:	07701
Home Telephone:	(732) 501-0005
Date of Birth:	02-28-2001
Gender:	Female
Occupation:	
Employer:	
Employer Telephone:	
Spouse:	
Spouse's Social Security #:	
Spouse's Employer:	
Spouse's Date of Birth:	

INSURANCE INFORMATION:

Patient Number:	Chach000
Place of Service:	In-patient hospital
Primary Insurance Plan:	CIGNA
Primary Insurance Plan ID #:	CC392678501
Group #:	923923
Primary Policyholder:	Cherie Chaney
Policyholder Date of Birth:	03-18-1976
Relationship to Patient:	Parent
Secondary Insurance Plan:	
Secondary Insurance Plan ID #:	
Secondary Policyholder:	

Patient Status   ☐ Married   ☐ Divorced   ☒ Single   ☐ Student   ☐ Other

DIAGNOSIS INFORMATION

Diagnosis	Code	Diagnosis	Code
1. Hepatic failure w/o coma	570	5.	
2.		6.	
3.		7.	
4.		8.	

PROCEDURE INFORMATION

Description of Procedure or Service	Date	Code	Charge
1. Initial in-patient hospital care - level 3	02-01-YYYY	99223	$175.00
2. Critical care services (30 - 74 mins)	02-01-YYYY	99291	$250.00
3. Critical care services (ea add'l 30 mins)	02-01-YYYY	99292	$225.00
4. Critical care services (ea add'l 30 mins)	02-01-YYYY	99292	$225.00
5.			
6.			

SPECIAL NOTES:

Physician spent a total of two hours dedicated to the critical care service of patient on 02-01-YYYY. Hooper Medial Center, 011 Hospital Drive, Toms River, NJ 08755, Facility NPI# 9900000011.

Case Study 23-1 (ICD-9)

SAL SILVER, M.D.

00039 Route 70 • Brick, NJ 08724 • (732) 469-0009

Tax ID# 11-4239900

NPI# 6003000700

Case Study

PATIENT INFORMATION:		INSURANCE INFORMATION:	
Name:	Chelsea Chaney	Patient Number:	Chach000
Social Security #:	090-92-0092	Place of Service:	In-patient hospital
Address:	0437 Kitty Court	Primary Insurance Plan:	CIGNA
City:	Howell	Primary Insurance Plan ID #:	CC392678501
State:	NJ		
Zip Code:	07701	Group #:	923923
Home Telephone:	(732) 501-0005	Primary Policyholder:	Cherie Chaney
Date of Birth:	02-28-2001	Policyholder Date of Birth:	03-18-1976
Gender:	Female		
Occupation:		Relationship to Patient:	Parent
Employer:		Secondary Insurance Plan:	
Employer Telephone:			
Spouse:		Secondary Insurance Plan ID #:	
Spouse's Social Security #:		Secondary Policyholder:	
Spouse's Employer:			
Spouse's Date of Birth:			

Patient Status   ☐ Married   ☐ Divorced   ☒ Single   ☐ Student   ☐ Other

DIAGNOSIS INFORMATION

	Diagnosis	Code		Diagnosis	Code
1.	Hepatic failure w/o coma	K72.90	5.		
2.			6.		
3.			7.		
4.			8.		

PROCEDURE INFORMATION

	Description of Procedure or Service	Date	Code	Charge
1.	Initial in-patient hospital care - level 3	02-01-YYYY	99223	$175.00
2.	Critical care services (30 - 74 mins)	02-01-YYYY	99291	$250.00
3.	Critical care services (ea add'l 30 mins)	02-01-YYYY	99292	$225.00
4.	Critical care services (ea add'l 30 mins)	02-01-YYYY	99292	$225.00
5.				
6.				

SPECIAL NOTES:

Physician spent a total of two hours dedicated to the critical care service of patient on 02-01-YYYY. Hooper Medial Center, 011 Hospital Drive, Toms River, NJ 08755, Facility NPI# 9900000011.

Case Study 23-2 (ICD-10)

GRETA GREEN, M.D.
01102 Neptune Blvd • Neptune, NJ 07070 • (732) 009-0049
Tax ID# 11-3499988
NPI# 3004005000

Case Study

PATIENT INFORMATION:

Name:	Frank Fender
Social Security #:	011-00-2121
Address:	0937 Kathy Court
City:	Brick
State:	NJ
Zip Code:	08724
Home Telephone:	(732) 505-0000
Date of Birth:	02-22-1942
Gender:	Male
Occupation:	Retired
Employer:	
Employer Telephone:	
Spouse:	
Spouse's Social Security #:	
Spouse's Employer:	
Spouse's Date of Birth:	

INSURANCE INFORMATION:

Patient Number:	Fenfr000
Place of Service:	Office
Primary Insurance Plan:	Medicare
Primary Insurance Plan ID #:	011-00-2121A
Group #:	
Primary Policyholder:	Frank Fender
Policyholder Date of Birth:	02-22-1942
Relationship to Patient:	Self
Secondary Insurance Plan:	
Secondary Insurance Plan ID #:	
Secondary Policyholder:	

Patient Status ☐ Married ☐ Divorced ☒ Single ☐ Student ☐ Other

DIAGNOSIS INFORMATION

	Diagnosis	Code		Diagnosis	Code
1.	Pain, finger	729.5	5.		
2.			6.		
3.			7.		
4.			8.		

PROCEDURE INFORMATION

	Description of Procedure or Service	Date	Code	Charge
1.	Arthrocentesis, small joint	07-22-YYYY	20600	$105.00
2.	Depo-medrol - up to 40 mg	07-22-YYYY	J1030	$40.00
3.				
4.				
5.				
6.				

SPECIAL NOTES:
Site of procedure is right hand, third digit.

Case Study 24-1 (ICD-9)

GRETA GREEN, M.D.
01102 Neptune Blvd • Neptune, NJ 07070 • (732) 009-0049
Tax ID# 11-3499988
NPI# 3004005000

Case Study

PATIENT INFORMATION:

Name:	Frank Fender
Social Security #:	011-00-2121
Address:	0937 Kathy Court
City:	Brick
State:	NJ
Zip Code:	08724
Home Telephone:	(732) 505-0000
Date of Birth:	02-22-1942
Gender:	Male
Occupation:	Retired
Employer:	
Employer Telephone:	
Spouse:	
Spouse's Social Security #:	
Spouse's Employer:	
Spouse's Date of Birth:	

INSURANCE INFORMATION:

Patient Number:	Fenfr000
Place of Service:	Office
Primary Insurance Plan:	Medicare
Primary Insurance Plan ID #:	011-00-2121A
Group #:	
Primary Policyholder:	Frank Fender
Policyholder Date of Birth:	02-22-1942
Relationship to Patient:	Self
Secondary Insurance Plan:	
Secondary Insurance Plan ID #:	
Secondary Policyholder:	

Patient Status   ☐ Married   ☐ Divorced   ☒ Single   ☐ Student   ☐ Other

DIAGNOSIS INFORMATION

	Diagnosis	Code		Diagnosis	Code
1.	Pain, finger	M79.644	5.		
2.			6.		
3.			7.		
4.			8.		

PROCEDURE INFORMATION

	Description of Procedure or Service	Date	Code	Charge
1.	Arthrocentesis, small joint	07-22-YYYY	20600	$105.00
2.	Depo-medrol - up to 40 mg	07-22-YYYY	J1030	$40.00
3.				
4.				
5.				
6.				

SPECIAL NOTES:
Site of procedure is right hand, third digit.

Case Study 24-2 (ICD-10)

GRETA GREEN, M.D.

01102 Neptune Blvd • Neptune, NJ 07070 • (732) 009-0049
Tax ID# 11-3499988
NPI# 3004005000

Case Study

PATIENT INFORMATION:

Name:	Helen Hurley
Social Security #:	002-00-0220
Address:	00973 Lakewood Road
City:	Neptune
State:	NJ
Zip Code:	07070
Home Telephone:	(732) 001-0222
Date of Birth:	04-01-1943
Gender:	Female
Occupation:	Retired
Employer:	
Employer Telephone:	
Spouse:	
Spouse's Social Security #:	
Spouse's Employer:	
Spouse's Date of Birth:	

INSURANCE INFORMATION:

Patient Number:	Hurhe000
Place of Service:	Office
Primary Insurance Plan:	Medicare
Primary Insurance Plan ID #:	002-00-0220A
Group #:	
Primary Policyholder:	Helen Hurley
Policyholder Date of Birth:	04-01-1943
Relationship to Patient:	Self
Secondary Insurance Plan:	
Secondary Insurance Plan ID #:	
Secondary Policyholder:	

Patient Status ☐ Married ☐ Divorced ☒ Single ☐ Student ☐ Other

DIAGNOSIS INFORMATION

Diagnosis	Code	Diagnosis	Code
1. Cyst, skin	706.2	5.	
2.		6.	
3.		7.	
4.		8.	

PROCEDURE INFORMATION

Description of Procedure or Service	Date	Code	Charge
1. Incision and drainage of cyst	04-27-YYYY	10060	$110.00
2.			
3.			
4.			
5.			
6.			

SPECIAL NOTES:
Site of procedure is left hand, thumb.

Case Study 25-1 (ICD-9)

GRETA GREEN, M.D.
01102 Neptune Blvd • Neptune, NJ 07070 • (732) 009-0049
Tax ID# 11-3499988
NPI# 3004005000

Case Study

PATIENT INFORMATION:		INSURANCE INFORMATION:	
Name:	Helen Hurley	Patient Number:	Hurhe000
Social Security #:	002-00-0220	Place of Service:	Office
Address:	00973 Lakewood Road	Primary Insurance Plan:	Medicare
City:	Neptune	Primary Insurance Plan ID #:	002-00-0220A
State:	NJ		
Zip Code:	07070	Group #:	
Home Telephone:	(732) 001-0222		
Date of Birth:	04-01-1943	Primary Policyholder:	Helen Hurley
Gender:	Female	Policyholder Date of Birth:	04-01-1943
Occupation:	Retired	Relationship to Patient:	Self
Employer:			
Employer Telephone:		Secondary Insurance Plan:	
Spouse:		Secondary Insurance Plan ID #:	
Spouse's Social Security #:			
Spouse's Employer:		Secondary Policyholder:	
Spouse's Date of Birth:			

Patient Status ☐ Married ☐ Divorced ☒ Single ☐ Student ☐ Other

DIAGNOSIS INFORMATION

Diagnosis	Code	Diagnosis	Code
1. Cyst, skin	L72.9	5.	
2.		6.	
3.		7.	
4.		8.	

PROCEDURE INFORMATION

Description of Procedure or Service	Date	Code	Charge
1. Incision and drainage of cyst	04-27-YYYY	10060	$110.00
2.			
3.			
4.			
5.			
6.			

SPECIAL NOTES:
Site of procedure is left hand, thumb.

Case Study 25-2 (ICD-10)

Appendix II
Forms

BLANK CMS-1500 FORM

Figure App II-1 is provided to make copies for completing the case studies in Appendix I.

E&M CODEBUILDER

Figure App II-2 contains guidelines used by the provider in determining the level of evaluation and management service to be coded for provider reimbursement.

EVALUATION AND MANAGEMENT CODES

Figure App II-3 lists commonly used codes found on the superbill/encounter form in the physician's office. Refer to this list for selecting the codes needed to complete the case-study exercises in Appendix I.

ADVANCE BENEFICIARY NOTICE (ABN) FORM

Figure App II-4 is the form used when a service or procedure is expected to be denied by Medicare. The patient has an option of checking "yes" or "no" as to receiving the service or procedure. If the patient checks "yes" and signs the form, the patient is agreeing to pay the physician for the service or procedure if it is denied.

NOTICE OF EXCLUSIONS FROM MEDICARE BENEFITS (NEMB) FORM

Figure App II-5 is the form used when a service or procedure is *not* a benefit covered by Medicare. By signing this form, the patient is agreeing to pay the physician for the service or procedure.

CMS OVERPAYMENT/REFUND FORM

Figure App II-6 is the form completed by the physician's office when Medicare has erroneously sent an overpayment to the physician. The form is sent along with a refund check to Medicare for the overpayment.

REQUEST FOR OPINION/CONSULT

Figure App II-7 is a sample of a form that may be used when an attending physician is requesting an opinion or consult from another physician regarding a patient.

REFUSAL TO AUTHORIZE PAYMENT

Figure App II-8 is a sample form letter from an insurance company to a physician stating a refusal to authorize payment on a procedure or service.

INFORMED REFUSAL

Figure App II-9 is a sample form letter written to the patient informing the patient that the insurance company has refused to authorize payment on a procedure or service.

CODE OF CONDUCT

Figure App II-10 contains sample guidelines, rules, and restrictions that may be used for employees in the medical office. They detail the conduct and ethics expected from employees in regard to Medicare and Medicaid and patient privacy.

THE UB-04 FORM

The UB-04 form (Figure App II-11) is used when billing for a facility. Examples might include:

- Hospital
- Nursing home
- Ambulatory surgical center

Guidelines and codes for billing on a UB-04 form are different from those used on a CMS-1500 form. To learn more about the UB-04, visit www.nubc.org.

HEALTH INSURANCE CLAIM FORM

APPROVED BY NATIONAL UNIFORM CLAIM COMMITTEE (NUCC) 02/12

PICA						PICA

1. MEDICARE   MEDICAID   TRICARE   CHAMPVA   GROUP HEALTH PLAN   FECA BLK LUNG   OTHER

(Medicare#)   (Medicaid#)   (ID#/DoD#)   (Member ID#)   (ID#)   (ID#)   (ID#)

1a. INSURED'S I.D. NUMBER   (For Program in Item 1)

2. PATIENT'S NAME (Last Name, First Name, Middle Initial)

3. PATIENT'S BIRTH DATE   MM DD YY   **SEX**   M   F

4. INSURED'S NAME (Last Name, First Name, Middle Initial)

5. PATIENT'S ADDRESS (No., Street)

6. PATIENT RELATIONSHIP TO INSURED   Self   Spouse   Child   Other

7. INSURED'S ADDRESS (No., Street)

CITY   STATE

8. RESERVED FOR NUCC USE

CITY   STATE

ZIP CODE   TELEPHONE (Include Area Code)   (   )

ZIP CODE   TELEPHONE (Include Area Code)   (   )

9. OTHER INSURED'S NAME (Last Name, First Name, Middle Initial)

10. IS PATIENT'S CONDITION RELATED TO:

11. INSURED'S POLICY GROUP OR FECA NUMBER

a. OTHER INSURED'S POLICY OR GROUP NUMBER

a. EMPLOYMENT? (Current or Previous)   YES   NO

a. INSURED'S DATE OF BIRTH   MM DD YY   **SEX**   M   F

b. RESERVED FOR NUCC USE

b. AUTO ACCIDENT?   PLACE (State)   YES   NO

b. OTHER CLAIM ID (Designated by NUCC)

c. RESERVED FOR NUCC USE

c. OTHER ACCIDENT?   YES   NO

c. INSURANCE PLAN NAME OR PROGRAM NAME

d. INSURANCE PLAN NAME OR PROGRAM NAME

10d. CLAIM CODES (Designated by NUCC)

d. IS THERE ANOTHER HEALTH BENEFIT PLAN?   YES   NO   *If yes*, complete items 9, 9a, and 9d.

READ BACK OF FORM BEFORE COMPLETING & SIGNING THIS FORM.

12. PATIENT'S OR AUTHORIZED PERSON'S SIGNATURE I authorize the release of any medical or other information necessary to process this claim. I also request payment of government benefits either to myself or to the party who accepts assignment below.

SIGNED _____   DATE _____

13. INSURED'S OR AUTHORIZED PERSON'S SIGNATURE I authorize payment of medical benefits to the undersigned physician or supplier for services described below.

SIGNED _____

14. DATE OF CURRENT ILLNESS, INJURY, or PREGNANCY (LMP)   MM DD YY   QUAL.

15. OTHER DATE   QUAL.   MM DD YY

16. DATES PATIENT UNABLE TO WORK IN CURRENT OCCUPATION   FROM MM DD YY   TO MM DD YY

17. NAME OF REFERRING PROVIDER OR OTHER SOURCE   17a.   17b. NPI

18. HOSPITALIZATION DATES RELATED TO CURRENT SERVICES   FROM MM DD YY   TO MM DD YY

19. ADDITIONAL CLAIM INFORMATION (Designated by NUCC)

20. OUTSIDE LAB?   YES   NO $ CHARGES

21. DIAGNOSIS OR NATURE OF ILLNESS OR INJURY Relate A-L to service line below (24E)   ICD Ind.

A. _____   B. _____   C. _____   D. _____
E. _____   F. _____   G. _____   H. _____
I. _____   J. _____   K. _____   L. _____

22. RESUBMISSION CODE   ORIGINAL REF. NO.

23. PRIOR AUTHORIZATION NUMBER

24. A. DATE(S) OF SERVICE						B. PLACE OF SERVICE	C. EMG	D. PROCEDURES, SERVICES, OR SUPPLIES (Explain Unusual Circumstances) CPT/HCPCS MODIFIER	E. DIAGNOSIS POINTER	F. $ CHARGES	G. DAYS OR UNITS	H. EPSDT Family Plan	I. ID. QUAL.	J. RENDERING PROVIDER ID. #
From MM	DD	YY	To MM	DD	YY									
1													NPI	
2													NPI	
3													NPI	
4													NPI	
5													NPI	
6													NPI	

25. FEDERAL TAX I.D. NUMBER   SSN EIN

26. PATIENT'S ACCOUNT NO.

27. ACCEPT ASSIGNMENT? (For govt. claims, see back)   YES   NO

28. TOTAL CHARGE $

29. AMOUNT PAID $

30. Rsvd for NUCC Use

31. SIGNATURE OF PHYSICIAN OR SUPPLIER INCLUDING DEGREES OR CREDENTIALS (I certify that the statements on the reverse apply to this bill and are made a part thereof.)

SIGNED _____   DATE _____

32. SERVICE FACILITY LOCATION INFORMATION

a. NPI   b.

33. BILLING PROVIDER INFO & PH #   (   )

a. NPI   b.

NUCC Instruction Manual available at: www.nucc.org   *PLEASE PRINT OR TYPE*

FIGURE APP II-1 Blank CMS-1500 form.

E&M CodeBuilder

SELECTING THE LEVEL OF HISTORY

HISTORY OF PRESENT ILLNESS (HPI) (place a check mark next to each documented HPI element)

_____ **Location** (of pain/discomfort; is pain diffuse/localized, unilateral/bilateral, does it radiate or refer)

_____ **Quality** (a description of the quality of the symptom [e.g., pain described as sharp/dull/throbbing/stabbing/ constant/intermittent/acute or chronic/stable/improving or worsening])

_____ **Severity** (use of self-assessment scale to measure subjective levels, 1–10, or comparison of pain quantitatively with previously experienced pain)

_____ **Timing** (establishing onset of pain and a rough chronology of pain development [e.g., migraine occurring mornings])

_____ **Context** (where is the patient and what is he doing when pain begins; is patient at rest or involved in an activity; is pain aggravated or relieved, or does it recur with a specific activity; has situational stress or some other factor been present preceding or accompanying the pain)

_____ **Modifying factors** (what has patient attempted to do to relieve pain [e.g., heat vs. cold—does it relieve or exacerbate pain; what makes the pain worse; have over-the-counter drugs been attempted—with what results])

_____ **Associated signs/symptoms** (clinician's impressions formulated during the interview may lead to questioning about additional sensations or feelings [e.g., diaphoresis associated with indigestion or chest pain, blurred vision accompanying a headache, etc.])

_____ **Total Score** (add the check marks and record the total; then place a check mark next to the history type below)

_____ BRIEF HISTORY (1–3 elements)   _____ EXTENDED HISTORY (4 or more elements)

REVIEW OF SYSTEMS (ROS) (place a check mark next to each documented ROS elements)

_____ Constitutional symptoms (e.g., fever, weight loss, etc.)   _____ Genitourinary

_____ Eyes   _____ Musculoskeletal

_____ Ears, nose, mouth, throat   _____ Allergic/Immunologic

_____ Cardiovascular   _____ Hematologic/Lymphatic

_____ Respiratory   _____ Neurological

_____ Gastrointestinal   _____ Psychiatric

_____ Integumentary (including skin and breast)   _____ Endocrine

_____ **Total Score** (add the check marks and record the total; then place a check mark next to the ROS type below)

_____ NONE

_____ PROBLEM-PERTINENT (1 body system documented)

_____ EXTENDED (2–9 body systems documented)

_____ COMPLETE (all body systems documented)

PAST, FAMILY, AND/OR SOCIAL HISTORY (PFSH) (place a check mark next to each documented PFSH element)

_____ Past history (patient's past experience with illnesses, operations, injuries, and treatments)

_____ Family history (review of medical events in the patient's family, including diseases that may be hereditary or place the patient at risk)

_____ Social history (an age-appropriate review of past and current activities)

_____ **Total Score** (add the check marks and record the total; then place a check mark next to the PFSH type below)

_____ NONE

_____ PERTINENT (1 history area documented)

_____ COMPLETE (2 or all 3 history areas documented)

FIGURE APP II-2   E&M CodeBuilder.   *(Continues)*

Circle the type of HPI, ROS, and PFSH and then select the appropriate level of history				
History of Present Illness	Brief	Brief	Extended	Extended
Review of Systems	None	Problem-pertinent	Extended	Complete
Past, Family, Social History	None	None	Pertinent	Complete
Select Level of History	**Problem-focused**	**Expanded problem-focused**	**Detailed**	**Comprehensive**

SELECTING THE LEVEL OF EXAMINATION

GENERAL MULTISYSTEM EXAM (refer to the general multisystem examination requirements in the HCFA *Guidelines for Evaluation and Management Services.* Place a tally mark for each bulleted item documented for each organ system/body area for up to the total number of allowed items [e.g., up to 2 marks can be made for the Neck exam])

_____ Constitutional (2)
_____ Eyes (3)
_____ Ears, nose, mouth, and throat (6)
_____ Neck (2)
_____ Respiratory (4)
_____ Cardiovascular (7)
_____ Chest (Breasts) (2)

_____ Gastrointestinal (5)
_____ Genitourinary (Male: 3; Female: 6)
_____ Lymphatic (4)
_____ Musculoskeletal (6)
_____ Skin (2)
_____ Neurological (3)
_____ Psychiatric (4)

_____ **Total Score** (add the tally marks and record the total; then place a check mark next to the exam type below)

_____ PROBLEM-FOCUSED EXAMINATION (1–5 elements identified by a bullet)
_____ EXPANDED PROBLEM-FOCUSED EXAMINATION (at least 6 elements identified by a bullet)
_____ DETAILED EXAMINATION (at least 2 elements identified by a bullet from each of 6 organ systems/body areas, *or* at least 12 elements identified by a bullet in two or more areas/systems)
_____ COMPREHENSIVE EXAMINATION (perform all the elements identified by a bullet in at least 9 organ systems or body areas and document at least 2 elements identified by a bullet from each of 9 organ systems/body areas)

SINGLE ORGAN SYSTEM EXAMINATION (refer to the single organ system examination documentation requirements in the HCFA *Guidelines for Evaluation and Management Services;* place a check next to the appropriate exam type below)

_____ PROBLEM-FOCUSED EXAMINATION (1–5 elements identified by a bullet)
_____ EXPANDED PROBLEM-FOCUSED EXAMINATION (at least 6 elements identified by a bullet)
_____ DETAILED EXAMINATION (at least 12 elements identified by a bullet; NOTE: for eye and psychiatric examinations, at least 9 elements in each box with a shaded border and at least 1 element in each box with a shaded or unshaded border is documented)
_____ COMPREHENSIVE EXAMINATION (all the elements identified by a bullet; document every element in each box with a shaded border and at least 1 element in each box with an unshaded box)

Select the appropriate level of medical decision making based upon the following criteria:			
Number of diagnoses or management options	*Amount/complexity of data to be reviewed*	*Risk of complications and/ or morbidity/mortality*	*Medical decision making*
Minimal	Minimal or none	Minimal	Straightforward
Limited	Limited	Low	Low complexity
Multiple	Moderate	Moderate	Moderate complexity
Extensive	Extensive	High	High complexity

Select the E/M code based on selection of level of history, examination, and medical decision making:					
History	Problem-focused	Expanded problem-focused	Expanded problem-focused	Detailed	Comprehensive
Examination	Problem-focused	Expanded problem-focused	Expanded problem-focused	Detailed	Comprehensive
Medical decision making	Straightforward	Low complexity	Moderate complexity	Moderate complexity	High complexity
Go to the appropriate E&M category and select the code based upon the information above					

FIGURE APP II-2 (*Continued*).

Office Visit Codes

New Patient

99201
99202
99203
99204
99205

Established Patient

99211
99212
99213
99214
99215

Office Consultation

New and Established Patients

99241
99242
99243
99244
99245

Inpatient Hospital Codes

Attending/Admitting Physician

Initial Visit	*Subsequent/Follow-up Visit*
99221	99231
99222	99232
99223	99233

Consulting Physician

Initial Visit	*Subsequent/Follow-up Visit*
99251	99231
99252	99232
99253	99233
99254	
99255	

Hospital Discharge

99238 30 minutes or under
99239 more than 30 minutes

ICU/Critical Care

99291 30 to 74 minutes
99292 each additional 30 minutes

Nursing Facility Services Codes

New and Established Patients

Initial Visit	*Subsequent/Follow-up*	*Discharge*
99304	99307	99315 (30 minutes or less)
99305	99308	99316 (more than 30 minutes)
99306	99309	
	99310	

FIGURE APP II-3 Evaluation and management codes.

A. Notifier:

B. Patient Name: **C. Identification Number:**

Advance Beneficiary Notice of Noncoverage (ABN)

<u>NOTE:</u> If Medicare doesn't pay for **D.** —————— below, you may have to pay.
Medicare does not pay for everything, even some care that you or your health care provider have good reason to think you need. We expect Medicare may not pay for the **D.** —————— below.

D.	E. Reason Medicare May Not Pay:	F. Estimated Cost

WHAT YOU NEED TO DO NOW:
- Read this notice, so you can make an informed decision about your care.
- Ask us any questions that you may have after you finish reading.
- Choose an option below about whether to receive the **D.** —————— listed above.
  Note: If you choose Option 1 or 2, we may help you to use any other insurance that you might have, but Medicare cannot require us to do this.

G. OPTIONS: Check only one box. We cannot choose a box for you.

☐ **OPTION 1.** I want the **D.** —————— listed above. You may ask to be paid now, but I also want Medicare billed for an official decision on payment, which is sent to me on a Medicare Summary Notice (MSN). I understand that if Medicare doesn't pay, I am responsible for payment, but **I can appeal to Medicare** by following the directions on the MSN. If Medicare does pay, you will refund any payments I made to you, less co-pays or deductibles.

☐ **OPTION 2.** I want the **D.** —————— listed above, but do not bill Medicare. You may ask to be paid now as I am responsible for payment. **I cannot appeal if Medicare is not billed**.

☐ **OPTION 3.** I don't want the **D.** —————— listed above. I understand with this choice I am **not** responsible for payment, and **I cannot appeal to see if Medicare would pay.**

H. Additional Information:

This notice gives our opinion, not an official Medicare decision. If you have other questions on this notice or Medicare billing, call **1-800-MEDICARE** (1-800-633-4227/**TTY:** 1-877-486-2048).
Signing below means that you have received and understand this notice. You also receive a copy.

I. Signature:	J. Date:

According to the Paperwork Reduction Act of 1995, no persons are required to respond to a collection of information unless it displays a valid OMB control number. The valid OMB control number for this information collection is 0938-0566. The time required to complete this information collection is estimated to average 7 minutes per response, including the time to review instructions, search existing data resources, gather the data needed, and complete and review the information collection. If you have comments concerning the accuracy of the time estimate or suggestions for improving this form, please write to: CMS, 7500 Security Boulevard, Attn: PRA Reports Clearance Officer, Baltimore, Maryland 21244-1850.

Form CMS-R-131 (03/11)   Form Approved OMB No. 0938-0566

From www.cms.gov

FIGURE APP II-4 Advance Beneficiary Notice (ABN) form.

NOTICE OF EXCLUSIONS FROM MEDICARE BENEFITS (NEMB)

There are items and services for which Medicare <u>will not pay.</u>

- Medicare does **not** pay for all of your health care costs. Medicare only pays for covered benefits. **Some items and services are not Medicare benefits and Medicare will not pay for them.**

- When you receive an item or service that is **not** a Medicare benefit, **you are responsible to pay for it,** personally or through any other insurance that you may have.

  The purpose of this notice is to help you make an informed choice about whether or not you want to receive these items or services, knowing that you will have to pay for them yourself. **Before you make a decision, you should read this entire notice carefully.**

  Ask us to explain, if you don't understand why Medicare won't pay.

  Ask us how much these items or services will cost you (**Estimated Cost: $**_____).

Medicare will not pay for: _____
_____ ;

☐ **1. Because it does not meet the definition of any Medicare benefit.**

☐ **2. Because of the following exclusion * from Medicare benefits:**

☐ Personal comfort items.	☐ Routine physicals and most tests for screening.
☐ Most shots (vaccinations).	☐ Routine eye care, eyeglasses and examinations.
☐ Hearing aids and hearing examinations.	☐ Cosmetic surgery.
☐ Most outpatient prescription drugs.	☐ Dental care and dentures (in most cases).
☐ Orthopedic shoes and foot supports (orthotics).	☐ Routine foot care and flat foot care.
☐ Health care received outside of the USA.	☐ Services by immediate relatives.
☐ Services required as a result of war.	☐ Services under a physician's private contract.

☐ Services paid for by a governmental entity that is not Medicare.

☐ Services for which the patient has no legal obligation to pay.

☐ Home health services furnished under a plan of care, if the agency does not submit the claim.

☐ Items and services excluded under the Assisted Suicide Funding Restriction Act of 1997.

☐ Items or services furnished in a competitive acquisition area by any entity that does not have a contract with the Department of Health and Human Services (except in a case of urgent need).

☐ Physicians' services performed by a physician assistant, midwife, psychologist, or nurse anesthetist, when furnished to an inpatient, unless they are furnished under arrangements by the hospital.

☐ Items and services furnished to an individual who is a resident of a skilled nursing facility (a SNF) or of a part of a facility that includes a SNF, unless they are furnished under arrangements by the SNF.

☐ Services of an assistant at surgery without prior approval from the peer review organization.

☐ Outpatient occupational and physical therapy services furnished incident to a physician's services.

* **This is only a general summary of exclusions from Medicare benefits. It is not a legal document. The official Medicare program provisions are contained in relevant laws, regulations, and rulings.**

From www.cms.gov

FIGURE APP II-5   Notice of Exclusions from Medicare Benefits (NEMB) form.

Medicare Part B Overpayment Refund Form

CMS
CENTERS for MEDICARE & MEDICAID SERVICES

This form, or a similar document, containing the following information should accompany every voluntary refund to properly record and apply a refund. Please complete and forward to the Medicare address listed below. Please submit separate forms for MSP and Non-MSP requests.

Name: _____

Address: _____

City: _____ State: __ Zip Code: _____

Provider Number: _____

NPI Number: _____

Contact Number: _____

For OIG Reporting Requirement:
Do you have a Corporate Integrity Agreement with OIG? ○ Yes ○ No

Patient's Name: _____

Medicare Number (HIC) (Include Suffix): _____

Claim Number(s): _____

Service Date(s): _____

Procedure Code: _____

Overpaid Amount: _____

Provider /Office Personnel Signature: (Print and Sign)
_____

Medicare Secondary Payer Reason for Overpayment

Must be completed for MSP Overpayments. Please check the appropriate number. For multiple overpayments, please attach detailed information. Please include a copy of the primary insurance remittance for the service(s) in question.

Medicare Secondary Payer (MSP)

☐ 01 Group Health Plan Insurance
☐ 02 No Fault Insurance
☐ 03 Liability Insurance
☐ 04 Workers Compensation
☐ 05 Black Lung
☐ 06 Veterans Administration
☐ 07 ESRD
☐ 08 Other Insurance Involvement (Please Identify)

Secondary Insurance:

If a box was checked in this section of the form, then an Insurance Name must be provided in the field below.

Insurance Name: _____
Insurance Address: _____
Insured's Name: _____
Employee's ID Number: _____
Primary Payer's Allowance: _____
Primary Payer's Payment: _____

Non-MSP Reason For Overpayment/Refund

Must be completed for non-MSP Overpayments. Please check the appropriate number. For multiple overpayments, please attach detailed information.

☐ 01 Incorrect Service Date (Specify Correct Date)
☐ 02 Duplicate Payment (Specify Correct Info)
☐ 03 Incorrect CPT Code (Specify Correct Code)
☐ 04 Not Our Patient(s)
☐ 05 Modifier Added/Removed (Specify Correction)

☐ 06 Billed in Error
☐ 07 Service Not Rendered
☐ 08 Medical Necessity Not Met
☐ 09 Patient Enrolled in HMO (Specify HMO)
☐ 10 Other (Please Identify)

Payment Options:

Please enclose a check addressed to Palmetto GBA or Medicare. Any checks addressed differently cannot be accepted for deposit.

The acceptance of a voluntary refund in no way affects or limits the rights of the Federal Government or any of its agencies or agents to pursue any appropriate criminal, civil, or administrative remedies arising from or relating to these or any other claims.   Rev. 09-2010

Medicare Part B Ohio/West Virginia
Palmetto GBA/Medicare
Medicare Part B - Finance & Accounting
P.O. Box 182934
Columbus, OH 43218-2934

Medicare Part B South Carolina
Palmetto GBA/Medicare
Medicare Part B - Finance & Accounting
P.O. Box 100280
Columbia, SC 29202-3280

From www.cms.gov

FIGURE APP II-6 CMS Overpayment/Refund form.

PRACTICE NAME
Practice Street Address
Suite X
Practice City, State Zip
Practice Phone Number

REQUEST FOR OPINION

Consultation request from: Doctor "A"
Doctor "B"
Doctor "C"

To: Consultant's Name: _____
     Specialty: _____

Re: Patient Name: _____
     Date: _____

Please provide an opinion and consult for the above-named patient. This patient is being sent to you for the following reasons:

_____

_____

_____

_____

_____

_____

_____

We understand that you may initiate treatment or perform medically necessary diagnostics for this patient. We look forward to your opinion and plan of care:

_____
Practice Name
"A", MD
"B", DO
"C", MD

FIGURE APP II-7   Request for opinion/consult.

Sample Letter
Refusal to Authorize Payment

Chairperson
Utilization Review Committee

Dear _____ ,

On ____(DATE)____ , I prescribed _____(TEST/PROCEDURE)_____ for _____(PATIENT'S NAME)_____ .

On ____(DATE)____ , you refused to authorize payment for that _____(TEST/PROCEDURE)_____ . I find that
I must take issue with your determination for the following reasons:

(List reasons and if applicable, include any prior examples where a payer
approved this recommendation and/or examples of how this
test/procedure was effective before.)

In my medical judgment, a _____(TEST/PROCEDURE)_____ is a very important part of my overall

care of __(PATIENT'S NAME)__ . __(PATIENT'S NAME)__ suffers from __(DESCRIBE CONDITION)__ .

The _____(TEST/PROCEDURE)_____ is necessary to ____(DESCRIBE WHY NECESSARY)____ .

Failure to perform the _____(TEST/PROCEDURE)_____ could result in the following problems:

(DESCRIBE PROBLEMS)

For these reasons, I urge you to reconsider your refusal to authorize payment for the procedure I have
prescribed.

By copy of this letter to _____(PATIENT'S NAME)_____ , I am reiterating my suggestion that

he/she obtain the ____(TEST/PROCEDURE)____ , despite your refusal to authorize payment, for the

reasons I have set forth in this letter and in prior discussions with _____(PATIENT'S NAME)_____ .

Yours truly,

(YOUR NAME)

cc: (PATIENT'S NAME)

FIGURE APP II-8   Refusal to authorize payment (sample letter).

Sample Letter
Informed Refusal

Patient Name
Patient Address

Dear _____ ,

On _____(DATE)_____ , I prescribed _____(TEST/PROCEDURE)_____ . On _____(DATE)_____ ,

_____(NAME OF PPO, IPA, HMO)_____ refused to authorize payment for same. On that basis, you

have informed me of your decision to forgo the _____(TEST/PROCEDURE)_____ I have prescribed.

I expressed my concerns regarding your decision during our discussion on _____(DATE)_____ about

the potential ramifications of your refusal to undergo the _____(TEST/PROCEDURE)_____ .

I recommend you appeal the _____(NAME OF PPO, IPA, HMO)_____ denial of benefits and

reconsider your decision to forgo the _____(TEST/PROCEDURE)_____ in light of the potential
consequences of your refusal. My staff can assist you with the appeal.

Please call _____(NAME OF STAFF PERSON)_____ if you would like our assistance.

Should you wish to discuss this further, please do not hesitate to contact me.

Sincerely yours,

(YOUR NAME)

FIGURE APP II-9   Informed refusal (sample letter).

[Practice Name]
CODE OF CONDUCT

I. INTRODUCTION

The medical practice of *[practice name]* will hereinafter be referred to as *[practice name]*.

This Code of Conduct sets forth *[practice name]*'s *Principles* and *Standards* for all *[practice name]* employees as those Principles and Standards specifically relate to *[practice name]*'s compliance efforts pursuant to federal laws, rules, and standards of the Medicare/Medicaid programs. The Principles articulate the policies of *[practice name]* and the Standards are intended to provide additional guidance to persons functioning in managerial or administrative capacities. The Principles set forth in this Code of Conduct shall be distributed to all physicians and employees. The Code of Conduct will be updated as necessary; *[practice name]* will distribute any change or update by sending each employee an individual copy. All employees are responsible to ensure that their behavior and activities are consistent with this Code of Conduct.

II. PURPOSE

This Code of Conduct has been adopted by the *[practice name]*, Inc. Board of Directors to provide standards by which employees of *[practice name]* will conduct themselves in order to protect and promote corporation-wide integrity and to enhance *[practice name]*'s ability to achieve *[practice name]*'s mission.

III. LEGAL COMPLIANCE

A. Principle

[Practice name] will strive to ensure that all activity by or on behalf of the professional corporation is in compliance with applicable federal and state laws and regulations, as they specifically relate to the prohibitions against the filing of false or fraudulent claims with Medicare, Medicaid, or other federally funded health care programs. All employees of *[practice name]* are expected to support the professional corporation in its commitment.

B. Standards

The following standards are intended to provide guidance to management and employees in administrative positions to assist them in their obligation to comply with applicable laws. These standards are neither exclusive nor complete. Employees are required to comply with all applicable laws, whether or not specifically addressed in this Code of Conduct. If questions regarding the existence, interpretation, or application of any law arise, they should be directed to *[practice name]*'s Compliance Officer or *[practice name]*'s respective Accounts Manager, who shall refer all legal issues to *[practice name]*'s outside legal counsel.

1. **Antitrust.** All employees must comply with applicable antitrust and similar laws that regulate competition. Examples of conduct prohibited by the laws include: (1) agreements to fix prices, bid rigging, and collusion (including price sharing) with competitors; (2) boycotts, certain exclusive dealing and price discrimination agreements; and (3) unfair trade practices, including bribery, misappropriation of trade secrets, deception, intimidation, and similar unfair practices. *[Practice name]* employees in managerial or administrative positions are expected to seek advice from *[practice name]*'s Compliance Officer, who shall refer the issue to *[practice name]*'s outside legal counsel when confronted with business decisions involving a risk of violation of the antitrust laws.

FIGURE APP II-10   Code of Conduct.   *(Continues)*

2. **Fraud and Abuse.** *[Practice name]* expects its employees to refrain from conduct that may violate the fraud and abuse laws. These laws prohibit (1) direct, indirect, or disguised payments in exchange for the referral of patients; (2) the submission of false, fraudulent, or misleading claims to any government entity, including claims for services not rendered, claims that characterize the service as different from the service actually rendered, or claims that do not otherwise comply with applicable program or contractual requirements; and (3) making false representations to any person or entity in order to gain or retain participation in a program or to obtain payment for any service. (For additional guidance, please refer to the *[practice name]* Fraud and Abuse Compliance Policy and the *[practice name]* Corporate Compliance Plan.)

3. **Discrimination.** *[Practice name]* believes that the fair and equitable treatment of employees, patients, and other persons is critical to fulfilling its vision and goals. It is a policy of *[practice name]* to treat patients without regard to the race, color, religion, sex, ethnic origin, age, or disability of such person, or any other classification prohibited by law. It is a policy of *[practice name]* to recruit, hire, train, promote, assign, transfer, lay off, recall, and terminate employees based on their own ability, achievement, experience, and conduct, without regard to race, color, religion, sex, ethnic origin, age, or disability, or any other classification prohibited by law. No form of harassment or discrimination on the basis of sex, race, color, disability, age, religion, ethnic origin, or disability, or any other classification prohibited by law will be permitted. Each allegation of harassment or discrimination will be promptly investigated.

4. **Stark.** All employees must comply with applicable Stark regulations and similar laws that regulate self-referral and compensation. Examples of provisions included in these laws are: (1) agreements for "kickbacks" between doctors and providers; (2) supervision by referring physicians of those providing designated health services to qualify for the in-office ancillary service exception; (3) managed care exemptions; (4) exception when no alternative provider is available; (5) reporting of provider financial relationships and those of their immediate families; and (6) a list of designated health services that are covered by the self-referral ban. *[Practice name]* employees in managerial or administrative positions are expected to seek advice from *[practice name]*'s Compliance Officer, who shall refer the issue to *[practice name]*'s outside legal counsel when confronted with business decisions involving a risk of violation of the self-referral and compensation laws.

5. **OSHA.** All employees must comply with *[practice name]*'s OSHA Policy Manual.

6. **ADA.** *[Practice name]* and *[practice name]*'s employees will comply with the Americans with Disabilities Act (ADA). The ADA prohibits discrimination on the basis of disability in employment. It also prohibits discrimination on the basis of disability for goods and services provided to *[practice name]* patients. Each allegation of discrimination will be promptly investigated.

IV. BUSINESS ETHICS

A. Principle

In furtherance of *[practice name]*'s commitment to the highest standards of business ethics and integrity, employees shall strive to accurately and honestly represent *[practice name]* and shall strive not to engage in any activity or scheme intended to defraud anyone of money, property, or honest services. Furthermore, any *[practice name]* employee who becomes aware of any potential violation of the federal fraud and abuse laws shall have the primary obligation to report such potential wrongdoing to the professional corporation.

FIGURE APP II-10

(Continues)

B. Standards

The standards set forth below are designed to provide guidance to ensure that *[practice name]*'s business activities reflect the highest standards of business ethics and integrity. Employee conduct not specifically addressed by these standards must be consistent with *[practice name]*'s Principle with respect to business ethics.

1. **Honest Communication.** *[Practice name]* requires candor and honesty from its employees in the performance of their responsibilities and in communication with *[practice name]*'s Compliance Officer. No employee shall make false or misleading statements to any patient, person, or entity doing business with *[practice name]* about other patients, persons, or entities doing business or competing with *[practice name]*, or about the products or services of *[practice name]* or its competitors.

2. **Misappropriation of Proprietary Information.** *[Practice name]* employees shall not misappropriate confidential or proprietary information belonging to another person or entity nor utilize any publication, document, computer program, information, or product in violation of a third party's interest in such product. All *[practice name]* employees are responsible to ensure that they do not improperly copy, for their own use, documents or computer programs in violation of applicable copyright laws or licensing agreements. Employees shall not utilize confidential business information obtained from competitors, including customer lists, price lists, contracts, or other information, in violation of a covenant not to compete, prior employment agreements, or in any other manner likely to provide an unfair competitive advantage to *[practice name]*.

3. **Fraud and Abuse.** *[Practice name]* expects its employees to refrain from conduct that may violate the fraud and abuse laws. These laws prohibit: (1) direct, indirect, or disguised payments in exchange for the referral of patients; (2) the submission of false, fraudulent, or misleading claims to any government entity, including claims for services not rendered, claims that characterize the service as different from the service actually rendered, or claims that do not otherwise comply with applicable program or contractual requirements; and (3) making false representations to any person or entity in order to gain or retain participation in a program or to obtain payment for any service. (For additional guidance, please refer to the *[practice name]* Fraud and Abuse Compliance Policy and the *[practice name]* Corporate Compliance Plan.) If a *[practice name]* employee becomes aware of any wrongdoing under the standards set forth in the *[practice name]* Compliance Program, whether committed by that employee or by someone else, that employee is obligated to report such wrongdoing to *[practice name]* in a manner procedurally consistent and in accordance with the *[practice name]* Corporate Compliance Plan and any and all written *[practice name]* compliance policies.

V. CONFIDENTIALITY

A. Principle

[Practice name] employees shall strive to maintain the confidentiality of patients and other confidential information in accordance with applicable legal and ethical standards.

FIGURE APP II-10   *(Continues)*

B. Standards

[Practice name] and its employees are in possession of and have access to a broad variety of confidential, sensitive, and proprietary information, the inappropriate release of which could be injurious to individuals, *[practice name]* business partners, and *[practice name]* itself. Every *[practice name]* employee has an obligation to actively protect and safeguard confidential, sensitive, and proprietary information in a manner designed to prevent the unauthorized disclosure of information.

1. **Patient Information.** All *[practice name]* employees have an obligation to conduct themselves in accordance with the principle of maintaining the confidentiality of patient information in accordance with all applicable laws and regulations. Employees shall refrain from revealing any personal or confidential information concerning patients unless supported by legitimate business or patient care purposes. If questions arise regarding an obligation to maintain the confidentiality of information or the appropriateness of releasing information, employees should seek guidance from *[practice name]* management or *[practice name]*'s Compliance Officer.

2. **Proprietary Information.** Information, ideas, and intellectual property assets of *[practice name]* are important to the corporation's success. Information pertaining to *[practice name]*'s competitive position or business strategies, payment and reimbursement information, and information relating to negotiations with employees or third parties should be protected and shared only with employees having a need to know such information in order to perform their job responsibilities. Employees should exercise care to ensure that intellectual property rights, including patents, trademarks, copyrights, and software, are carefully maintained and managed to preserve and protect the value of the intellectual property.

3. **Personnel Actions/Decisions.** Salary, benefit, and other personal information relating to employees shall be treated as confidential. Personnel files, payroll information, disciplinary matters, and similar information shall be maintained in a manner designed to ensure confidentiality in accordance with applicable laws. Employees will exercise due care to prevent the release or sharing of information beyond those persons who may need such information to fulfill their job functions.

VI. ADMINISTRATION AND APPLICATION OF THIS CODE OF CONDUCT

[Practice name] expects each person to whom this Code of Conduct applies to abide by the Principles and Standards set forth herein and to conduct the business and affairs of *[practice name]* in a manner consistent with the general statement of principles set forth herein.

Failure to abide by this Code of Conduct or the guidelines for behavior that the Code of Conduct represents may lead to disciplinary action. For alleged violations of the Code of Conduct, *[practice name]* will weigh relevant facts and circumstances, including, but not limited to, the extent to which the behavior was contrary to the express language or general intent of the Code of Conduct, the egregiousness of the behavior, the employee's history with the corporation, and other factors that *[practice name]* deems relevant. Discipline for failure to abide by the Code of Conduct may, in *[practice name]*'s discretion, range from oral correction to termination.

Nothing in this Code of Conduct is intended to nor shall be construed as providing any additional employment or contract rights to employees or other persons.

Although *[practice name]* will generally attempt to communicate changes concurrent with or prior to the implementation of such changes, *[practice name]* reserves the right to modify, amend, or alter the Code of Conduct without notice to any person or employee.

FIGURE APP II-10 *(Continued)*.

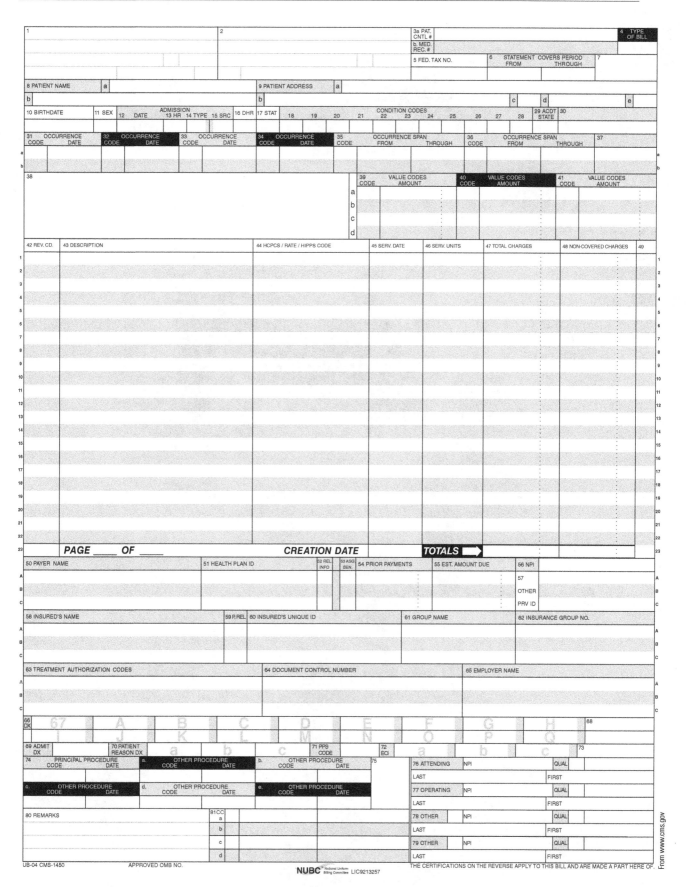

FIGURE APP II-11   UB-04 form.

Appendix III
Commonly Used Acronyms in Medical Billing and Coding

AAPC	American Academy of Professional Coders
ABN	Advance Beneficiary Notice
ACA	Affordable Care Act
AHIMA	American Health Information Management Association
AMA	American Medical Association
AMBA	American Medical Billing Association
BA	body area
BLK LUNG	black lung
C	comprehensive
CAP	Claims Assistance Professional
CC	chief complaint
CCA	Certified Coding Associate
CCS	Certified Coding Specialist
CCYY	year: indicates entry of two digits each for century and year
CEU	continuing education unit
CHAMPUS	Civilian Health and Medical Program of the Uniformed Services
CHAMPVA	Civilian Health and Medical Program of the Department of Veterans Affairs
CHRS	Certified Healthcare Reimbursement Specialist
CLIA	Clinical Laboratory Improvement Amendments
CMRS	Certified Medical Reimbursement Specialist
CMS	Centers for Medicare and Medicaid Services
CPB	Certified Professional Biller
COB	coordination of benefits
CPT	Current Procedural Terminology
D	detailed
DD	day: indicates entry of two digits for the day
DHHS	Department of Health and Human Services
DME	durable medical equipment

Dx	diagnosis
E&M	evaluation and management
EDI	electronic data interchange
EFT	electronic funds transfer
EHR	electronic health record
EIN	Employer Identification Number
EMG	Emergency
EOB	explanation of benefits
EP	established patient
EPF	expanded problem-focused
EPSDT	early and periodic screening, diagnosis, and treatment
ERA	electronic remittance advice
EX	Exam
F	Female
FECA	Federal Employees' Compensation Act
GTIN	Global Trade Item number
H	high
HCFA	Health Care Financing Administration
HCPCS	Healthcare Common Procedure Coding System
HIBCC	Health Industry Business Communications Council
HIC	health insurance claim
HIPAA	Health Insurance Portability and Accountability Act of 1996
HMO	health maintenance organization
HPI	history of present illness
HX	history
ICD-9-CM	Internal Classification of Diseases, 9th Revision, Clinical Modification
ICD-10-CM	International Classification of Diseases, 10th Revision Clinical Modification
ICN	internal control number
ID or I.D.	identification
INFO	information
IP	inpatient
IPPE	initial preventive (preventative) physical examination
L	low
LMP	last menstrual period
M	male
M	moderate
MCO	managed care organization
MDM	medical decision making
MFS	Medicare fee schedule
MM	month: indicates entry of two digits for the month
NCQA	National Committee for Quality Assurance
NDC	National Drug Codes
NEBA	National Electronic Biller Alliance
NEMB	Notice of Exclusion from Medicare Benefits
NHA	National Healthcareer Association
No.	number
NONPAR	nonparticipating provider
NP	new patient

NPI	National Provider Identification
NUCC	National Uniform Claim Committee
NUCC-DS	National Uniform Claim Committee Data Set
OCR	optical character reader (*or* recognition)
OMB	Office of Management and Budget
OP	outpatient
OS	organ system
OZ	product number (Health Care Uniform Code Council)
PAR	participating provider
PCP	primary care provider
PF	problem-focused
PFSH	past family and social history
PH	phone number
PHI	protected health information
PIN	provider identification number
POS	point of service
PPMP	physician-performed microsurgery procedures
PPO	preferred provider organization
QUAL	qualifier
REF	reference
ROS	review of systems
Rx	prescription
SF	straightforward
SOF	signature on file
SPR	standard paper remittance
SSN	Social Security Number
UCR	usual and customary rate
UPC	Universal Product Code
UPIN	unique provider identification number
USIN	universal supplier identification number
VP	vendor product number
YY	year: indicates entry of two digits for the year (see also CCYY)

Appendix IV
Medicare Part B Carriers by State

AK	Noridian Administrative Services, LLC, (02102, MAC Part B), 900 42nd Street S., PO Box 6740, Fargo, ND 58108-6740
AK	Noridian Administrative Services, LLC, (02101, A and B MAC, J-F), 900 42nd Street S., PO Box 6740, Fargo, ND 58108-6740
AK	Noridian Administrative Services, LLC, (02102, A and B MAC, J-F), 900 42nd Street S., PO Box 6740, Fargo, ND 58108-6740
AL	Cahaba Government Benefit Administrators, (10102, MAC Part B) PO Box 13384 Birmingham, AL 35202-3384
AR	Novitas Solutions, Inc. (07102, MAC Part B) Suite 1200, 9330 Lyndon B Johnson Fwy, Dallas, TX 75243
AZ	Noridian Administrative Services, LLC, (03102, MAC Part B), 900 42nd Street S., PO Box 6740, Fargo, ND 58108-6740
AZ	Noridian Administrative Services, LLC, (03102, A and B MAC, J-F), 900 42nd Street S., PO Box 6740, Fargo, ND 58108-6740
AZ	Noridian Administrative Services, LLC, (03101, A and B MAC, J-F), 900 42nd Street S., PO Box 6740, Fargo, ND 58108-6740

CA	Noridian Administrative Services, LLC, (01111, A and B MAC, J-E), 900 42nd Street S., PO Box 6740, Fargo, ND 58108-6740
CO	Novitas Solutions, Inc. (04112, MAC Part B) Suite 1200, 9330 Lyndon B Johnson Fwy, Dallas, TX 75243
CT	National Government Services, Inc. (13102, MAC - Part B), PO Box 7108, Indianapolis, IN 46207-7108
CT	National Government Services, Inc. (13101, A and B and HHH MAC, J-K), PO Box 7108, Indianapolis, IN 46207-7108
CT	National Government Services, Inc. (13102, A and B and HHH MAC, J-K), PO Box 7108, Indianapolis, IN 46207-7108
FL	First Coast Services Options, Inc., (09102, MAC - Part B), 532 Riverside Avenue, Jacksonville, FL 32202
GA	Cahaba Government Benefit Administrators, (10202, MAC Part B) PO Box 13384 Birmingham, AL 35202-3384
ID	Noridian Administrative Services, LLC, (02202, MAC Part B), 900 42nd Street S., PO Box 6740, Fargo, ND 58108-6740
ID	Noridian Administrative Services, LLC, (02201, A and B MAC, J-F), 900 42nd Street S., PO Box 6740, Fargo, ND 58108-6740
ID	Noridian Administrative Services, LLC, (02202, A and B MAC, J-F), 900 42nd Street S., PO Box 6740, Fargo, ND 58108-6740
IL	National Government Services, Inc. (06102, MAC, Part B), PO Box 7108, Indianapolis, IN 46207-7108
KY	Cahaba Government Benefit Administrators, (10402, MAC Part B) PO Box 13384 Birmingham, AL 35202-3384
LA	Novitas Solutions, Inc. (07202, MAC Part B) Suite 1200, 9330 Lyndon B Johnson Fwy, Dallas, TX 75243
MA	National Government Services, Inc. (14212, MAC - Part B), PO Box 7108, Indianapolis, IN 46207-7108
MA	National Government Services, Inc. (14211, A and B and HHH MAC, J-K), PO Box 7108, Indianapolis, IN 46207-7108
MA	National Government Services, Inc. (14112, A and B and HHH MAC, J-K), PO Box 7108, Indianapolis, IN 46207-7108

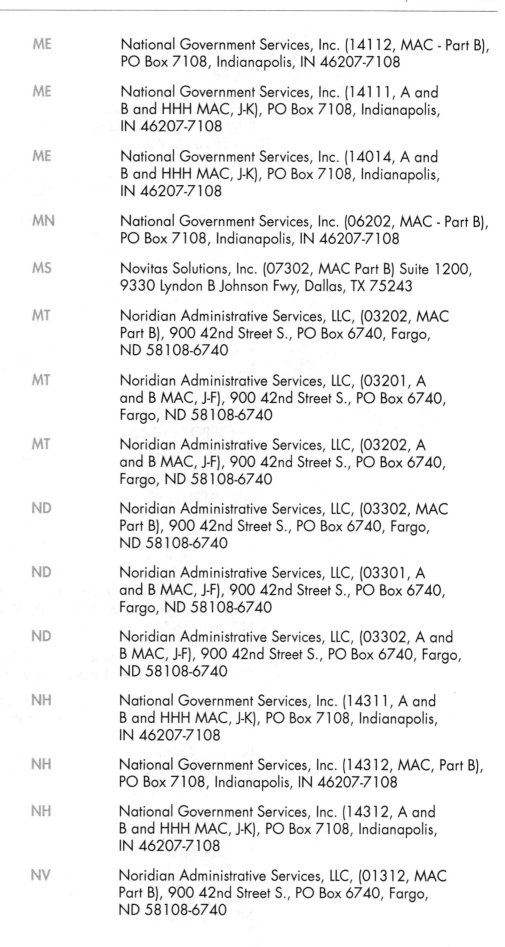

ME	National Government Services, Inc. (14112, MAC - Part B), PO Box 7108, Indianapolis, IN 46207-7108
ME	National Government Services, Inc. (14111, A and B and HHH MAC, J-K), PO Box 7108, Indianapolis, IN 46207-7108
ME	National Government Services, Inc. (14014, A and B and HHH MAC, J-K), PO Box 7108, Indianapolis, IN 46207-7108
MN	National Government Services, Inc. (06202, MAC - Part B), PO Box 7108, Indianapolis, IN 46207-7108
MS	Novitas Solutions, Inc. (07302, MAC Part B) Suite 1200, 9330 Lyndon B Johnson Fwy, Dallas, TX 75243
MT	Noridian Administrative Services, LLC, (03202, MAC Part B), 900 42nd Street S., PO Box 6740, Fargo, ND 58108-6740
MT	Noridian Administrative Services, LLC, (03201, A and B MAC, J-F), 900 42nd Street S., PO Box 6740, Fargo, ND 58108-6740
MT	Noridian Administrative Services, LLC, (03202, A and B MAC, J-F), 900 42nd Street S., PO Box 6740, Fargo, ND 58108-6740
ND	Noridian Administrative Services, LLC, (03302, MAC Part B), 900 42nd Street S., PO Box 6740, Fargo, ND 58108-6740
ND	Noridian Administrative Services, LLC, (03301, A and B MAC, J-F), 900 42nd Street S., PO Box 6740, Fargo, ND 58108-6740
ND	Noridian Administrative Services, LLC, (03302, A and B MAC, J-F), 900 42nd Street S., PO Box 6740, Fargo, ND 58108-6740
NH	National Government Services, Inc. (14311, A and B and HHH MAC, J-K), PO Box 7108, Indianapolis, IN 46207-7108
NH	National Government Services, Inc. (14312, MAC, Part B), PO Box 7108, Indianapolis, IN 46207-7108
NH	National Government Services, Inc. (14312, A and B and HHH MAC, J-K), PO Box 7108, Indianapolis, IN 46207-7108
NV	Noridian Administrative Services, LLC, (01312, MAC Part B), 900 42nd Street S., PO Box 6740, Fargo, ND 58108-6740

NV	Noridian Administrative Services, LLC, (01311, A and B MAC, J-E), 900 42nd Street S., PO Box 6740, Fargo, ND 58108-6740
NV	Noridian Administrative Services, LLC, (01312, A and B MAC, J-E), 900 42nd Street S., PO Box 6740, Fargo, ND 58108-6740
NY	National Government Services, Inc. (13202, MAC - Part B), PO Box 7108, Indianapolis, IN 46207-7108
NY	National Government Services, Inc. (13201, A and B and HHH MAC, J-K), PO Box 7108, Indianapolis, IN 46207-7108
NY	National Government Services, Inc. (13202, A and B and HHH MAC, J-K), PO Box 7108, Indianapolis, IN 46207-7108
NY	National Government Services, Inc. (13202, A and B and HHH MAC, J-K), PO Box 7108, Indianapolis, IN 46207-7108
OH	Cahaba Government Benefit Administrators, (10502, MAC Part B) PO Box 13384 Birmingham, AL 35202-3384
OR	Noridian Administrative Services, LLC, (02302, MAC Part B), 900 42nd Street S., PO Box 6740, Fargo, ND 58108-6740
OR	Noridian Administrative Services, LLC, (02301, A and B MAC, J-F), 900 42nd Street S., PO Box 6740, Fargo, ND 58108-6740
OR	Noridian Administrative Services, LLC, (02302, A and B MAC, J-F), 900 42nd Street S., PO Box 6740, Fargo, ND 58108-6740
PR	First Coast Services Options, Inc., (09202, MAC - Part B), 532 Riverside Avenue, Jacksonville, FL 32202
RI	National Government Services, Inc. (14412, MAC - Part B), PO Box 7108, Indianapolis, IN 46207-7108
RI	National Government Services, Inc. (14411, A and B and HHH MAC, J-K), PO Box 7108, Indianapolis, IN 46207-7108
RI	National Government Services, Inc. (14412, A and B and HHH MAC, J-K), PO Box 7108, Indianapolis, IN 46207-7108
SD	Noridian Administrative Services, LLC, (03402, MAC Part B), 900 42nd Street S., PO Box 6740, Fargo, ND 58108-6740

SD	Noridian Administrative Services, LLC, (03401, A and B MAC, J-F), 900 42nd Street S., PO Box 6740, Fargo, ND 58108-6740
SD	Noridian Administrative Services, LLC, (03402, A and B MAC, J-F), 900 42nd Street S., PO Box 6740, Fargo, ND 58108-6740
TN	Cahaba Government Benefit Adminstrators, (10302, MAC Part B) PO Box 13384 Birmingham, AL 35202-3384
UT	Noridian Administrative Services, LLC, (03502, MAC Part B), 900 42nd Street S., PO Box 6740, Fargo, ND 58108-6740
UT	Noridian Administrative Services, LLC, (03501, A and B MAC, J-F), 900 42nd Street S., PO Box 6740, Fargo, ND 58108-6740
UT	Noridian Administrative Services, LLC, (03502, A and B MAC, J-F), 900 42nd Street S., PO Box 6740, Fargo, ND 58108-6740
VI	First Coast Services Options, Inc., (09302, MAC - Part B), 532 Riverside Avenue, Jacksonville, FL 32202
VT	National Government Services, Inc. (14512, MAC - Part B), PO Box 7108, Indianapolis, IN 46207-7108
VT	National Government Services, Inc. (14511, A and B and HHH MAC, J-K), PO Box 7108, Indianapolis, IN 46207-7108
VT	National Government Services, Inc. (14512, A and B and HHH MAC, J-K), PO Box 7108, Indianapolis, IN 46207-7108
WA	Noridian Administrative Services, LLC, (02402, MAC Part B), 900 42nd Street S., PO Box 6740, Fargo, ND 58108-6740
WA	Noridian Administrative Services, LLC, (02401, A and B MAC, J-F), 900 42nd Street S., PO Box 6740, Fargo, ND 58108-6740
WA	Noridian Administrative Services, LLC, (02402, A and B MAC, J-F), 900 42nd Street S., PO Box 6740, Fargo, ND 58108-6740
WI	National Government Services, Inc. (06302, MAC Part-B), PO Box 7108, Indianapolis, IN 46207-7108
WI	National Government Services, Inc. (06302, MAC Part-B), PO Box 7108, Indianapolis, IN 46207-7108

WY	Noridian Administrative Services, LLC, (03602, MAC Part B), 900 42nd Street S., PO Box 6740, Fargo, ND 58108-6740
WY	Noridian Administrative Services, LLC, (03602, MAC Part B), 900 42nd Street S., PO Box 6740, Fargo, ND 58108-6740
WY	Noridian Administrative Services, LLC, (03601, A and B MAC, J-F), 900 42nd Street S., PO Box 6740, Fargo, ND 58108-6740
WY	Noridian Administrative Services, LLC, (03602, A and B MAC, J-F), 900 42nd Street S., PO Box 6740, Fargo, ND 58108-6740

Appendix V

Insurance Commissioners by State

Note: Please remember that this information is subject to change. You can obtain the most current information online at http://www.naic.org

Alabama

Alabama Department of Insurance
201 Monroe Street, Suite 502
Montgomery, AL 36104
http://www.aldoi.gov

Alaska

Alaska Division of Insurance
550 West 7th Avenue, Suite 1560
Anchorage, AK 99501-3567
http://www.commerce.alaska.gov

Arizona

Arizona Department of Insurance
2910 North 44th Street, Suite 210
Phoenix, AZ 85018-7256
http://www.id.state.az.us

Arkansas

Arkansas Department of Insurance
1200 West 3rd Street
Little Rock, AR 72201-1904
http://insurance.arkansas.gov

California

California Department of Insurance
300 Capitol Mall, Suite 1700
Sacramento, CA 95814
http://www.insurance.ca.gov

Colorado

Colorado Division of Insurance
1560 Broadway, Suite 850
Denver, CO 80202
http://www.dora.state.co.us

Connecticut

Connecticut Department of Insurance
PO Box 816
Hartford, CT 06142-0816
http://www.ct.gov

Delaware

Delaware Department of Insurance
Rodney Building
841 Silver Lake Boulevard
Dover, DE 19904
http://www.delawareinsurance.gov

District of Columbia

Department of Insurance, Securities Regulation and Banking
Government of the District of Columbia
810 First Street, N.E., Suite 701
Washington, DC 20002
http://disr.dc.gov

Florida

Office of Insurance Regulation
J. Edwin Larson Building
200 East Gaines Street, Room 101A
Tallahassee, FL 32399-0305
http://www.floir.com

Georgia

Office of Insurance and Safety
Fire Commissioner
2 Martin Luther King, Jr. Drive
Floyd Memorial Building
704 West Tower, Suite 704
Atlanta, GA 30334
http://oic.ga.gov

Hawaii

Hawaii Insurance Division
Department of Commerce & Consumer Affairs
PO Box 3614
Honolulu, HI 96811-3614
http://www.hawaii.gov

Idaho

Idaho Department of Insurance
700 West State Street, 3rd Floor
Boise, ID 83720-0043
http://www.doi.idaho.gov

Illinois

Department of Financial and
Professional Regulation
Illinois Department of Insurance
122 S. Michigan Ave. 19th Floor
Chicago, IL 60603
http://www.idfpr.com

Indiana

Indiana Department of Insurance
311 W. Washington Street, Suite 103
Indianapolis, IN 46204-2787
http://www.in.gov

Iowa

Iowa Insurance Division
Two Ruan Center
601 Locust, 4th floor
Des Moines, IA 50319-3438
http://www.iid.state.ia.us

Kansas

Kansas Department of Insurance
420 S.W. 9th Street
Topeka, KS 66612-1678
http://www.ksinsurance.org

Kentucky

Kentucky Office of Insurance
PO Box 517
Frankfort, KY 40602-0517
http://insurance.ky.gov

Louisiana

Louisiana Department of Insurance
PO Box 94214
Baton Rouge, LA 70804-9214
http://idi.la.gov

Maine

Department of Professional & Financial Regulation
Maine Bureau of Insurance
34 State House Station
Augusta, ME 04333-0034
http://maine.gov

Maryland

Maryland Insurance Administration
200 St. Paul Place, Suite 2700
Baltimore, MD 21202
http://www.mdinsurance.state.md.us

Massachusetts

Massachusetts Office of Consumer
Affairs and Business Regulation
Division of Insurance
1000 Washington Street, 8th floor
Boston, MA 02110
http://state.ma.gov

Michigan

Michigan Department of Insurance
and Financial Service
Attn: Office of the Commissioner
PO Box 30220
Lansing, MI 48909-7720
http://www.michigan.gov

Minnesota

Minnesota Department of Commerce
85 7th Place East, Suite 500
St. Paul, MN 55101-2198
http://insurance.mn.gov

Mississippi

Mississippi Insurance Department
PO Box 79
Jackson, MS 39205
http://www.mid.state.ms.us

Missouri

Financial Institutions and Professional Registration (DIFP)
PO Box 690
Jefferson City, MO 65102-0690
http://www.insurance.mo.gov

Montana

Montana Department of Insurance
840 Helena Avenue
Helena, MT 59601
http://csi.mt.gov

Nebraska

Nebraska Department of Insurance
Terminal Building, Suite 400
941 "O" Street
Lincoln, NE 68508
http://doi.nebraska.gov

Nevada

Department of Business and Industry
Division of Insurance
1818 East College Parkway, Suite 103
Carson City, Nevada 89706
http://doi.state.nv.us

New Hampshire

New Hampshire Insurance Department
21 South Fruit Street, Suite 14
Concord, NH 03301
http://nh.gov/insurance

New Jersey

New Jersey Department of Insurance
20 West State Street CN325
Trenton, NJ 08625-0325
http://www.state.nj.us

New Mexico

Office of Superintendent of Insurance
PO Box 1689
Santa Fe, NM 87501
http://osi.state.nm.us

New York

New York State Department of Financial Services
One state Street
New York, NY 10004
http://dfs.ny.gov

North Carolina

Department of Insurance
State of North Carolina
1201 Mail Service Center
Raleigh, NC 27699-1201
http://www.ncdoi.com

North Dakota

North Dakota Department of Insurance
600 East Avenue, 5th floor
Bismarck, ND 58505-0320
http://nd.gov

Ohio

Ohio Department of Insurance
50 West Town Street
3rd floor, Suite 300
Columbus, OH 43215-1067
http://insurance.ohio.gov

Oklahoma

Oklahoma Department of Insurance
7645 E. 63rd Street, Suite 102
Tulsa, OK 74133
http://ok.gov

Oregon

Oregon Insurance Division
PO Box 14480
Salem, OR 97309-0405
http://oregon.gov

Pennsylvania

Pennsylvania Insurance Department
1326 Strawberry Square, 13th Floor
Harrisburg, PA 17120
http://insurance.pa.gov

Puerto Rico

Office of the Commissioner of Insurance
B5 Calle Tabonuco Street
Suite 216 PMB 356
Guaynabo, Puerto Rico 00968-3029
http://www.gobierno.pr/GPRPortal

Rhode Island

Department of Business Regulation
Rhode Island Insurance Division
1511 Pontiac Ave. Building 69-2
Cranston, RI 02920
http://www.dbr.state.ri.us

South Carolina

South Carolina Department of Insurance
PO Box 100105
Columbia, SC 29202-3105
https://www.doi.sc.gov

South Dakota

South Dakota Division of Insurance
Department of Revenue and Regulation
445 East Capitol Avenue, 1st Floor
Pierre, SD 57501-3185
http://dlr.sd.gov

Tennessee

Tennessee Department of Commerce & Insurance
Davy Crockett Tower, 5th Floor
500 James Robertson Parkway
Nashville, TN 37243-0565
http://tn.gov/commerce

Texas

Texas Department of Insurance
PO Box 149104
Austin, TX 78714-9104
http://www.tdi.state.tx.us

Utah

Utah Department of Insurance
3110 State Office Building
Salt Lake City, UT 84114-1201
http://www.insurance.utah.gov

Vermont

Department of Financial Regulation
89 Main Street
Montpelier, VT 05620-3101
http://www.bishca.state.vt.us/

Virgin Islands

Office of the Lieutenant Governor
Division of Banking & Insurance
1131 King Street, Suite 101
Christiansted
St. Croix, VI 00820
http://www.ltg.gov.vi

Virginia

State Corporation Commission
Bureau of Insurance
Commonwealth of Virginia
PO Box 1157
Richmond, VA 23218
http://www.scc.virginia.gov

Washington

Washington State
Office of the Insurance Commissioner
PO Box 40256
Olympia, WA 98504-0256
http://www.insurance.wa.gov

West Virginia

West Virginia Department of Insurance
PO Box 50540
Charleston, WV 25305-0540
http://www.wvinsurance.gov

Wisconsin

State of Wisconsin
Office of the Commissioner of Insurance
PO Box 7873
Madison, WI 53707-7873
http://oci.wi.gov

Wyoming

Wyoming Department of Insurance
106 East 6th Ave.
122 West 25th Street, 3rd East
Cheyenne, WY 82002-0440
http://doi.wyo.gov

Glossary

accounts receivable   monies owed to a provider for his or her services.

adjudication   the actual processing of the claim by the insurance carrier.

adjustment   the dollar amount adjusted off the patient's account, reflecting the difference between the fee for services billed and the allowed amount determined by the insurance company.

admit   term used when the provider admits the patient into the hospital.

admit/discharge sheet   a sheet generated by the hospital listing all patient information, including demographics and insurance information.

Affordable Care Act (ACA)   landmark health reform legislation intended to lower health care costs and provide health care coverage to millions of uninsured Americans. It was signed into law by President Barack Obama in March 2010.

age   grow old.

allowed amount   the dollar amount an insurance company deems fair for a specific service or procedure.

American Academy of Professional Coders (AAPC)   organization of professionals dedicated to educating physician-based coders.

American Health Information Management Association (AHIMA)   organization of professionals dedicated to advancing the field of health information management and coding.

ANSI-X12   standardized encryption of patient and provider information completed on a CMD-1500 form.

appeal   a formal way of asking the insurance carrier to reconsider the decision regarding the payment of a claim.

assignment of benefits   when the provider receives reimbursement directly from the payer.

audit   a formal examination of an individual's or organization's accounts.

authorization   a patient's signed approval for the medical office to use the PHI for billing purposes when submitting a health insurance claim to the insurance company.

batch   a set of claims.

beneficiary   term used for a patient who has Medicare coverage.

carrier   a company that has contracted with the CMS to pay Part B claims.

cash flow   a stream of cash (income) used for disbursements.

Centers for Medicare and Medicaid Services (CMS)   a government agency that oversees the Medicare and Medicaid programs.

certification   a professional status or level earned by successful completion of an examination; a person who is certified may subsequently list the designated credentials after her or his name.

Certified Billing and Coding Specialist (CBCS)   a certification offered by the National Healthcareer Association.

Certified Coding Associate   an entry-level coding certification offered by AHIMA.

Certified Medical Reimbursement Specialist (CMRS)   a certification offered by the American Medical Billing Association.

Certified Professional Biller (CPB)   exam offered through the American Academy of Professional Coders

Certified Professional Coder   coding certification exam offered by the American Academy of Professional Coders.

check forgery   is a false writing or alteration of a document.

claim attachment   additional information submitted with the health insurance claim (e.g., progress notes).

clean   describes a claim with no errors.

clean claim   is a claim that has no data errors when submitted to the insurance company.

clearinghouse   an entity that forwards claims to insurance payers electronically.

coder   the person whose job it is to assign CPT, HCPCS, and ICD-9 codes on the superbill, based on the provider's documentation.

codes   assigned letters, numbers, or a combination of both used to report procedures, services, supplies, durable medical equipment, and diagnoses.

co-insurance   a percentage the patient is responsible to pay of the cost of medical services. This is associated with indemnity, traditional, and commercial health insurance plans.

collection agency   an agency retained by the practice for the purpose of collecting debts.

commercial   another term for indemnity or traditional health insurance plans.

consultation   term used when a provider calls upon another physician to evaluate and make an assessment on a patient in the hospital setting.

consulting provider   the provider called upon to provide a consultation regarding a patient who is in the hospital.

continuing education unit (CEU)   a level of measurement of noncredited education.

contract   an agreement between two or more parties.

co-payment   a flat fee the patient pays each time for medical services. This is associated with managed care plans.

coverage   existence and scope of existing health insurance.

CPT modifier   a two-character numeric descriptor used only with CPT codes.

critical care   direct delivery by a physician of medical care for a critically ill or critically injured patient.

Current Procedural Technology (CPT)   codes used to report services and procedures. These are level I codes under HCPCS.

decipher   to interpret the meaning of.

deductible   the amount the patient is responsible to pay before any reimbursement is issued by the insurance company. This is usually associated with indemnity, traditional, or commercial plans.

demographics   statistical information about a patient.

denied   claim is refused to grant payment due to an insurance coverage issue.

Department of Insurance   the governmental agency in charge of controlling and regulating insurance companies.

dependents   persons covered under the policyholder's plan.

disability insurance   insurance providing income to a policyholder who is disabled and cannot work.

discharge   the patient's release from the hospital.

documentation   the process of recording information in the medical chart, or the materials in a medical chart.

E codes   codes used to describe external causes of injury, poisoning, or other adverse reactions affecting the patient's health.

electronically   via a computer modem.

electronic claims submission   the process of submitting health insurance claims via computer modem.

electronic data interchange (EDI)   a mutual exchange of data via computer modem.

electronic funds transfer (EFT)   payment method in which funds are deposited directly into the provider's bank account.

electronic health record (EHR)   electronic medical record-keeping system, replacing paper medical records.

electronic medical record (EMR)   digital version of a patient record, usually limited to its location site.

eligibility category   a category listing requirements for a person to be covered by a specific plan.

emergency room visits   an encounter in the emergency room.

employee   a person employed who is covered under an employer's group health plan.

employee/significant other (E/S) coverage   health insurance covering the employee and the employee's significant other.

encounter form   another name for the superbill.

encrypted   information that is converted into code for security purposes.

established patient   a patient who has been seen in the past 36 months.

explanation of benefits (EOB)   the form sent to a provider or patient detailing benefits paid or denied by the insurance company.

family coverage   health insurance coverage for the individual employee, the employee's spouse, and the employee's children.

fee schedule   a list of allowed amounts for all services and procedures payable by the insurance company.

file   an element of data storage.

fiscal agent   a company that contracts with CMS to pay Medicaid claims.

follow-up   the process of checking the status of a claim.

follow-up visit   subsequent visit made by the physician following an admission.

forgery   a false writing or alteration of a document.

government plan   a health insurance plan funded by the government.

group number   the number on the identification card that identifies the patient's employer group health plan.

guarantor information   states who is financially responsible for the patient's account.

HCPCS   a coding system used to report procedures, services, supplies, medicine, and durable medical equipment. Comprised of CPT (level I) and national (level II) codes.

HCPCS modifier   a two-character alphabetic or alphanumeric descriptor used with both CPT level I and level II national codes.

HCPCS national codes   alphanumeric codes used to identify categories not included in HCPCS level I codes. These codes are considered level II codes.

health insurance   a contract between the subscriber and the insurance company to pay for medical care and preventive services.

health insurance identification card   card given to subscriber as proof of insurance.

Health Insurance Portability and Accountability Act of 1996 (HIPAA)   mandates government regulations that govern patient privacy, security, and electronic record transactions.

health maintenance organization (HMO)   a prepaid medical service plan that provides services to plan members.

HIPAA the Health Insurance Portability and Accountability Act of 1996, a law that stipulates patients' privacy rights regarding their PHI.

home-based billing the ability for an experienced biller to work from their home office.

home visit a visit made by the provider to the patient's home.

hospital billing sheet form used by the provider to record hospital codes for inpatient visits.

husband/wife (H/W) coverage health insurance covering both the husband and wife.

ICD-9-CM *International Classification of Diseases, 9th Revision, Clinical Modification.* The ICD-9 codes are used to report diagnoses, signs, and symptoms of a patient.

ICD-10-CM *International Classification of Diseases, 10th Revision, Clinical Modification.* ICD-10 will replace ICD-9 in the United States on October 1, 2015. This will be an updated improvement on ICD-9-CM.

identification number the number listed on the identification card that identifies the patient to the insurance company.

identify confirmation proof of identification prior to receiving services, usually in the form of a driver's license or state-issued identification card.

indemnity plan a type of insurance plan in which reimbursement is made at 80 percent of the allowed amount. The patient is then responsible to pay the remaining 20 percent.

individual the one and only person covered under a health insurance plan.

initial hospital care the first hospital inpatient encounter with a patient by the admitting physician.

in network medical care sought from participating providers within a managed care plan.

inpatient a patient who has been admitted to a hospital.

insurance aging report shows monies owed to the provider from insurance companies.

insured another term for policyholder or subscriber.

intelligence-free does not carry information about health care providers, such as the state in which they practice or their specialization.

intermediate care facility an institution that provides health-related care and services to individuals who do not require the degree of care and treatment that a hospital or nursing facility is designed to provide.

level of visit is decided by looking at the last digit of the CPT Evaluation and Management code. Example: Code 99201 is a level one, code 99214 is a level four.

long-term care facility a facility that provides medical services and assistance to patients over an extended period of time, and is designed to meet the medical, personal, and social needs of the patient.

maintaining keeping current.

managed care plan a health insurance plan that includes financing, management, and delivery of health care services.

manual claims submission the process of submitting health insurance claims via mail. The claim may be either handwritten or printed from the computer.

Medicaid a government plan for financially indigent people.

medical biller the person responsible for submitting a provider's charges to the appropriate party.

medical billing company an offsite company hired to process medical bills for the provider.

medical chart a confidential document that contains detailed and comprehensive information on the individual patient and the care given to that patient.

Medicare a government health insurance plan primarily covering persons aged 65 and older.

Medicare Part B coverage for physician and outpatient services.

Medicare Part C Medicare Advantage Plans approved by Medicare but managed by private entities.

Medigap supplemental insurance for patients with Medicare as their primary. These plans may pick up the Medicare deductible and co-insurance.

military treatment facility (MTF) a place where Tricare members receive medical treatment.

modifier a two-character alphabetic, numeric, or alphanumeric descriptor used to signify that a procedure or service has been altered by an unusual or specific circumstance, although the code itself has not changed. Additional use includes referencing a specific body site.

National Healthcareer Association organization that specializes in the certification of health care professionals, including coders.

National Provider Identifier (NPI) a 10-digit, intelligence-free, numeric identifier.

National Uniform Claim Committee (NUCC) is a voluntary organization that represents providers, payers, designated standards maintenance organizations, and vendors. It is chaired by the American Medical Association (AMA), with the Centers for Medicare and Medicaid Services (CMS) as a critical partner.

new patient a patient who has never been seen before, or who has not been seen in the past 36 months.

noncovered service or procedure not listed as a covered benefit in the payer's master benefit list.

nursing facility a facility that provides continuous medical supervision via 24-hour-a-day nursing care and related services, in addition to food, shelter, and personal care.

nursing home visit a visit made by the provider to a patient who resides in a nursing home.

office visit an encounter in the provider's office.

online-based medical billing the process of submitting health claims through a website on the Internet.

Original Medicare the Medicare plan in which reimbursement for most services and procedures is paid at 80 percent of the allowed amount.

out of network medical care sought from nonparticipating providers; those providers who have not contracted with specific managed care plans.

out of pocket the patient's share of the cost of health care services. This can include co-payment, co-insurance, or a deductible.

outpatient services performed at a facility where the patient stays less than 24 hours and is not admitted to the facility; also, the term for the patient receiving such services.

outsource send work offsite.

outstanding not yet paid.

overhead a business expense.

paper trail a written or printed evidence of someone's activities.

parent/child coverage health insurance coverage for a parent and child.

patient aging report shows monies owed to the provider from patients (patient balances due).

patient registration form a form used to gather all patient information, including demographics and insurance information.

payer synonym for insurance company.

plan type a specific name assigned by the insurance company designating a specific plan for that type of insurance. For example, Oxford has a "liberty" plan.

point-of-service (POS) plan a health insurance plan in which the patient pays a co-payment when staying in network.

policyholder the person who has (carries) the health insurance.

post-dated check a check dated for the future.

posting the act of making an entry in the patient's account.

preferred provider network (PPN) a group of civilian medical providers that has contracted with Tricare.

preferred provider organization (PPO) this type of plan offers discounts to insurance company clients in exchange for more members.

prescription drugs medications prescribed by a physician (or other licensed prescriber).

primary the insurance plan that is billed first for medical services.

primary care provider (PCP) a physician (or other health care provider) who is responsible for a patient's main health care.

protected heath information (PHI) any information that identifies a patient, including age, sex, ethnicity, or demographics, or that describes his or her health status.

provider-based pertaining only to a provider.

rebill to resubmit a claim.

referral permission from the primary care physician to seek services from a specialist for an evaluation, testing, and/or treatment. Managed care plans require this.

rejected claim refused to accept.

revenue cycle starts when a patient calls to schedule and appointment with a provider and ends with payment is appropriately posted to the patient's account.

scrubbing reviewing a claim for errors or missing information.

secondary the insurance plan that is billed after the primary has paid or denied payment.

self-pay a patient with no health insurance who must pay out of pocket for medical care.

soft collections mailing patient-due statements or calling patients to remind them of their past-due balances.

specialist physician who concentrates on a particular area of medicine (for example, cardiology or gastroenterology).

state insurance commissioner the appointed official in charge of each state's Department of Insurance.

subscriber another term for policyholder.

subsequent hospital care care provided to a patient (per day) following the initial hospital care.

superbill a form listing CPT, HCPCS, and ICD-9 codes used to record services performed for the patient and the patient's diagnosis(es) for a given visit.

supplemental another name for secondary insurance. A supplemental plan usually picks up the patient's deductible and/or co-insurance.

tickler file also called a suspense or follow-up file, tracks all correspondence a biller has made on any pending or resubmitted insurance claims.

traditional another term for indemnity or commercial health insurance plans.

Tricare health insurance provided for retired military personnel, active military personnel, and their dependents.

Tricare Extra a Tricare plan available only to retired military service members and their families. This plan is not available overseas.

Tricare Prime the only Tricare plan offering coverage for active-duty service members. Retired members may also select this plan.

Tricare Standard a Tricare plan available only to retired military service members and their families. This plan is available both in the United States and overseas.

turnaround time the time it takes for the insurance carrier to process a claim

unauthorized authorization or approval not obtained prior to treatment.

V codes ICD-9 codes assigned for preventive medicine services, and for reasons other than disease or injuries.

write off to adjust the dollar amount due from the patient or insurance company to reflect a zero balance due on the claim in question, or sometimes the patient's entire balance. The amount adjusted is called a *write-off*.

Index

Printed in the USA
CPSIA information can be obtained
at www.ICGtesting.com
JSHW052152180524
63175JS00003B/13